D0555328

RENEWALS 458-4574

DATE DUE

SEP 28			
OCT 11			
OCT 25			
NOV 15			
DEC 27			
Jan 10			
AUG 31			
AUG 13 2008			
AUG 14 2008			
GAYLORD		PRINTED IN U.S.A.	

Dedicated to the memory of
Belle Ruth Witkin (1917-1998)

For contributions to the art and practice
of needs assessment, for collegiality and support
offered to so many other professionals,
and for being a dear friend.

James W. Altschuld
Belle Ruth Witkin

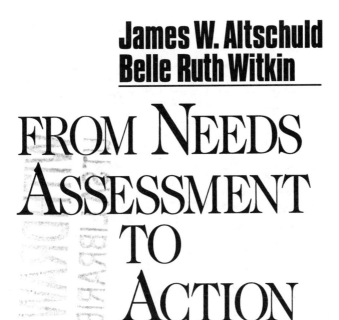

FROM NEEDS ASSESSMENT TO ACTION

Transforming
Needs Into
Solution
Strategies

Sage Publications, Inc.
International Educational and Professional Publisher
Thousand Oaks ▪ London ▪ New Delhi

Library
University of Texas
at San Antonio

Copyright 2000 by Sage Publications, Inc.

All rights reserved. No part of this book may be reproduced or utilized in any form or by any means, electronic or mechanical, including photocopying, recording, or by any information storage and retrieval system, without permission in writing from the publisher.

For information:

Sage Publications, Inc.
2455 Teller Road
Thousand Oaks, California 91320
E-mail: order@sagepub.com

Sage Publications Ltd.
6 Bonhill Street
London EC2A 4PU
United Kingdom

Sage Publications India Pvt. Ltd.
M-32 Market
Greater Kailash I
New Delhi 110 048 India

Printed in the United States of America

Library of Congress Cataloging-in-Publication Data

Altschuld, James W.
  From needs assessment to action: Transforming needs into solution strategies / by James W. Altschuld, Belle Ruth Witkin.
    p. cm.
  Includes bibliographical references and index.
  ISBN 0-7619-0931-1 (cloth: acid-free paper)
  ISBN 0-7619-0932-X (pbk.: acid-free paper)
  1. Strategic planning. 2. Needs assessment. I. Witkin, Belle Ruth, 1917- . II. Title.
  HD30.28.A388 1999
  658.4'012-dc21   99-6773

00 01 02 03 04 05 10 9 8 7 6 5 4 3 2 1

Acquiring Editor:	C. Deborah Laughton
Editorial Assistant:	Eileen Carr
Production Editor:	Diana E. Axelsen
Editorial Assistant:	Patricia Zeman
Typesetter/Designer:	Janelle LeMaster
Indexer:	Virgil Diodato
Cover Designer:	Michelle Lee

**Library
University of Texas
at San Antonio**

CONTENTS

FOREWORD

        s a person who generally enjoys doing needs assessments but seldom relishes reading about them, I found that this book provided a refreshing change. Starting with some sticking points and ambiguities of the needs assessment process left over after their landmark 1995 book, Witkin and Altschuld have taken a flashlight to the dark corners of the needs assessment closet and have done so in a way that is both insightful and entertaining.

What are these dark corners? And why is it important that they be examined anyway? From my viewpoint, there have been three obscure areas, and their elucidation as provided in this book represents a major step forward for the field.

The major one in my mind is the prioritization of needs, often passed over lightly in practice but in fact at the heart of the analysis process. The current book provides guidance in using four alternative ways of prioritizing needs and gives examples of instances where they have been used. One of these (Sork's procedure) has only recently been publicized in U.S. circles. While certainly not the last word on this subject, this chapter tackles the problem head on and provides some alternatives for practitioners never available before.

Another dark corner, unfortunately, has been the underutilization of needs assessment findings. As is indicated in the book's title, the intent of the book is to propel practitioners from the study of needs to putting those results into action. Just as the evaluation community discovered "utilization-focused evaluation" two decades ago, needs assessors are coming to grips with the tremendous waste involved when a perfectly good needs assessment study gathers dust on some administrator's bookshelf. This book helps practitioners take the crucial extra steps to make certain that results are used effectively, and not just ignored.

Another corner in the needs assessment closet, it seems to me, has been the problem of incorporating both qualitative and quantitative methodologies into the same needs assessment effort. The current book devotes an entire chapter to multiple- (mixed-) methods needs assessments. This chapter was particularly encouraging to me, because it showed five case studies in which multiple methods were profitably used. For me it was encouraging, because, while acknowledging the increased complexity involved, the book offers hope to practitioners that such needs assessments are feasible, if handled with expertise, and, by providing a holistic picture, the resulting studies can have a positive impact on the organizations involved.

The net result is a book that provides a forthright addition to the authors' earlier work. It is not a "makeover," but rather a substantial addition.

I have always believed that the skills needed for research in general and for needs assessment in particular are generic problem-solving skills. This book shows how those skills can be honed beyond the basic levels to provide accurate and insightful information—findings that are extremely useful to the process of systematic planning. I found the final chapter delightful as the authors acknowledge their continuing astonishment at how complex assessing needs has become. Given the complexity of their objects of inquiry, human organizations, how could they have found otherwise?

On a more personal note, having maintained friendships with both Jim Altschuld and Belle Ruth Witkin over nearly two decades, I was saddened by the news of Belle Ruth's passing in February 1998. She was a key contributor to the field, imaginative and inspiring, over a major proportion of my professional life. I have been encouraged by Jim's continuation of their joint enterprise, completing a book that would have made Belle Ruth justly proud. To both of them I say "Bravo" for a job well done.

Nick Eastmond
Utah State University

PREFACE

sad thing happened halfway through the writing of this book. Belle Ruth Witkin died on February 2, 1998. Please allow me a short digression. I had worked closely with her for a period of 5 years. We had become more than collaborators; we had become good friends. Her family and I also became close.

I have pondered about what to put into this part of the preface. Would it be best to recite the milestones of a very productive career? Should the focus be on professional achievements that continued unabated for many years after retirement? Would it be even wise to try to explain how a high school English and composition teacher had somehow been employed in a technical capacity for Boeing during World War II? And what about the interests in the arts, music, opera, literature, and the ability to be cheerful and strong in the face of a lifelong battle with polio? It was a very rich life, and a lot of time could be spent on any of the above topics.

A better way to honor Belle Ruth is to describe how her presence affected this book. Four chapters were done in draft when she passed away. Yet all of the remaining text has been written as though we were sitting in the same room working on ideas and critiquing each other's efforts. In a very real sense, Belle Ruth was there.

In our first book, she was very critical of my drafts, often asking, Is this necessary or are you sure that this topic is relevant? As the relationship grew, I noticed that what was criticized was usually incorporated into the book, although in altered and improved form. In time, I did the same thing to her drafts, and we came to a point where the other person's work was changed without much discussion between the two of us. Trust was the nature of the collaboration.

Belle Ruth always insisted that we should question what we were doing. She was demanding, and her standards were very high. So, in completing this book, I pretended that we were still writing together. She was constantly probing my reasoning and chiding me to live up to those standards. Therefore, the best way to honor her is to say that *I hope in some small way that this book is of the quality that was the hallmark of the work of Belle Ruth Witkin.*

POINT OF VIEW

For some time, we perceived that there was an increasing gap between current and ideal practice in needs assessment (NA). Although we were pleased with our first book (Witkin & Altschuld, 1995), it did not deal with many subtle dimensions of the NA process. Most of our attention in that book was devoted to a three-phase model for assessing needs, an extensive treatment of NA methods, and the causal analysis of needs. If somehow we contributed to the gap in practice 4 years ago, it was not our intent, and we apologize.

Now we will provide guidance for what we perceive to be omissions in the NA process. To illustrate the types of problems that concern us, we have embedded many real-world examples drawn from varied fields throughout the text. The book is not a cookbook with detailed lists of procedural steps; rather, our emphasis is to develop an understanding of how the results of an NA are transformed into action plans for an organization and procedures for facilitating that transformation.

Implicit in the last statement is the idea that NA should be viewed from the standpoint of the organization, not from that of an individual. We think of organizations as having the resources to fully study needs and to develop programs to resolve them. Do not infer from this stance that a "top-down" approach is being favored or promoted. We believe that data must be collected from multiple constituencies (i.e., from individuals or groups who have needs and who would be the direct recipients of subsequent services from a program). Such "Level 1" needs are prime in making prioritized decisions about resources, programs, and services. Furthermore, because needs and their assessment are complex, we recommend that a committee be formed to guide the process and that it includes representatives from many of the concerned stakeholding groups. This will increase buy-in to results and is consistent with the idea of democratic decision making.

In regard to content, we have tried to reach an equilibrium between the level of depth and the number of methods and procedures that are covered in the book. This means that some topics (survey design and analysis, Sork's prioritizing strategy) have been discussed in more detail than others. Such choices were based on our work in NA and what we felt would be most relevant to bridging the gap in practice. Several topics are in the text because we believe that they will become more prominent in NA in the next 5 to 10 years.

AUDIENCES FOR THIS BOOK

If you work as a needs assessor or have leadership roles in NA, you will find this book to be valuable. It is applicable to fields such as health, education, business, mental health, social services, library services, and others. If you teach about NA, you will be able to use many of the concepts in your instruction. One of us has successfully incorporated many of the concepts in this book into two NA courses taught at the graduate level. Preliminary student response has been very positive.

For those of you who are managers or administrators, we have dealt extensively with your role in relation to the NA process. If you are a member of a needs assessment committee (NAC), the book describes the role of the committee and specific activities for it to consider and possibly implement. Having a few copies of the book available for NAC use would be worthwhile.

ORGANIZATION AND CONTENT

This text is a sequel to our 1995 book. We start by examining the gap in the NA process itself (Chapter 1) and by taking a fresh look at the three-phase model we proposed in 1995, especially in regard to management considerations that will help to ensure the success of the assessment (Chapter 2). When should management be involved, and what is its responsibility in regard to resources, potential snags, and so forth? We also discuss how to get the NA process going, the initial composition of the NAC, and the potential for changing its composition toward the end of the assessment. A checklist has been provided at the end of Chapter 2 to enable an NAC to monitor its progress through the three phases.

Chapters 3 through 6 represent the core of activities necessary to transform needs into solution strategies. The focus of Chapter 3 is on problems commonly encountered in NA data, the design of surveys that are the predominant methodology in NA, and the analysis of survey data. In Chapter 4, other sources of quantitative information and data generated from qualitative methods are described followed by strategies for combining data from multiple-methods NAs. From there, setting needs-based priorities and selecting solution strategies are covered in Chapters 5 and 6, respectively.

Once a solution is selected, it must be translated into an organizational plan for action. In Chapter 7, a specific case is used to illustrate how this process occurs and the importance of NAC leadership at this point in time.

We have consistently advocated the use of multiple (mixed) methods in NA; therefore, in Chapter 8, five multiple-methods NAs are reviewed and then followed by a cross-case analysis. The last chapter (Chapter 9) contains some final observations about NA and areas of need for the field. A brief glossary of terms is also appended.

UNIQUE FEATURES AND HOW TO USE THIS BOOK

A number of unique contributions are being made in this text in relation to management's role vis-à-vis the NA process, typical problems occurring in NA data, dealing with data from multiple methods, alternatives for setting needs-based priorities and selecting solutions, the translation of solutions into action plans, analysis of multiple-methods NAs, and the glossary of terms. We feel that the linkage of much of this content to the NA context has not been done to any great extent before.

To use this book, the first two chapters should be read for an overview of the NA process. With understandings derived from those chapters, it should be fairly easy to determine what other parts of the book would be of benefit. If NA data are of concern, go to Chapters 3 and 4; if solution strategies have to be selected, go to Chapter 6, and so forth. The choice depends on where you are in the NA process and what activities have not yet been completed. At the same time, our message is not meant to dissuade anyone from reading the entire book, because many special features in it would be of interest to all individuals involved in NA.

ACKNOWLEDGMENTS

We are very grateful to the colleagues and friends who have shared their wisdom and suggestions with us. The book is rich in examples based on works that were used with the permission of other needs assessors. Their willingness to share such efforts with us and our readers is appreciated. Their names are cited where appropriate in the text.

Many current and former graduate students (now colleagues) from The Ohio State University have offered suggestions for this book and thereby enhanced its quality. In alphabetical order, they are Carol Cullen, Gwo-Jen Guo, Mary Sue Hamann, David Hansen, Rosemary Lysaght, Craig McGuire, Phyllis Thomas, Gary Timko, and Jung Sook Yoon. On a related note, Suwimon Wongwanich and Amornwich Nakornthap have used ideas from their graduate work to develop an NA curriculum and research program in Thailand. To all of these individuals we express our gratitude for your interest in and many insightful ideas about NA.

The work, patience, and perseverance of Barbara Heinlein must be cited. She was able to take rough, word-processed material and somehow turn it into a polished final product. Her spirit was indomitable. Melissa Campbell-Nemeth was very helpful in the early stages of the library work, as was Marla Mayerson in regard to producing special figures and illustrations for the book. Kudos to all of you.

A word is in order about Dan Ruth, senior editor at Sage Publications. Dan was so patient and supportive, especially when tragedy hit the writing team. That kindness deserves recognition, as does that of C. Deborah Laughton, who succeeded Dan as our editor and continued to assist in the same thoughtful manner. Our appreciation is also extended to Diana Axelsen (production editor), Stephanie Caballero (promotion manager), Eileen Carr (editorial assistant), Gillian Dickens (copy editor), Janelle LeMaster (typesetter/designer), and our reviewers, Nick Eastmond (Utah State University) and Marybelle Keim (Southern Illinois University) for all of their efforts on our behalf.

Then there are our families. It is difficult to put into words the appreciation that is due on the Altschuld side to Ruth, Steven and his wife and infant son, Karen and Andrew, and to David and Racheal. They have been so understanding and patient during the mood swings that accompany writing a book. Thanks for caring.

Special acknowledgment must be also given to Joe Witkin, Sheryl (Witkin) and David Killman, and Lorin. Joe, without your help neither this book nor the first one would have been completed. Your involvement and assistance with so many details paved the way for the success of this endeavor. Thanks from both of our hearts.

Finally, to Belle Ruth for wise counsel, mentorship, and for being such a good friend—Godspeed.

THE NEED

WOULD YOU BELIEVE THIS STRANGE TALE?

Picture this scenario: two authors discussing a second book on needs assessment (NA). It is a beautiful summer day, and they are spending most of their time sitting outside, enjoying the weather, and playing with ideas.

Is another book really needed? What is missing from the prior effort? What kinds of problems bedevil needs assessors? Hadn't we provided enough specifics in the first book to guide the process? Do we, ourselves, fully understand the process? What kinds of difficulties do people have in conducting NA studies? The interchange is spirited and lively, and the authors argue with each other and question whether they should consider going any further.

Then a story is suggested to us by a friend (V. Pace, personal communication, July 1996). From that story we developed the following dialogue that was part of the prospectus for this book.

From Beans to Baristas: Dialogue on a Summer Afternoon

(Overheard as the authors get together for some brainstorming in the Northwest. Believe it or not, the sun is shining.)

He: Don't you think it is about time we considered writing another book on NA?

She: Not really. Well, OK, after we finished our first one, we did note several topics that we had not touched on.

He: Right. We really went into some detail about how to do an NA, but we didn't answer the question, Where do you go from here?

She: That's true. Remember all those NAs that we found that never really resulted in any action? The number of NA reports that have landed on a high shelf, never to see the light again, almost rivals the piles of *National Geographics* stored in basements and attics in this land.

He: Hey, that's the old problem of utilization. Can we do something that won't put the reader into a coma?

She: I've got it. No one has really dealt with bridging the gap between the NA and planning solutions or programs to meet the need. We can call it *From Beans to Baristas.*

He: What the heck are baristas?

She: Don't you have espresso stands in Ohio? The barista serves you your espresso or latte—out here they come in all kinds of flavors.

He: So what about the beans?

She: That's the Starbucks story—Starbucks is the company that triggered the national mania for coffee and coffee bars. Its mission is to be known as the maker of the finest coffee in the world. It fundamentally changed the way Americans buy coffee. Prior to Starbucks, people bought the coffee beans, whole or ground, and made their own coffee at home, and the company originally just sold the whole beans. A young fellow who was hired to manage the retail marketing of the beans became obsessed with the idea of bringing the romance and culture of Italian coffee bars to America, specifically through Starbucks. He set up a coffee bar offering brewed drinks and espresso beverages made from Starbucks beans. Finally he bought out his old bosses, merged his coffee bar with their assets, and the rest is history. Those fellows have made millions, and now you find espresso bars in hospitals, supermarkets, corporate lobbies, on downtown streets, and all over.

He: So your point about NA is—

She: Come on—use your imagination. Starbucks saw a need and filled it. They made the jump from just selling the beans to selling the brewed coffee, and they did it in a way no one else in this country had done. They really bridged the gap.

He: OK. So we'll show how you go from beans to baristas and the field of NA will never be the same.

She: You've got it. Care for an espresso before we start?

He: Sure. How about a mocha decaf, double tall, hold the whip.

Through discussions like this we began to question if NAs really led to change in organizations. On the basis of the dialogue, we dreamed up a catchy title, *From Beans to Baristas: Bridging the Gap From Needs to Solutions.* Indeed, that name was part of our book prospectus. But the strange tale continues. Our ideas were accepted but not the title. The publishers felt that the book would be indexed under foods rather than in a more desirable academic location; thus, this text was born, albeit with its current title.

WHAT SPECIFICALLY IS MISSING?

Many NAs (our own efforts included) simply do not result in action being taken to resolve problems. Difficulties are encountered in the NA process that impede the development of meaningful action plans—plans that, if implemented, would help to resolve high-priority needs.

Examples of several of these difficulties are briefly described below.

1. Limited Guidance Regarding a Number of Key Procedures in the NA Process. Although there is a rapidly expanding base of references related to NA, there are limitations to it. They include a lack of published discussion on the subtleties of survey design for use in obtaining data about needs, multiple ways that survey data can be analyzed and portrayed, alternative techniques for setting needs-based priorities and issues inherent in those techniques, mechanisms for identifying and selecting solution strategies for high-priority needs, and how solutions can be transformed into action plans for organizations that have a reasonable chance of success.

2. *How to Deal With Multiple Sources of NA Data.* The concepts of need and NA are complicated and value laden. The meanings of needs will vary from one stakeholding group to another. Data regarding needs are often collected from a variety of individuals and groups by different methodologies (surveys, focus group interviews, small and large group techniques, existing databases and records, etc.). The needs assessor then must analyze such data, interpret them, and create, if possible, a holistic, meaningful picture of needs. This is not easy to achieve, and there are not many concrete illustrations in the literature of how to proceed in such situations.

3. *NA and the Organization.* NAs may take on the appearance of activities that exist by themselves, dissociated from the "real" life of the organization. NAs may deal with multiple data sets; working with them is time-consuming, with potentially long delays before results become available; they require sizable expenditures of resources that may be resented by some constituencies in the organization; they may appear to reflect a "top-down" philosophy leading to subtle (or not so subtle) attempts to sabotage or downplay their outcomes; and so forth.

Thus, a common result is that the final NA report is consigned to a dusty shelf, languishing away to a slow, easily forgotten death. At best, the report may lead to an incremental amount of utilization (either direct or conceptual) of results. For success, the needs assessor must strive to keep the administration and staff involved in the NA process. Involvement is a necessary condition for serious attention to be paid to the findings of the NA and their implications for action to be taken by the organization.

4. *Getting Tired of the Whole Thing.* We have participated in a number of NAs that were well implemented and technically sound but that led to virtually no change in the way the organization went about its business. This is analogous to the situation in which the operation was a success but the patient died. Some factors affecting inattention to results were beyond our control (change of administrators, delays in obtaining clearance for the project, a competing survey coming out at the same time as ours).

On the other hand, NA results may not be used due to maturation as a source of invalidity (Campbell & Stanley, 1963). Numerous NA projects require time, resources, and the expenditure of a great deal of energy. Enthusiasm, which is usually present at the start, begins to wane with the passage of time. As the NA is progressing, the organization still conducts its continuing, normal activities, and because of that, attention to and interest in the NA sometimes takes a backseat. As time elapses, the original impetus for the NA shifts toward other endeavors. Boredom with NA can easily emerge.

Moreover, the novelty of the enterprise may be short-lived and erodes in kind of a Hawthorne effect fashion. People simply get tired of the "whole NA thing" and no longer are able to invest their psychological and physical energies in it. In turn, the effectiveness of the NA effort is seriously reduced.

Problems such as these are symptomatic of gaps in the NA process. Definitions of need and approaches to assessing needs are fairly clear and generally well accepted. There are books and other writings on NA, as well as about methods and data collection procedures, that are highly applicable to NA. But the gap between assessing needs, prioritizing them, and then moving into the selection and design of solution strategies within the organizational context represents a major problem for the needs assessor (see Figure 1.1). These kinds of concerns are the main themes of this book. This book is about going from need to action.

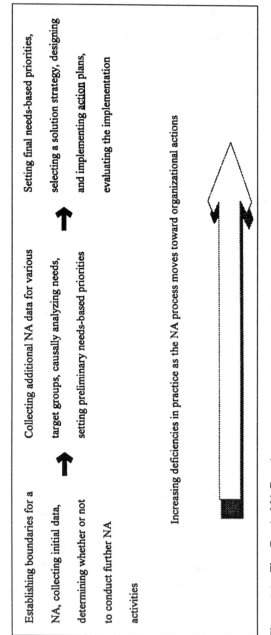

Establishing boundaries for a NA, collecting initial data, determining whether or not to conduct further NA activities

Collecting additional NA data for various target groups, causally analyzing needs, setting preliminary needs-based priorities

Setting final needs-based priorities, selecting a solution strategy, designing and implementing action plans, evaluating the implementation

Increasing deficiencies in practice as the NA process moves toward organizational actions

Figure 1.1. The Gap in NA Practice

THIS BOOK AS A SEQUEL
TO OUR PRIOR ONE

This book is a sequel to and builds on ideas presented in our 1995 book. Let us make the appropriate connections here.

First, we defined need as a noun representing the difference or discrepancy between two states—current status in regard to the area or topic in consideration (the *what is* condition) and the desired status for that topic (the *what should be* condition). (Some may argue that dealing with discrepancies places a negative cast on program development, and it would be better to focus on asset building—that is, identifying and enhancing strengths instead of emphasizing deficiencies. No matter what view is taken, some form of discrepancy analysis will be part of the program planning process. Taking an already strong area and making it even stronger contains elements of thinking about a gap between current status and desirable status.)

Is discrepancy analysis really at the core of NA? Do people actually work with discrepancies when they carry out the process and work with problems in real-world situations? In 1991, Hansen conducted research to determine if discrepancies were the underlying basis of the NA process. Through interviews with professionals in five fields, he determined that the analysis of discrepancies between the what is and what should be states was integral to how interviewees routinely identified and dealt with problems or needs (see also Hansen, Altschuld, & Sage, 1991). Defining a discrepancy was the step most often mentioned by the professionals when they discussed how they approached problematic situations. The idea of need as a discrepancy is fundamental to all work in NA.

Second, in 1995, NA was defined as "a systematic set of procedures undertaken for the purpose of setting priorities and making decisions about programs or organizational improvement and allocation of resources. The priorities are based on identified needs" (Witkin & Altschuld, 1995, p. 4). In accord with the definition, we stressed that NAs are carried out in an organizational framework and must take into account that context if results are to be used. Our current thinking remains consistent about this point; therefore, aspects of conducting, presenting, and using NAs in the organizational milieu are found throughout the text.

We continue to emphasize the use of a needs assessment committee (NAC) to provide leadership and guidance for the NA. It is wise to select some committee members from constituencies that might be affected by the results of the NA. The NAC should consist of from 6 to 20 or more persons who, in addition to being involved in all major policy decisions, may participate in some of the actual NA work. (Note: smaller groups are easier to facilitate, but larger ones can be divided into subcommittees.) Since the NAC may participate in the actual NA procedures, it would be desirable for several of its members to have methodological understandings and skills.

Members of the NAC represent different constituencies; therefore, it is to be expected that they would have varied opinions in regard to the focus of the NA. They should be encouraged to express their views, with all perspectives being valued and given due respect. At the same time, it is important that the group has a strong orientation toward working together to ensure that the NA becomes a reality. Debate and consideration of different positions are healthy, but heated confrontations will quickly lead to a group that becomes ineffective and counterproductive. Cooperation must characterize the spirit of the group instead of ideological posturing and conflict.

NAs are generally conducted by organizations (school systems, businesses, social service agencies, government offices) to determine the nature of problems affecting them and to seek ways that the problems can be overcome. Because NAs lead to organizational change, the NAC should have either a representative or two from the leadership of the organization, or it should maintain communication with management. This does not mean that the NA is "top-down" in nature or controlled. The NA should collect data from varied grass-roots constituencies, and the information so derived should play a major role in the NA.

THREE OTHER IMPORTANT
IDEAS REGARDING NA

Three other ideas are critical to understanding the nature of need and conducting NAs. These other ideas—the three levels of need, the main phases of NA activity, and systems and subsystems—are briefly examined as follows.

THREE LEVELS OF NEED AND TARGET GROUPS

There are three levels of need, with different target groups associated with each (Witkin, 1984, 1994; Witkin & Altschuld, 1995). The levels are as follows:

Level 1 (the primary level) consists of those individuals who would be the direct recipients or receivers of services. The services would be a result of a program developed to resolve a high-priority need. Examples of these target groups would be students, clients, patients, customers, and so on.

Level 2 (the secondary level) is composed of individuals or groups who deliver services to Level 1 (and sometimes Level 2 is used to refer to a treatment provided to Level 1 target groups). Examples would be teachers, social workers, counselors, health care professionals, librarians, policymakers, administrators, and others.

Level 3 (the tertiary level), which is substantially different from Levels 1 and 2, focuses on resources and inputs into solutions. Examples of this level of need are buildings, facilities, classrooms, transportation systems, salaries and benefits, program delivery systems, and the like.

NAs should always be directed toward Level 1 target groups. Level 1 individuals and groups are the very reason for the existence of Levels 2 and 3, not vice versa. In education, social work, health care, and most other fields, Level 1 needs are the "raison d'être" for service deliverers and delivery systems. Therefore, the initial data to be collected or that which are readily available from databases and other existent sources should provide insights into the problems faced by Level 1 target groups. This self-evident statement would seem to add little value to this discussion.

Research shows, however, that even though Level 1 concerns should be prime in NA, they are not! Most NAs are conducted at Levels 2 and 3 (Witkin, 1994). Level 1 needs can almost become lost in the shuffle or be relegated to secondary status in NA. This may simply reflect the fact that NAs are conducted under the aegis of organizations and routinely carried out by Level 2 personnel within them. Is it any surprise, given these circumstances, that the results may not fully represent Level 1 needs? The significance placed on Level 1 here is to remind the needs assessors that the needs of the Level 1 target groups are the rationale for the existence of Levels 2 and 3. Needs assessors should remember to ask questions about whose needs are being assessed and for what purpose.

A minor point of confusion sometimes occurs in regard to a Level 2 NA and the assumption that dealing with Level 2 needs will automatically have an effect on the needs of service recipients (Level 1). Suppose the NA was conducted in regard to the staff development needs of teachers, professors, physicians, nurses, social workers, counselors, or some other professional group of service deliverers. Based on the assessment, decisions could be made to hold staff development seminars or to support attendance at professional conferences. The intent of these activities would be to help staff maintain a sense of professionalism, keep them abreast of developments in their fields, enhance feelings of self-worth and the value of their work, improve morale, and reduce turnover by creating a positive image that the organization cares about its employees.

It could be argued that Level 1 groups will ultimately benefit from such activities and that these strategies will be a means for alleviating Level 1 needs, but it is somewhat of a stretch to do so. In cases such as this, it might be better to think of the service deliverers as a pseudo-Level 1 target group for whom the NA is being conducted. True Level 1 needs may or may not be taken care of by resolving those

PHASE 1	PHASE 2	PHASE 3
Preassessment	*Assessment*	*Postassessment*
(exploration)	*(data gathering)*	*(utilization)*
Set up management plan for NA	Determine context, scope, and boundaries of the NA	Set priorities on needs at all applicable levels
Define general purpose of the NA	Gather data on needs	Consider alternative solutions
Identify major need areas and/or issues	Set preliminary priorities on needs—Level 1	Develop action plan to implement solutions
Identify existing information regarding need areas	Perform causal analyses at Levels 1, 2, and 3	Evaluate the NA
Determine • Data to collect • Sources • Methods • Potential uses of data	Analyze and synthesize all data	Communicate results
Outcomes: Preliminary plan for Phases 2 and 3 and plan for evaluation of the NA	**Outcomes:** Criteria for action based on high-priority needs	**Outcomes:** Action plan(s), written and oral briefings, and reports

Figure 1.2. Three-Phase Plan for Needs Assessment
SOURCE: Witkin & Altschuld (1995). Used by permission.

of service deliverers. This is why it would be appropriate to examine periodically how the above activities relate to Level 1 needs.

THE THREE PHASES OF NA

In Figure 1.2, a general model for conducting an NA is provided. It shows NA as consisting of three phases—Phase 1 (preassessment), Phase 2 (assessment), and Phase 3 (postassessment). The initial set of tasks to be accomplished is to focus the effort and obtain information that is already available about the area(s) of concern. Thus, the preassessment phase is occupied with simply starting the process and determining if enough information is on hand to preclude expending resources in a more costly, time-consuming, and full-blown NA. In many situations, tons of such data exist and, if located, offer enough details about the nature of important discrepancies without necessitating further work. In this book, it is assumed that, to a great degree, many Phase 1 activities have been completed with a decision having been made to proceed into the activities and steps of Phases 2 and 3.

Therefore, although some features of Phase 1 will be included later, the main body of the text will focus on important parts of Phases 2 and 3. Phase 2 is concerned with the methods for collecting data about needs, setting preliminary needs-based priorities, analyzing and synthesizing all data, and determining the causes underlying needs. Ideally, as noted previously, the NA would deal with Level 1 needs first before progressing to the second and third levels of needs—service provider and system needs, respectively. Phase 2 sets the stage for Phase 3, in which final needs-based priorities are set, solution strategies are selected, and action plans are developed and implemented.

The methodology of NA, how to perform causal analyses, numerous examples of how methods could be applied (or adapted) to NA, and the strengths and weaknesses in those applications have been described previously by us and others. They can readily be located in the literature (see the reference list for this text). These sources are very useful, but they tend to give more attention to method and less to priority setting, selecting solution strategies, and action planning. Because these areas are less well explained in the praxis of the field, Chapters 3 through 6 are designed to explore their nature specifically in relation to NA.

SYSTEMS AND SUBSYSTEMS

Organizations are composed of subsystems that, although interconnected, often tend to function independently of each other. This causes a problem in the NA process in that the identification of needs and subsequent actions in one subsystem will affect other subsystems. In

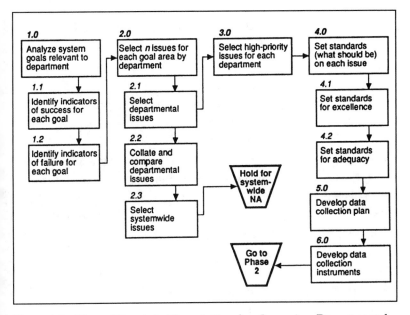

Figure 1.3. Flow of Events in Phase 1, Based on Issues in a Departmental System
SOURCE: Witkin and Altschuld (1995). Used by permission.

these circumstances, a way to avoid getting "hung up" here would be to limit the scope of the assessment to only well-defined, highly important subsystem areas. As the assessment moves forward, needs relating to other subsystems or the total organization itself will emerge and should be noted in the final NA reports, perhaps even in a special section. Key administrators and managers should be informed about such needs, and they may be incorporated into a systemwide NA carried out at a subsequent time. Figure 1.3 is a flowchart of a subsystem assessment in which systemwide issues have been observed and held for future consideration.

NAs can rapidly become too large and fragmented if the above course is not followed. They will be too broad in scope and try to cover so much territory that the whole enterprise will become chaotic and have little chance of success. Narrowing the scope of an NA may miss some things, but overall it is a better way to go.

ADMINISTRATIVE COMMITMENT TO NA

An assumption being made in any NA is that there is a willingness to explore ideas and problems and an openness to change on the parts of management and staff. The NA can be quickly torpedoed by an NAC that is just going through the motions or by an administration that may, through its subtle body language, convey the stance that deep down it is not committed to modifying how the organization functions. Therefore, it is imperative for the administration at the start of the process to make clear why it is interested in needs and what it would do with the results of the endeavor.

Needs can lead to different ways of operating and managing activities. Power bases can be threatened, and control can be diminished. Such change can be frightening not just for administrators but for anyone. People like to be in control of their environments and efforts. Dealing with needs will require some honest soul searching. Without an initial public statement from the administration about its commitment to and support for the NA, the NAC and other staff members may begin to suspect that other motives (politics and co-opting as opposed to trust and improvement) are in play.

As an example of how to deal with such a concern, one of us participated in a situation in which internal evaluation teams composed of teachers were established to evaluate programs in a school district. The teams began to question the rationale underlying their formation, the role and contribution of administrators, and the freedom of a team to pursue the evaluation in the manner it desired. The coauthor felt that if the administrators did not make their position known in a direct and forthright manner and if the enterprise was constrained or controlled by them, it was not going to be successful. To their credit, after serious deliberation, the administrators agreed to serve in advisory and support capacities (i.e., they became partners in the evaluation). They stated their position in a public forum with the involved teachers. The observation was that this was a necessary condition for success and would apply equally to conducting NAs.

WHAT IS THE CONTENT
OF THE REST OF THE BOOK?

In Chapter 2, the major operational activities for each of the three phases of NA are discussed, with special emphasis being given to the role of management in the NA. The description of the activities should help needs assessors and NACs to develop a clear understanding of what is operationally necessary for conducting an NA. Included with the activities of Phase 1 is an example of the output of a group process that would be useful for guiding Phase 2 activities. It depicts the way in which a group process can be integral to NA decision making, aid in selecting methods for Phase 2, and establish a positive tone for the NA. The discussion then moves into important activities of Phases 2 and 3.

Chapter 3 deals with problems found in NA data, the design of NA surveys, and the analysis of survey data. Chapter 4 then moves to other sources of data and some ideas for handling data from multiple sources. Chapter 5 focuses on setting needs-based priorities and the subtleties inherent in such techniques. In Chapter 6, five approaches for selecting solution strategies based on needs-based priorities are offered. It is our perception that collectively the methods in these four chapters have not been placed in the NA context to an extensive degree before. Chapter 7 concludes "bridging the gap" by looking at how solution strategies can be translated into concrete action plans.

Chapter 8 is rather unique. Its content is based on an analysis of five case studies of NAs that employed multiple (mixed) methods. For a number of years, we have been on a multiple-methods bandwagon. There was a strong need, given this predisposition, to depict how multiple methods have been used and issues associated with such use. It is our hope to be objective in the treatment of multiple methods instead of giving a self-serving confirmation of our position. Chapter 9 contains some final observations about NA.

Lastly, a glossary of terms has been appended. We felt it would be valuable to clarify terms and, by so doing, to continue to improve and advance the practice of NA. The definitions in the glossary are connotative rather than denotative. As the practice of NA evolves, it is perceived that these early attempts at definitions will be updated and changed.

THE THREE PHASES OF
NEEDS ASSESSMENT

A Closer Look

uality planning is essential for a needs assessment (NA) to be successful.[1] Let us examine the rationale underlying this simple declaration.

NAs have many complex features and dimensions. They take place within the political and social environments of organizations. They are often based on information obtained from a wide array of constituencies. They work best when key decision makers are committed to the endeavor and when a dedicated committee conducts and guides the endeavor. The NA process can become difficult, especially when its focus is on very public and contentious topics in education, health care, social services, urban development, business, and other areas.

NAs are political. When resources are allocated to one need over another, NAs become political (see Fiorentine, 1994, for a discussion of policies that guide needs-based distribution of resources). Resources—human, financial support, and time—are finite, and attending to one prioritized need will preclude attention being paid to others. In a biblical sense, someone's ox will be gored. Some NAs may be complicated and require a lengthy period of time to complete. When all of the above aspects are considered, they indicate that we must enter into the NA process carefully and only after serious thought about whether it would be worthwhile.

Even how NAs start is somewhat murky. A group or organization may become concerned about the value or attractiveness of its services or products and feel that further investigation should be undertaken. An organization may have a cyclical management information system that has detected recurring problems that demand attention. Perhaps complaints are coming from staff members or from individuals who are intimately familiar with organizational products and services. The complaints could represent obstacles that hamper the ability of the organization to serve its clientele.

No matter how the process begins, some kind of structure must be set up to study the nature of problems and to determine if action should be taken to resolve them. This observation is the basis for key Phase 1 (preassessment) activities. A person or group is given responsibility for initiating the NA effort. Some sort of guiding committee is formed to provide insight and direction for the NA. Commitment to the endeavor has to be there at the beginning and nurtured throughout the process. Concrete ties to key administrators have to be established and maintained. Adequate funding to carry out NA activities has to be secured. Phase 1 is the foundation, the building block for NA.

PHASE 1 (PREASSESSMENT)

Table 2.1 contains a description of the major operational steps involved in Phase 1 and management considerations, as well as general comments regarding the steps. No matter how it arises, once a decision is made to conduct an NA, two important initial activities occur. A needs assessor is selected to lead the NA, and a needs assessment

Table 2.1 An Overview of Key Operational Activities in Phase 1 (Preassessment) of NA

Major Operational Activities	Management Considerations	Comments
Determine the organizational interest and commitment to looking at problems (needs). (Interest comes from informal meetings/discussions or formal mechanisms such as evaluation reports, MIS systems, etc.)	Management must stay tuned to the pulse beat of concerns and see if sufficient internal or outside interest exists to pursue an NA. If interest is not there, time and money will be wasted in a futile and frustrating effort.	Initial and continuing commitment is essential, especially if it is necessary to proceed into Phases 2 and 3.
Leadership responsibility is assigned to a needs assessor to start a formal process of identifying and exploring needs.	Bring in outside expertise for this role or select a knowledgeable internal person to lead the effort.	In a large NA that requires a major expenditure of funds or one that is politically charged, it is better to consider an outsider (or outsiders) for this role.
Form an NAC to guide the work on Phase 1 (and Phases 2 and 3 if they become necessary).	Choose individuals who can commit time to the effort and have the knowledge, skills, and personality to contribute.	The choice of NAC members is critical because if they develop ownership in the process and if concerns of importance are identified, they will be key supporters of change.
Conduct initial NAC meetings in such a way that all future NA activity is focused on major concerns.	Allot sufficient time and funding to this activity. Assume at least a month and, more realistically, 2 months for the focusing part of Phase 1 to occur.	This seemingly simple step is the bedrock of the NA process. See the text for an illustration of how this activity might take place.

(continued)

Table 2.1 Continued

Major Operational Activities	Management Considerations	Comments
The needs assessor and NAC locate and collect available data and information about concerns during periods between formal meetings of the group.	As described earlier, this activity requires time and resources to complete. Make sure that reasonable resources are provided.	Information that is located often extends beyond the focus of a particular NA. Valuable sources of information that are routinely collected by the organization or easily accessible from external sources are usually identified and procured.
Information is synthesized by the needs assessor to aid the NAC in making decisions related to further NA activity.	The needs assessor may request additional support for assembling and interpreting collected materials in a manner that will facilitate decision-making processes. Management should provide such resources if asked.	Tables and information produced here reveal a great deal about the needs of the organization. They also may point to economical ways of obtaining information that might be useful for other organizational activities. Findings and results of Phase 1 are conveyed in writing and in a debriefing presentation to key administrators or decision makers for consideration.
An overall decision is made to proceed into Phase 2 activity, to jump ahead to Phase 3, or to go no further.	If the decision is to enter into Phases 2 or 3, adequate resources must be provided for the tasks of those phases.	Retain and organize the materials and reports generated in Phase 1 to document the NA process.

committee (NAC) is chosen. Without the right kind of leadership and a strong, sustained commitment to the endeavor, the likelihood of the NA resulting in organizational change is seriously diminished.

Within the organization, experienced and knowledgeable staff members could be recruited for the leadership role. In general, we do not recommend using them. NAs are political in nature and can become quite emotionally charged (see the disaggregated priority-setting example in Chapter 5). Internal consultants are cheaper and, in some situations, might work well. Conversely, they might come with organizational "baggage," could be perceived as being biased in favor of one need over others, and could represent management's position.

Most of the time, it is our suggestion to hire external consultants to facilitate or lead the NAC. They have skills in the NA process, experience in working with small groups, familiarity with methods used in NA, and a reputation for fairness. They probably will not have vested interests in a particular area of need.

Facilitators can be found in consulting firms that specialize in the social sciences or in work related to business settings. They also are at universities in disciplines such as public policy and administration, communication, education, and social work. Indeed, a small but growing number of individuals view NA as the main focus of their professional work and, if available, they should be considered for the leadership of not only Phase 1 activities but possibly for most of the other two phases. Their specialized knowledge, coupled with their objectivity, would be worth the additional cost, especially if the NA is politically sensitive. (It should be noted that NAs tend to require more time than the organization or an external consultant may initially realize. Therefore, both parties must exercise caution in estimating the time and costs necessary for an NA, and provisions for contingencies should be built into agreements between them.)

The NAC should consist of a cross section of individuals who represent distinct constituencies that could be affected by the results of the NA. Choose individuals based on their reputation for express-ing their opinions and perceptions as well as their ability to cooperate and contribute to a group endeavor such as this one. If they have some knowledge and awareness of methods, view it as an added bonus. For example, if a professional population were chosen to be on an NAC, there would be more likelihood of methodological knowledge as compared to an NAC composed of consumers of mental health services, who generally would not be familiar with methodology.

Two other concerns about the NAC are important. First, how big should it be? A smaller group (6-10 persons) is more manageable, but then again there are less human resources with which to work. One could consider starting with a larger group of 20 or so members and then divide it into smaller working subcommittees. The choice depends on the local circumstances, the nature of the NA to be undertaken, and the experience of the needs assessor in working with either small or large groups. Second, in Phase 1, the NAC will have to meet often and on a fairly tight schedule. Due to this press, it is absolutely critical at the very first meeting to ascertain the true availability of members for regular meetings over the next 2 months. Members have to make a strong commitment to staying on task and attending meetings. (It is for this reason that a small, dedicated group may be better able to meet deadlines and achieve results than a larger one.)

The first NAC meeting might begin with the leader indicating the charge to the group (general areas of focus) and the three phases of the NA. (A bit of prefocusing is frequently used to "jump-start" Phase 1 activities.) The NAC could then review and possibly prioritize goals for the area of concern that had been supplied to them. Another option would be to have the NAC generate and rank order concerns for each goal and subsequently deal only with the highest-ranking concerns. Although many procedures for getting the initial deliberations of an NAC started have been explained in depth elsewhere (Eastmond, Burnham, & Witkin, 1987; Wickens, 1980; Witkin & Altschuld, 1995), one recent illustration of the process would be informative.

To get started, the NAC could work with a form such as the one shown in Figure 2.1 and fill it in with what they feel is known about each highly ranked concern, where that information is located, and ideas about additional information that would be desirable to gather. (This underscores the need to carefully select individuals for NAC

Goal:			
Concern:			

What Is Known		Data to Gather	
Facts	**Sources**	**Facts**	**Sources**
		Opinions	**Sources**

Figure 2.1. Blank Data Resources List Format for Preassessment

SOURCE: Witkin & Altschuld (1995). Used by permission.

NOTE: Additional columns may be added to indicate who will be responsible for gathering the data and target dates.

Goal:	Expand AEA membership in accord with criteria developed by a membership committee.		
Concern:	To what extent does the membership represent the diversity and nature of practicing evaluators? What are potential other sources of AEA members?		

What Is Known		Data to Gather	
Facts	**Sources**	**Facts**	**Sources**
Number of members	Membership lists	AEA prime	Surveys
Highest degree	Topical interest	organization	Interviews at
Gender	group lists	Evaluation as a	conference
Countries	Registration	prime focus	FGIs
Area of specialization	Evaltalk list	Nature of practice	
		Other organizations	
		Opinions	**Sources**
		Why join	See above
		What value	
		When	

Figure 2.2. Completed Data Resources List Format for Preassessment

SOURCE: Altschuld & Witkin (1995). Used by permission.

NOTE: Additional columns may be added to indicate who will be responsible for gathering the data and target dates.

membership. Many times, the NAC will be knowledgeable about the organization and its problems and will be able to identify ways in which information can be generated in a quick and economical fashion.)

In 1995, Altschuld and Witkin used the form in an NA workshop conducted at the annual meeting of the American Evaluation Association (AEA). Workshop participants were presented with the situation that the AEA was considering an NA about the future of the organization. They were provided with some description of the background of AEA, issues affecting the organization, and its future. Then they were given a goal, concerns related to the goal, and a brief orientation to the use of the form in Figure 2.1. In small groups they deliberated about concerns, agreed on a key concern or two, and produced a completed form. Figure 2.2 represents the efforts of one small group after about 25 minutes of discussion.

The results in Figure 2.2 were remarkable considering how little time was available for the activity. The group developed a rich set of ideas about what was already known and what information would be of value to locate. When challenged about the methods for collecting information, their imagination was up to the charge. Not only were they able to suggest what would be of importance, but they also suggested alternative ways to find or produce the data. Their ideas for data collection were innovative and cost-effective (translation: cheap to implement). Although there is some bias in this example because the workshop participants had extensive training and methodological experience, the activity is generalizable. The procedure has been successfully used by one of the coauthors in a variety of group environments. It is immediately apparent that an outcome such as the one depicted in Figure 2.2 would have tremendous value for the subsequent work of virtually any NAC.

Continuing with Phase 1, the responsibility for the NAC and needs assessor(s) will be to seek out, collect, and synthesize existing information—in other words, compiling information (in tables or short written summaries) based on the initial brainstorming work. This activity will last from 2 weeks to several months depending on the nature of the specific NA. The NAC could also be asked to help collect the data. When this activity is completed, the group must examine what the information says about the goal and its underlying concern(s). Questions to guide deliberations are as follows:

- Does the NAC perceive that it knows enough about the concern from the tables and summaries of the data?
- Does the information collected seem to be sufficient for decision-making purposes?
- Does the NAC feel uneasy or uncertain about the concerns for a goal?
- Do they feel strongly enough to make a decision to move to Phase 2 or 3 of the NA?
- Is the need area of sufficient importance to warrant more attention?

If the NAC decides to move to Phase 2, content such as shown in Figure 2.2 will come into play. With the suggestions for additional information to be collected and how that data could be obtained as a basis for discussion, the needs assessor leads the NAC into Phase 2 activities and could even suggest other methods for gathering data. Thus, Phase 1 lays the groundwork for the next two phases of NA.

Before moving to Phase 2, it is important to stress one feature critical to the completion of the form given in Figure 2.1. Groups tend to quickly generate concerns for a goal that represent self-fulfilling, data-oriented questions rather than focusing on issues. Stated alternatively, "data exist, and we know that this particular data set is there, so let's posit a question for which something already is available and can easily be found." It is a fine distinction but nevertheless an important one. Data-oriented questions are not bad, but they may not lead to the consideration and development of a full slate of goal-related concerns. It is the responsibility of the needs assessor to keep the group on track and appropriately focused.

Here is how that can be done. We started the AEA workshop with the following goal about the professional society in the next century: "To expand the membership of AEA according to criteria developed by a membership committee." Using that goal as a starting point, it was then explained that concerns deal with problematic aspects, issues, values, or perspectives regarding the goal. Samples of the concerns were provided as follows:

- To what extent does the current membership of the AEA represent the diversity and nature of practicing evaluators?
- What kinds of diversity do we want to see in the organization in terms of age, fields represented, and so forth?
- What are potential sources of AEA members?
- How many people became involved as graduate students, and how many of those have maintained their AEA membership (and also what is the retention rate for all AEA members)?

By using examples of concerns, we were able to keep the small groups from not falling into the trap of the self-fulfilling types of questions. In most cases, to facilitate the process, the needs assessor will have to employ a strategy similar to the one used in the workshop.

PHASE 2 (ASSESSMENT)

In Phase 2, the NAC determines what additional data will be collected, specifies the procedures that will be used for obtaining data, analyzes and interprets data, looks at causes of needs, and makes decisions relative to Phase 3. As the NA proceeds into Phase 2, it is important to recognize that a lot of effort has already been devoted to the focus of the NA. The NAC has met numerous times, amassed a lot of data, and examined results, and the needs assessor has periodically recapped for the group what has transpired to the present time.

Now the NAC should catch its breath and look at where it is in the process to ensure that there is agreement on the general themes and boundaries for subsequent data collection. (NAs sometimes are so broad in scope that nothing gets done or so narrow that they deal with only a small part of the need. Therefore, a review of the overall process is warranted. See Eastmond et al., 1987, in this regard.)

After agreement on boundaries has been achieved, the expenditure of funds and resources for the collection of more data should be carefully scrutinized. How will such data fit into the overall understanding of needs? How will it relate to Level 1, 2, and 3 concerns? What methods might be appropriate for obtaining it? How much will the methods cost, and what special kinds of expertise will be required?

In other words, a different set of decisions now faces the NAC. This is the point where the needs assessor might describe other methodological options based on his or her expertise and familiarity with the NA literature. Eventually, the NAC determines whether additional data about needs would be beneficial. If such data are obtained, they are analyzed and synthesized for further use in NA. In addition, the NAC may look at the potential causes of the observed discrepancies or needs (see Witkin & Altschuld, 1995; Witkin & Stephens, 1973, for causal analysis techniques).

Table 2.2 contains a summary of Phase 2 activities. The table was constructed in a manner similar to Table 2.1. Phase 2 could be thought of as the engine that propels the NA vehicle (i.e., new information, if mandated, is generated). This information, in conjunction with the outcomes from Phase 1, helps the NAC see what might be the preliminary priorities for action planning in Phase 3.

Although the entries in the table are self-explanatory, some facets of Phase 2 require amplification. First, conditions do change, so keep in mind that the information from Phase 1 may be dated, often having come from archived sources. So it may be important to seek other, more up-to-date information. Second, consider alternative ways in which data might be collected. It is simply too easy to fall into the "Law of the Hammer" type of thinking (the hammer is the tool we know and understand, hence everything will need hammering). What this means is that we are familiar and comfortable with a certain method or set of methods, so that is what will be used. Be open to options before making final decisions about the methodology.

Be alert to adapting methods to local conditions. Perhaps a Delphi technique (an iterative set of questionnaires) would be of value for obtaining data about a specific area of need, but a mailed Delphi

Table 2.2 An Overview of Key Operational Activities in Phase 2 (Assessment) of NA

Major Operational Activities	Management Considerations	Comments
Review the activities and results of Phase 1 at the first NAC meeting of Phase 2.	Management personnel should attend this session and observe the deliberations for this phase. The collection of more data will be critical for future actions, and every attempt should be made to stay informed.	Management attendance is solely for the purpose of learning about the reasons for Phase 2 activities. It is crucial that the tone be facilitative rather than constraining. Commitment must be made to taking a supportive rather than a directing role.
Determine the level (1, 2, and/or 3) of the NA and the desired end states (the "what should be") for those levels.	Recognize that consensus regarding end states will take time to establish, especially if standards do not currently exist or if existing standards do not fit the local situation.	End states have value beyond this specific NA and could be used later in the evaluation of programs designed to alleviate needs. They may also point toward important variables to include in a program evaluation.
Identify and select appropriate methods for conducting the assessment phase.	This activity reflects the importance of the choice of the individual to lead the NA. Experienced needs assessors understand the range of methods, time and costs involved, and trade-offs among methods. Some methods may require specialized statistical or analytical skills necessitating additional expenditures.	Many options are available for data collection: archived sources of information (records, logs, rates under treatment, census reports), various types of communicative approaches (surveys, interviews, the Delphi technique, community forums, and others), and so forth.
Implement the selected methods and gather data about needs. Keep the focus on Level 1 needs first before considering Levels 2 and 3.	This set of activities almost always requires more time than planned. Anticipate that timelines will have to be extended. Be cool; don't lose patience.	How to use methods has been documented in numerous literature sources and books. They should be reviewed for the best ways to implement methods.

28

Analyze the data and identify discrepancies with an eye toward establishing preliminary priorities for Level 1 first and then for looking at Level 2 and 3 needs.	This is an important step in NA, so resist the temptation to prematurely push the process to closure. More effort is required before resources should be committed to certain needs and especially before devoting resources to organizational actions.	Many subtle issues make it difficult to derive meaning from NA data and, in turn, to specify priorities. These problems are described in Chapter 3, along with a look at surveys and survey data. Other sources of data and ways to combine data from multiple methods are examined in Chapter 4, and priority setting is discussed in Chapter 5. Note: the highest needs in terms of size of discrepancy may not represent the highest priority for action. Other factors play a role in determining priorities.
Perform causal analyses for the needs with the highest preliminary priorities at each of the three levels.	It might be advantageous for management to become part of the NAC for this activity. Causal analyses reveal what is at the heart of the discrepancy and whether it is feasible for the organization to attend to it.	Causal analyses, with information obtained for Phases 1 and 2, may indicate that resolving some needs are beyond the ability of the organization or that collaborative efforts might be required to deal with them. Hence, some high-priority needs will not be considered for action by the organization in Phase 3.
Synthesize all data collected and summarize the results of all major Phase 2 activities.	See above entries.	See above entries.

procedure with all of its complexity is beyond what the NAC and needs assessor can handle. Or there may be insufficient resources for hiring someone else to carry out the procedure. Ask then, "Is there some adaptation of the technique that would fit here and yield useful results?" For example, if you have an intact group that meets regularly, a modification of the Delphi technique, the group Delphi, could be used to take advantage of this fortuitous local circumstance. All NA methods in well-known texts are, for the most part, general frameworks, not rigid approaches that cannot be cleverly altered to fit the context of the local NA. They are robust and flexible, and they should be thought of in that light.

Costs play a large role here as well. After choosing methods for the NA, the NAC might ask if there are simpler ways to collect these data or very similar data (e.g., could sample size be reduced without compromising the quality of information?). NAs can be expensive, and the needs assessors and the NAC should be careful with regard to the expenditure of funds.

One other caution is that regardless of how needs are assessed, specific NA questions should be as free from bias or "leading the witness" as possible. Suppose that a survey required respondents to select possible solution strategies for resolving a prioritized need. It would be best to include an array of as many realistic solutions as feasible and, at the same time, allow the respondent the option of adding his or her own suggestions. This would be desirable and fairer than simply focusing on a narrow range of choices favored by the NAC.

The time required for Phase 2 activities also warrants attention. In our work, NAs always seemed to take longer than anticipated, with frequent and subtle shifts in direction routinely occurring. NAs get into values and bring to the surface deep-seated perspectives, especially when the NAC first looks at the topics of interest. Seeking agreement about the focus of the NA (i.e., specifics regarding the *what should be* questions and what are reasonable standards or levels for current status or end states) frequently will be a difficult experience for the NAC. NAs sometimes take groups into the very heart and soul of the organization.

Because of the valuing dimensions embedded in NA, numerous references to or hints about time are included in the management considerations in Tables 2.1 and 2.2. Put bluntly, NA is not like making widgets. It is a dynamic, interactive process that is filled with many unknowns. Within reasonable limits, the NA enterprise must be viewed with patience and a sense of stoicism.

PHASE 3 (POSTASSESSMENT)

In Phase 3, final priorities are established, solution strategies are selected, and an action plan is developed, implemented, and evaluated. This is where the gap in the process described in Chapter 1 is most noticeable.

Phase 3 would be closest to what Rodriguez (1988) identified as needs analysis. Needs analysis takes place after needs have been identified and prioritized. It consists of defining criteria (costs, fit to the local situation) for solution strategies, examining alternative solutions in terms of the needs, and selecting and implementing the strategy that has the highest potential of resolving the need. As Rodriguez pointed out, there is confusion in terminology in that a need cannot be analyzed before it has been identified. Assessment (identification) of needs therefore has to precede needs analysis. We agree. We do not differentiate among the terms other than noting that our thinking about NA starts with the initial identification of needs and then proceeds into what others would term *needs analysis*.

Table 2.3 provides an overview of Phase 3. Although setting final priorities is the first step, its placement was arbitrary. If the NA has gone well, priority setting could appropriately be the culminating event in Phase 2. Wherever it is placed, it is a crucial NA step and should be done by rating a need against explicit criteria that have been

Table 2.3 An Overview of Key Operational Activities in Phase 3 (Postassessment) of NA

Major Operational Activity	Management Considerations	Comments
Set final priorities on needs at all three levels.	It would be advisable that management be notified when the NAC reaches this point in the process. Consideration should be given to becoming involved in prioritization and to including other individuals or groups.	Identifying criteria for priorities may be difficult. It, like earlier activities in Phases 1 and 2, tends to require some soul searching by key players. In Chapter 5, a number of different techniques are described.
Identify and consider alternative solutions for the high-priority needs.	Management could consider participating in this aspect of the NA but as full participants, not as managers. Because solutions are carried out internally, management may see it as desirable to shift the leadership of the NAC to someone inside the organization.	Emphasizing alternative solutions tends to focus the NAC into more divergent, expansive thinking. Openness to new ideas and ways to handle problems can be exciting. Needs represent problems, but dealing with them also provides opportunities for the organization (see Chapter 6).
Assess human and material resources.	Management should be active here and should be able to provide valuable information about the resource picture.	Often there are more resources available in the organization or in the local environment than anticipated. All groups involved in the NA process should be alert to such possibilities.
Select an optimum solution strategy, develop action plans for implementation, and prepare a final NA report.	See above considerations.	At this point, a critical decision is made about redirecting resources and staff or seeking new resources. Note the next activity.

Inform all staff of progress and allow them the opportunity to offer suggestions and input.	Provide appropriate situations for staff members to be fully updated in regard to the NA process. Be open to new ideas and thoughts about final directions. It is important for staff to know that NA is a dynamic process and one that they can affect. Avoid any inclination to close off further staff input.	Staff buy-in beyond the NAC and management builds a broader base of support for change. This activity must convey a receptivity to staff ideas.
Evaluate the results of the NA process and look for ways to periodically reassess needs.	Management and the NAC need to review the entire NA effort and the results so obtained. Be a *loving critic*: What lessons were learned that would help to guide similar, future endeavors, and what are some pitfalls to avoid?	Many ways of collecting NA information were used that could be of value at a later date. In addition, some less important needs at this time might become more prominent in the future. Evaluations of the NA process and outcomes often are not undertaken.
Document the entire process and communicate results. (Note: in Figure 1.2, communication was the last part of Phase 3, whereas now we have placed it, as expressed above, earlier in the phase.)	In Phases 1 and 2 and throughout the NA, it is desirable to maintain an audit trail. Summaries of major events, reports, and copies of instrumentation will be useful. Documentation will potentially reduce the resources needed for the next NA. Management should allot time and resources for this activity and require that it be completed before signing off on the NA.	The placement of communication activity in an earlier part of this table seems to be more appropriate.

established and agreed on by the NAC prior to thinking about priorities. In many NAs, the procedures for setting priorities are far from ideal.

Because priorities determine future organizational directions and actions, a question arises as to who should do the prioritizing. The NAC is obviously one logical choice. By virtue of its involvement during the whole NA process, it has intimate knowledge of all deliberations, procedures, and results. The NAC should definitely be one of the groups that prioritizes. NAC membership could be expanded by the inclusion of a few key managers and informal power brokers in the organization. New members of the group would be less familiar with the NA, and therefore it would be helpful if they were supplied with a brief summary of the NA process and findings prior to their prioritizing.

Perhaps an even better alternative would be to have the managers, informal decision makers, and even outside constituencies (consumers, concerned citizens) constituted as independent rating groups. After briefing them, their independent ratings could be obtained and compared to those of the NAC. If the results were similar, the idea that priorities were commonly held across the organization would be strengthened. If not, it would be incumbent for the needs assessor and the NAC to find out why priorities differed and to reconcile those differences before the organization proceeds into developing action plans.

With prioritized needs in hand, the NAC turns its attention to identifying solution strategies and selecting one of them. A number of things are important here. First, the NAC can very quickly gravitate toward one solution and not seek or meaningfully consider others. Groups tend to want to move rapidly to a solution strategy without identifying and examining alternatives. The NAC may be tired and have a predisposition to get its work wrapped up as fast as possible. This does not represent the best situation for doing good analytical work in NA.

The problems we find in society, education, health, the delivery of health services, and many other areas in which NAs have been conducted can be complex and not easily resolved. Criteria for solutions will be numerous and multifaceted, and no one approach could fully meet all of them. Most techniques (see Chapter 6) for choosing a solution from among many alternatives require that weighted criteria for making that final selection be specified in advance. Each solution would then be rated in terms of the criteria, with the one receiving the highest ratings being the most likely choice.

Second, recognize that in Phase 3, the NA shifts from an externally guided process to one that has become internal and dependent on a strong internal buy-in by staff. Witkin (1984) described an NA that had been well implemented from a technical standpoint but failed due to being perceived as more in the domain of the outside consultant rather than being relevant to internal staff.

Third, commitment from administrators is essential. In 1985, Thomas and Altschuld conducted an NA that collected data for a nationwide business and industry consortium. To gain internal support, they included members of the central consortium staff in various parts of the NA. Staff developed ownership in the data and results that unfortunately could not be capitalized on due to a change in the leadership of the organization. The new administrators did not feel that the original reason for commissioning the NA fit their perceptions of what the organization should be doing at this time. Despite internal, lower-level support, the findings of the NA were tabled, and no actions were taken. (Thomas and Altschuld felt that the organization missed an opportunity that could have netted it millions of dollars in earnings.)

Fourth, although consultants have tremendous value early in the NA process in terms of their knowledge and expertise, that worth begins to diminish the further into Phase 3 the process moves. The organization is now developing action plans that require internal leadership. A possible way to deal with this problem would be to transfer leadership of the NAC in the middle of the phase to employees of the organization. They would assume responsibility for implementing any changes emanating from the results of the NA. It would be still desirable to maintain some involvement of the consultants but in more of a supportive role. The transfer of leadership is important, and it should be thought out and made explicit well before it takes place. Without it, the likelihood increases that the NA may have been a good exercise for the organization but one that accomplished little.

Fifth, along with a change in leadership, additional attention should be given to the composition of the NAC. Its task has changed from that of assessment to one of developing concrete plans for new directions for the organization. Does the NAC have the right mix of individuals to deal with what are now implementation concerns? If the answer is no, then with a small NAC it would be easy to expand membership by several individuals who have the expertise that would help with Phase 3 types of concerns. Such expansion may have been envisioned at the start of the NA process, and this course of action should have been made clear to the NAC at its initial meeting. If the NAC is large, adding members probably will not make much sense, and the group may have to be reconstituted. In either instance, there should be some continuing members who understand the history of what has taken place and the rationale behind important NAC decisions.

The choice of new members should be based on expertise and potential contributions and, of equal importance, on their personal characteristics. When they join the NAC, its members have been meeting and interacting for months or longer. Group chemistry has developed. Members understand each other and how to react to and interpret the comments, suggestions, and even the body language of their comembers. New individuals who do not get along well with others or who do not really perform well in group settings could easily upset the balance of what has become a productive, task-oriented working team. Much progress in the NA process would be lost by choosing the wrong persons. Therefore, new members should be included only if needed, and they should be selected with the greatest of care.

Another alternative that we would not recommend would be to include the action planners in the NAC right at the start of the NA. A point made earlier was that groups have a tendency to want to move quickly into solution strategies before needs or problems have been sufficiently analyzed and studied. Placing action planners on the NAC at the beginning would, in our judgment, exacerbate the press for premature closure and be detrimental to the NA process. Of course, local environments and the players in them are different, and the choice of NAC members and the timing of their involvement are always tempered by the specific context.

In Table 2.3, the third activity is really an overview of a more detailed set of steps. The NA is coming to fruition. A final report has been generated, and a solution, one with a high likelihood of resolving a priority need, has been identified, examined, and chosen. Information gained from Phases 1 and 2 has guided many of the steps in the NA process and continues to be of value for and influences the design of the action plan produced in Phase 3. There is, however, one aspect of all three phases of NA that is problematic, and it deals with developing awareness and support throughout the organization for the NA and the organizational activities that will result from it. Hence, it will be particularly important to focus on how such support can be achieved (the fourth activity in the table).

Modern institutions, especially in a technology- and information-driven society, are complex and limited in what can be accomplished by a top-down approach. To use education as an example, not so long ago a principal was considered to be the educational leader of the school (i.e., the individual who had extensive understanding of what was taught and how it was taught). That premise is no longer tenable. High school science now includes content that, until recently, was part of the undergraduate curriculum. Even at the elementary level, there are teachers who have specialized in mathematics and science instruction. The elementary or secondary principal frequently has to rely on teachers, supervisors, or staff at the district level for content knowledge and, as another example, for expertise in regard to computers (software, hardware, and computer-assisted instruction). The principal cannot be the fount of knowledge, and the role has gravitated more toward that of an administrator than the "educational leader" of another generation.

This observation easily extends to many business and industry situations as well as governmental services. With fast-moving technologies and rapid access to numerous sources of data and information, it is probable and indeed likely that the top levels of the organization will not be as well informed as they were in the past.

How, then, should the NA proceed to obtain staff involvement and support? (See Altschuld, Yoon, & Cullen, 1993, for ways of establishing administrative involvement and support.) First, regular communication to staff should be a goal. Short memos about progress or key events taking place are helpful. Second, activities in Phases 1 and 2 often require that data be collected from staff members via surveys, interviews, the use of databases they are responsible for, and so on. Thank you notes could be sent (even personalized where appropriate), and summaries generated from information provided by staff could be circulated back to them. People, for the most part, are curious and want to be informed about what is happening around them. Even simple ways of keeping them involved will be appreciated.

Lastly, in regard to communication, the use of formal meetings or debriefing sessions for staff is encouraged. The tone of the sessions should be open and characterized by a willingness to receive input and commentary about the NA process and its subsequent results. If possible, keep the size of each session to 25 or fewer so that discussion is facilitated. Start the meeting by briefly explaining the NA process, representation on the NAC, the major findings, the needs-based priorities, solutions that were considered, and final action plans. Some of the key aspects of NAC deliberations also should be described. Keep in mind that the results of an NA process are not set in stone. New ideas and thoughts should be considered as important additions to a dynamic ongoing endeavor.

The final two activities in Table 2.3 deal with evaluation of the NA project and its documentation. In most NAs, the end of the process is reached, physical and psychological energy are low, and no one wants to invest more time in evaluating and documenting everything that has taken place. After all, aren't the final NA report and the action plan documentation enough? Perhaps, but institutional memories are short, and the lessons learned from the NA may be lost when the organization next decides (3-4 years down the road) that it is time to reexamine its needs. Major players are no longer there, the consultant has moved on, and so forth. Without evaluation and adequate documentation, the long-term value of the NA has been severely reduced.

The need for adequate documentation cannot be overemphasized. Surveys may have been produced; sources of important, routinely kept, and easily available information have been located and accessed; key variables have been identified and operationalized; top and lower priorities have been determined with some of the latter possibly becoming high priorities 4 years in the future; and a myriad of other important NA activities have been completed. Clearly, the first place to start a new NA would be to review what was done previously. Can the NA instruments be updated and used anew? Are there variables from the first effort that ought to be examined again in relation to trends that are affecting the organization? Are there variables that we should routinely monitor? Have constituent groups changed enough that perhaps new ones should be included in Phase 2 activities at this time? To answer questions such as these, records would be invaluable, and management should insist that an NA documentation file be developed and several copies (electronic and hard) be archived.

Beyond documentation, what problems did the first NA encounter, how were they resolved, and what might be done differently in the new NA? These questions demonstrate why the evaluation of the NA itself is so important. NA does not conform to a rigid set of rules and specifications. Each NA must be adapted to fit the dimensions and subtleties of the organizational milieu in which it is conducted. Each one is unique and represents a learning experience for the organization. Certainly, the costs of the NA, the time required, and problems encountered have been observed, and an audit trail of what has transpired should be maintained for future endeavors. Minutes of meetings provide valuable insights about decisions that were made and the factors that influenced them. The minutes should be included in the archived materials from the NA.

Another useful way to evaluate the NA might be to conduct focus group interviews (FGIs) that are primarily debriefing sessions for the NAC. They should take place several weeks after the NA is completed and the NAC has had time to reflect on the experience. NAC members would be given a list of questions to think about several days or a week before the actual interviews. They would be directed to review the list and to come to the FGI with written notes about topics. Questions might include the following:

- What part of the NA process worked well, and why do you think it was successful?
- What part of the NA did not work well, and what do you think contributed to its unfavorable outcome?
- What information from the NA most influenced subsequent decisions and why?
- If we were to do the NA over, what would you have changed?

A summary from the FGIs in the form of recommendations to a future NAC could become a very good way to help them begin their deliberations.

CHAPTER SUMMARY

The three phases described in this chapter comprise the basic structure of NA. A great deal of emphasis here has been placed on management concerns, several subtle hidden issues in the process, and how some of the specific phase-related activities might be operationalized. Figure 2.3, a checklist for the three phases, has been provided to help facilitate keeping track of the NA process.

Undertaking an NA seems overwhelming, especially when the activities in Tables 2.1, 2.2, and 2.3 are viewed collectively. We understand that perception. It was a deliberate decision to present a comprehensive picture of the NA endeavor while acknowledging that the

Phase/Activities	Activity Completion		Notes, Issues, Comments
	Yes	No	
Phase 1—Preassessment			
Organizational interest is there			
Management is committed to the NA effort and to change			
NA leader has been identified			
NAC members representing diverse perspectives have been identified and selected			
Planning for first NAC meeting is completed			
NAC meetings provided a clear focus for the NA			
NAC and needs assessor have located sufficient information about the focus of the NA			
Data have been synthesized into a meaningful picture related to the needs area			
Phase 1 has been concluded			
Decisions to stop or move to Phase 2 or 3 have been made			
Results have been communicated to management			
Reasonable records have been kept and archived			
Phase 2—Assessment			
Phase 2 activities have been summarized by the needs assessor and reviewed by the NAC			
The target group focus (Levels 1, 2, and/or 3) for the NA have been specified			
End states for the levels have been specified			
Methodological options for collecting additional NA data have been considered			
Methods have been selected			
Additional NA data have been collected			
The data have been analyzed/collated/synthesized			
Preliminary priorities have been determined			
Causal analyses (even crude ones) have been performed			

Figure 2.3. Checklist for NA Activities

(continued)

41

Phase/Activities	Activity Completion		Notes, Issues, Comments
	Yes	No	
Phase 2 has been concluded			
Decisions regarding Phase 3 have been made			
Reasonable records have been kept			
Records have been archived			
Phase 3—Postassessment			
Nature of the NAC has been reconsidered			
NAC has been reconstituted, if necessary			
Final priorities have been set			
Solution options have been identified			
Criteria for selecting solutions have been specified			
Human and material resources have been assessed			
The solution that most satisfies the criteria has been selected			
Action plans for the solution have been developed			
Overview of the NA process and plans have been prepared for communicating with staff members and seeking their input			
Results have been communicated to staff in open forums			
Final plans have been developed based on input			
Strategies for evaluating the plans and the NA have been developed			
NA process and results have been evaluated			
Phase 3 has been concluded			
Decision to implement action plans is in progress			
Reasonable records have been kept			
All key results (including those from the evaluation of the NA itself) have been archived			

Figure 2.2 Continued

resources will not always be available to conduct all aspects of the NA process. Knowledge of the full process helped us as we made adaptations to specific contexts and levels of support. Organizations and individuals obviously have to do the same thing—tailor the process to fit local conditions and finances rather than being constrained by what might seem to be ideal parameters.

Chapter 3 begins about midway into Phase 2. It is guided by the assumption that Phase 1 activities have been completed and a decision has been made to collect additional data and information—in other words, to conduct Phase 2 activities. The first part of the chapter is focused on problems found in NA data, and from there it goes into the design and analysis of surveys.

NOTE

1. There are numerous sources in the literature that deal with how to plan and implement NA studies. For more perspectives on the NA process, we recommend that you also consult Kaufman (1992); Kaufman, Rojas, and Mayer (1993); McKillip (1987); Reviere, Berkowitz, Carter, and Ferguson (1996); Soriano (1995); Warheit, Bell, and Schwab (1979); and Witkin (1984).

DATA-RELATED ISSUES
AND SURVEY METHODS

SOME INITIAL THOUGHTS ABOUT NA DATA

Although some may think of needs assessment (NA) as research, to us it has always been a decision-oriented process that uses an array of techniques and procedures. Needs assessors are confronted with many subtle data-related problems emanating from the methods used and the definition of need as the measurable discrepancy between the *current* status and the *desirable* (or "what should be or ought to be") status. These problems could be classified into the categories described below.

ISSUES IN DETERMINING ESTIMATES OF CURRENT STATUS

1. *Many important variables in the assessment of social or educational needs are difficult to measure.* How do we determine current status regarding diet, drug abuse, smoking, alcoholism, drunk driving, child abuse, mental health, and other similar types of variables? Further-

more, if multiple methods are employed to ascertain current status, vastly different estimates of baseline conditions often are observed. This compounds our ability to understand what is happening. Look at how the current status is measured for one variable, driving while under the influence of alcohol (DUI), where most of the information comes from arrest records with DUI as the offense. The records indicate only how many people were caught DUI, not how many were on the road at any given time (Fitzpatrick, 1992). If data about the prevalence of DUI as derived from these records were extrapolated to the entire population, the predicted number of drunk drivers out there would seriously underestimate the actual number (kind of a scary proposition!).

2. *The measurement of current status may be neither valid nor reliable.* Many times, *self-report* data are the source of current status information. If people were asked (via survey or interview) about behaviors such as smoking, drinking, using drugs, exercising, and other related variables, would they tell the truth, and would their responses vary so much over time that it is not possible to develop a clear and reliable picture of current status? (See Anderson, Jesswein, & Fleischman, 1990, for a discussion of the problems in self-report data obtained from service recipients and service providers and cautions that should be used in interpreting them.) Suppose we measured weekend eating patterns by asking individuals on Monday what they had eaten over the prior 2 days. Would they honestly tell us? Would they give us the same information if asked again? (Isn't it convenient to "forget" that candy bar you snacked on the other day?)

3. *The determination of current status comes from different information sources that do not agree.* Work done by Goering and Lin (1996) provided a good illustration of this problem. They determined the current status of mental health treatment in Ontario (Canada) by accessing multiple independent databases and found that although relationships across the bases were apparent, different ways of collecting data led to varied approximations of current status. For example, in one base, the estimation of current status was derived from interviews of the general

population, whereas in another it came from physician records, and there was disagreement across the two sets of information.

ISSUES IN DETERMINING THE WHAT IS
DESIRABLE OR WHAT SHOULD BE CONDITION

1. What is the standard for a what should be condition? In the health field, as an illustration, standards for blood pressure, pulse rates, and immunization levels for children are straightforward and arise from years of research and practice. Yet even in health, it is not always a simple matter to arrive at standards. What is a reasonable level of physical activity or wellness? In other fields, it is more difficult to come up with reasonable, agreed-on standards. What are desirable levels of mathematics or science achievement for American students? In many NAs, the standards for the what is desirable ("what should be") condition come from judgments or comparisons to other situations rather than empirical study.

2. Confusing what should be conditions with wants. When individuals or groups are asked "what should be," they often respond with wants and wish lists. The real world, whatever it is, does not seem to be pertinent to their what should be conditions. If questions were worded in a manner that asked about "what ought to occur" or "what is likely to be expected," the responses may be less in terms of wants or wishes and more in regard to realistic expectations. Still, there would be a tendency to drift to the want or wish list side of the equation. (This may not necessarily be bad. Sometimes in NA, we dream and shoot for the moon. In education, as a case in point, some would argue that to strive for the achievement of minimum standards will lead to just that—the attainment of only minimum standards.) For most NA situations, however, it is probably better to use wording that reduces the tendency toward wish list responses.

3. Obtaining consistently high survey ratings for all what should be questions. NA surveys usually contain prestructured, scaled questions that call for ratings regarding the importance of the items in a set. The needs assessor or NAC has spent a great deal of time studying the area of concern and identifying potentially important aspects of it to be included on the survey. Because of this *prestructuring*, respondents tend to give high ratings to all of the what should be questions so that little differentiation is observed between the means of items. That is, the ratings of items are clustered on the positive end of the scale (usually toward 5 on a Likert scale), and negatively skewed distributions result for the what should be condition.

ISSUES IN DETERMINING DISCREPANCIES

1. *Discrepancies are determined in terms of wants and/or relative what should be status.* It is sometimes difficult to know if needs have been identified, especially if the what should be status reflects wants rather than realistic expectations. The size of discrepancies tends to be enlarged when the former condition exists.

2. *What about the size and nature of a discrepancy before it can be considered a need?* NA procedures will uncover many discrepancies, some of which may or may not require attention. What are the decision rules that help us to determine whether a discrepancy really represents a high-priority need? (See Chapter 5 in regard to setting needs-based priorities and subsequent aspects of this chapter that deal with indices of needs.)

3. *Developing discrepancies from multiple sources of input.* In the NA carried out by Goering and Lin (1996), four sources of data were used to define the current level of treatment in mental health. In many NAs, this is a typical situation, with data coming from a variety of groups and methodological techniques. The needs assessor somehow has to construct meaning from disparate sources of information.

4. *It may not be possible to calculate discrepancies.* Not all NA data can be transformed into discrepancies. Qualitative techniques (e.g., the nominal group technique, focus group interviews, individual interviews, etc.) do not produce discrepancy-type data. Needs are inferred rather than directly calculated from the data generated from these techniques. At times, even quantitative data may not lead to discrep-

ancies. Surprisingly, many NA surveys do not contain what is and what should be scales, and therefore the calculation of discrepancies is not possible.

ISSUES THAT CUT ACROSS ALL ASPECTS OF NA

1. Multiple sources, multiple groups, multiple headaches. We have consistently advocated the use of multiple (mixed) methods for NA and collecting data from multiple groups. We feel that it is not possible to fully understand the nature and extent of either the current or desired status from a single source of information. To us, NA is a prime candidate for the use of multiple methods. It is not uncommon for one NA to include focus group interviews, interviews with key informants, nominal groups, surveys, analyses of existing records, census reports and public databases, databases compiled by commercial institutions, planning groups, United Way projections, observations, and so forth.

The needs assessor seeks pertinent information from wherever it is available. That information, however, may neither triangulate nor be complementary in the sense proposed by Greene, Caracelli, and Graham (1989). Moreover, existing data sets, reports, and summaries may have been collected for purposes other than the assessment of need. Subtlety in definitions and data collection procedures (e.g., sampling, instrumentation, wording of questions, return rates, etc.) will require care in interpreting how the information relates to the area of need. Does it really relate? Does it truly fit the focus of the NA? Further complicating this mix is the fact that each source has error inherent in it.

In addition, subtle variations in one technique might be employed to obtain information from varied constituencies and groups. In an educational NA, surveys might be administered to four distinct groups—parents, students, teachers, and community leaders. Although the same general questions will be used, they tend to be slightly different, with the wording and format tailored to the perspectives of each constituent group. This within-method variation could be contrasted with a between-methods NA in which different methods were used with each group. Keeping in mind that different methods or variations within a method might produce different outcomes, the complex landscape of NA becomes immediately apparent.

Interpretation of data from different constituencies may be difficult. Anderson et al. (1990) compared responses about needs given by service providers to those from members of the general community. They suggested that in certain categories, providers tended to overstate needs (transportation), whereas community members may have understated them in others (spousal, substance abuse). They postulated that needs assessors may have to weight responses by respondent group, depending on the specific content of questions included in surveys and interviews.

Multiple methods (between-methods), within-method variations, and data from multiple constituencies are part of the practical world of NA. They make NA difficult and exciting at the same time. The needs assessor has to assemble a coherent picture from data that, in the worst of cases, may be in conflict. Despite issues with their use, multiple methods reduce reliance on the single measure and help us to more fully comprehend and appreciate the nature of needs.

2. Placing undue emphasis on numerical data. This problem is not to be seen as an attack on numbers or statistics for we routinely incorporate numerical data and statistical analyses in our NAs. Instead, our point is that it is easy to overemphasize the value and quality of numerical information.

Several examples will make this clear. In 1997, counselors at The Ohio State University favored a system of reporting sexual assault that would include incidents described to them as well as those on official signed complaints (Caruso, 1997). Undoubtedly, the current system leads to a lower (by some unknown magnitude) prevalence of sexual assault than would the proposed one. (Similarly, Fisher noted that in 1998, Ohio University changed the way it calculated rape and assault statistics so that a higher and probably a truer prevalence of this crime would be reported. This honesty could affect the university's enrollment, for it would appear to have an unusually high rate of such crimes when compared to other institutions.)

Other examples relating to problems associated with numerical data have been cited in articles in the *Wall Street Journal*. In 1997, the *Journal* carried two articles dealing with hospital billing practices and how the consumer price index (CPI) is determined. Both of the articles emphasized caution when interpreting numerical data.

Lagnado (1997) defined the upcoding of illnesses by hospitals as "upgrading the seriousness of a medical malady by filing Medicare bills under the DRG (diagnosis related group) code that will carry the highest price" (p. B1). According to Lagnado, upcoding appeared to be endemic in billing procedures. If one were conducting an NA that relied on a sampling of hospital billing records, then the severity of health problems would be overestimated. Without understanding upcoding and the process by which records are created, the records would be misinterpreted.

Duff (1997) commented on the problems associated with the CPI, a critical statistic affecting all U.S. citizens. She observed that the CPI may not realistically reflect consumer prices and may exaggerate inflation by as much as 1.1%. Because the CPI has an impact on Social Security, the Federal Reserve, benefits to individuals, salary increases in companies, and many other dimensions of the government and life, a 1.1% differential would have a serious ripple effect on the entire U.S. economy. But the political consequences of changing the CPI would be enormous.

Aside from arguments about the formulas and models used to estimate the CPI, an even more basic problem is the nature of the data used to produce the index and how the data are obtained. Critics point out that when the price of a commodity such as chicken rises, consumers begin to substitute beef in their diets if its price has remained stable during the same time period. By the same token, the index does not take into account that although the cost of a new computer has not changed in 2 years, the newer model is more powerful and sophisticated than the one purchased earlier.

Duff (1997) also described how CPI data are collected. Part-time employees are paid $12.50 per hour to comparison shop and conduct field interviews. Because some latitude is given to the employees and the list of 207 categories of goods tracked for the CPI is updated once every 10 years, the potential for error in data collection and thus in the index itself is sizable. The ubiquitous cellular phones that are now everywhere are not included in the current CPI. (Note: Kadlec, in 1998, indicated that the Bureau of Labor Statistics has compiled a new list of market basket goods for the CPI.)

As a last thought here, consider statistics about crime. For years readers of newspapers have been bombarded with conflicting ideas about the rate of crime in the country. The problems in interpreting what are seemingly rudimentary numbers caught the attention of the late columnist Mike Royko. In a playful, tongue-in-cheek vein, he suggested that "it's simple: Crime is down because prison population is up" (Royko, 1997, p. 9A). We are neither as imaginative, cynical, skeptical, nor as creative as Royko. Our position with regard to numerical data is that they are an important source of information, but interpretation and meaning should be assigned to them only when needs assessors understand how the data were collected.

MOVING BEYOND ISSUES
TO KEY QUESTIONS

The following are five key questions that are frequently asked about NA methods and data analysis:

What methods are available?

How do the methods fit into the NA I am conducting, or what would be my best choices for conducting this specific NA?

Are there special ways to handle the data from the most commonly used NA method, the survey?

How do I begin to work with and understand needs from quantitative sources other than surveys and from data generated through the use of qualitative methods? (In the latter instance, needs will be inferred rather than directly measured.)

How do I pull together this jigsaw puzzle of results into a usable body of information for making needs-based decisions and developing programs to resolve high-priority needs?

For the first two questions, McKillip (1987), Witkin and Altschuld (1995), and Berkowitz (1996) have provided extensive listings of NA methods. McKillip described a large number of them and developed a flowchart for their selection within the NA context. Similarly, Witkin and Altschuld discussed more than 22 methods, including the causal analysis of needs, and their book contained the steps necessary to implement procedures, summaries of how to analyze data, and illustrative cases regarding the methods. Berkowitz posed questions that are asked in NA and related them to methods for collecting data.

It is not necessary to repeat what has been covered elsewhere. The earlier writings are recommended as guides for selecting and learning how to use numerous methods. Many other references are available for a host of methods that could be applied to NA situations, although the methods were not solely designed for NA work. Given the richness of existing sources, the remainder of this chapter is focused as follows.

For the third question, the technique most often used in NA is the survey (Witkin, 1994). Somewhere between 60% and 70% of all NAs employ the technique. Therefore, the nature of survey design in NA will be examined at some length. Well-constructed NA surveys contain (at a minimum) double-scaled items that ask for ratings about current and desired status, in accord with the definition of need (the measurable discrepancy between . . .). With two scores for each item, it is possible to calculate a numerical discrepancy or an index of need. Many ways of analyzing survey data and deriving the index of need are treated next in this chapter.

(The fourth and fifth questions are dealt with in Chapter 4. It ends with brief vignettes of results arising from the use of multiple methods in NA. We look at interpretation when results agree and what might be done when they do not. We hope that our suggestions about the latter situation will be helpful.)

SOME POINTERS REGARDING
CONSTRUCTION OF THE NA SURVEY

One way of constructing an NA survey is to take advantage of double-scaled items. Double scaling requires ratings of both the current and the desired status for an item. Hamann (1997) distinguished these "discrepancy" items from "preference" items that use a single-scale format that ascertains only the importance of goals or a sense of need (e.g., "Which of the following activities need to be undertaken?"). Discrepancies cannot be determined from the single-scale preference format. Preference items are frequently used in NA. In general, Likert-type (5-point) scales are employed for the single-scale and double-scaled formats.

In 1997, Hamann and Altschuld conducted a study that compared the two formats. The priorities determined from the double-scaled format were markedly different from those obtained from the preference format. This outcome is supportive of the idea that the double-scaled format is superior for NA. It has higher face validity and fits the definition of need, but there are subtle problems with its use that will be explained shortly.

The format of NA items does not have to be limited to two dimensions. Misanchuk (1982) suggested that more scales could be added, and in this vein, Scissons (1982) felt that three components of a need should be assessed—desired status, current status, and motivation to deal with a problem area. Other scales might relate to the costs of resolving a need and the likelihood of needs continuing into the future. In Figures 3.1a and 3.1b, two ways of presenting double-scaled questions are shown. (If three or more scales are used, place the

Figure 3.1a

The What Should Be Scale 1 2 3 4 5	Item Number and Stem	The What Is Scale 1 2 3 4 5
	1. _____	
	2. _____	
	3. _____	
	4. _____	
	5. _____	
	6. _____	
	7. _____	

Figure 3.1b

Item Number and Stem	The What Should Be Scale 1 2 3 4 5	The What Is Scale 1 2 3 4 5
1. _____		
2. _____		
3. _____		
4. _____		
5. _____		
6. _____		
7. _____		

Figure 3.1. Alternative Versions of the Double-Scaled NA Survey Format

content in the stem of the item on the left side of the page and the scales on the right.)

In developing versions of an NA instrument for comparing the single-scaled and double-scaled formats, Hamann (1997) paid careful attention to the overall organization of the instrument and how questions were framed (presented to the respondents). Both of these aspects are important for the design of any NA survey.

In regard to organization, respondents should rate items placed in self-contained, distinct categories denoted by category headings. For example, if the NA focused on school achievement, items dealing with mathematics, science, and reading should be clustered together. Items should be kept within their categories and not mixed. This simple and apparent detail of design, which should reduce respondent confusion, is often overlooked. Hamann (1997) used the following categories in an NA survey in mental health: consumer satisfaction with services, consumer involvement in treatment, psychological symptoms, relationships with other people, independent functioning and well-being, and family involvement.

It may be desirable to have participants rank order or weight the relative importance of the categories themselves. With rankings, it would be possible to weight the value of the needs in different categories. Altschuld et al. (1985) used a double-scaled NA format in an evaluation of administrative performance. The instrument was divided into six major categories. When the overall mean ratings of importance ratings for the categories were reviewed, it was evident that some categories were of much higher value (priority) than others. If the calculation of an index of need for an item were weighted in accord with the value of a category, subsequent needs-based decisions would be affected.

When should respondents be asked to rank order or weight categories? In the Hamann (1997) study, respondents ranked the categories prior to actually looking at the items in each category. Hamann (personal communication, 1997) felt that it would be better to have respondents do the ranking after they had completed the survey and thereby gained greater understanding of its content. We agree that rankings would be more meaningful if respondents were to rank order categories at the end of the survey.

Wording of the scales is also critical for producing high-quality NA data. Sometimes needs assessors use scales labeled "Importance" (desired status) and "Achievement" (current status) and then develop discrepancies accordingly. This process is based on the assumption that subtracting the results of one scale from the other is reasonable, is easy to do, and makes good common sense. *It may not be so reasonable!*

Importance and achievement are, after all, two different entities, and subtracting one from the other may be neither legitimate nor logical. One way to partially get around this difficulty is through the wording of the scales. Instead of importance and achievement, the two scales should contain many of the same words or very similar wording. One illustration of such scaling, adopted from Witkin and Altschuld (1995), is shown as follows:

What should students in your grade be able to do now? (Desired status)

What are students in your grade currently able to do? (Current status)

(Students provided two responses for each of a series of 5-point, behaviorally anchored items.)

Another example required students to specify how many hours should be spent daily on school-related activities (what should be) versus how many hours are actually spent on such activities (current status).

Hamann (1997) developed items that reflect this concern for scale wording. Respondents were required to rate the extent to which it was important to measure a certain aspect of mental health and the extent to which it was currently being measured.

Many other features of instrument design enhance the survey process in NA. Attending to the nature of cover letters, appeal of the topic to respondents, visual layout, logical flow of questions, sampling procedures, follow-up strategies, and 101 other aspects of surveys in general (and NA surveys specifically) all contribute to the successful implementation of a survey study. For considerations like these, well-known survey texts such as those by Salant and Dillman (1994) and Fowler (1993) should be consulted for additional guidance on the development and use of surveys.

Many other options for structuring scaled NA questions are possible. Likert-type scales do not necessarily have to be used. Witkin, Richardson, Sherman, and Lehnen (1979) provided excellent examples of behaviorally anchored types of scales that have been implemented in NAs. One such scale is depicted in Figure 3.2.

Circle two answers for each item. Example:

What you can do now   A Ⓑ C D E

What students in your grade should be doing   A B C Ⓓ E

In the library, I find books...					
25	A only with someone's help.	B Between A and C	C by using the card catalog.	D Between C and E	E by using the card catalog and reference guides.	A B C D E
In the library, students in my grade should find books...						A B C D E
Information about different careers or jobs: I know...						A B C D E
26	A little or nothing about jobs or careers.	B Between A and C	C something about the skills required.	D Between C and E	E all about the rewards and requirements.	A B C D E
Information about different careers or jobs: Students in my grade should know...						A B C D E
Plans for future career and training: I have...						A B C D E
27	A no ideas for a career or training.	B Between A and C	C some ideas for careers and training.	D Between C and E	E a future career picked out; detailed plans for training.	A B C D E
Plans for future career and training: Students in my grade should have...						A B C D E
Consumer education: I know how to...						A B C D E
28	A open a checking account.	B Between A and C	C A, and cash checks using proper ID.	D Between C and E	E A, C, and balance a checkbook.	A B C D E
Consumer education: Students in my grade should know how to...						A B C D E
Foreign language class: I understand my teacher...						A B C D E
29	A only when teacher speaks English.	B Between A and C	C only when teacher speaks slowly, simply.	D Between C and E	E however quickly teacher speaks, no matter what is said.	A B C D E ☐ I don't take this subject.
Foreign language class: Students in this subject should understand their teacher...						A B C D E

Figure 3.2. Behaviorally Anchored Rating Scales (BARS) Using a Two-Response Discrepancy Format

SOURCE: Witkin et al. (1979). Used by permission.
NOTE: From the APEX Needs Assessment Survey for Secondary School Students.

Another option would be for the needs assessor and the NAC to consider using magnitude estimation scaling (MES). When a Likert-type scale is employed, the difference between a 4 and a 5 may be much greater for many respondents than the difference between a 2 and a 3. In other words, equidistances on the scale are not equidistances in the minds of respondents. For both of the authors, the difference between 4 and 5 is of a much greater magnitude than circling 3 instead of 2. Indeed, some respondents may be thinking in ratio terms rather than equal intervals when they select scale points.

MES is a form of scaling that allows surveyors to capitalize on this ratio way of thinking. In MES, the first item or anchor is given an arbitrary value such as 50. Then the respondent is asked to compare each of the remaining items to the anchor. If the respondent feels that the item is twice as important as the anchor, he or she is instructed to give it a value of 100, or a 25 if it is perceived as being one half as important, a 10 if of one fifth the importance, and so forth. The responses are always in terms of ratios of the anchor item value. Because ratio scores are involved, a modified version of a geometric mean is calculated for each item.

MES tends to work best when a group is trained through a series of cross-modality exercises in which they are taught to think in terms of ratios. Cross-modality training might start with looking at the length of lines (this line is twice as great as the length of the anchor line) and then move into other examples tied to the specific content focus of the NA. Due to the sensitivity gained through training, MES may not work well for mail surveys or phone interviews.

Yet another way to set up scale points is to have them represent the *percentage* or degree to which an area should be achieved and the extent to which it is achieved. Even further, Witkin (1975) proposed putting a short, factually oriented paragraph describing some of the background about a set of questions prior to having respondents answer the questions. This type of explanatory paragraph, which would be placed before each new section of the survey, would tend to ensure that respondents' ratings come from a common frame of reference. Although this approach has the advantage of creating some level of equal knowledge on the part of respondents, it increases the length of the survey and the time necessary to complete it, and it could possibly attenuate the return rate for a mailed survey.

All of these options (as well as many others) for scaling and formatting surveys are viable choices for and have been used in NA contexts. Certainly, as the survey is being planned, all options should be considered.

ANALYZING THE DATA: CALCULATING A NUMERICAL NEEDS INDEX

THE SIMPLEST WAY: DIFFERENCES BETWEEN MEANS

The easiest way to analyze survey data is to produce a table such as Table 3.1. In the table, the current status mean has been subtracted from the desired status mean for each item, and then the items have been placed in rank order, beginning with the largest positive discrepancies down to the highest negative discrepancies. (A negative discrepancy, one in which current status is higher than desired status, usually raises a red flag about resources that are perhaps being expended for overachievement of the particular emphasis of the item.) The table should include the numbers of individuals completing both scales for each item, which would be especially important for interpreting results.

There are several caveats to stress in regard to the table. First, if the survey has been distributed to multiple constituencies, separate tables should be constructed for each and then compared. Combining all the groups into one table blurs what may be important distinctions or similarities among them. Second, P. Thomas (personal communication, March 1997) observed that many times with the double-scaled format, respondents do not complete one or both of the scales for an item. For example, suppose that 75 respondents rate the desired status for an item, whereas only 45 provide ratings for the "what is" scale. Calculating the discrepancy by subtracting the mean for what is based

Table 3.1 Differences Between Means

Item Number and Stem	Mean for the What Should Be Status	Number of Respondents	Mean for the What Is Status	Number of Respondents	Size of Discrepancy[a]	Rank Order of Discrepancy
14. _____	4.45	52	2.85	41	1.60	1
8. _____	4.76	55	3.19	38	1.57	2
23. _____	3.67	43	2.35	28	1.32	3
3. _____	4.42	53	3.20	44	1.22	4
_____						
_____						
15. _____	2.85	51	3.78	35	-.93	34

a. Based on the subtraction of unweighted means.

on 45 individuals from the mean based on 75 individuals introduces bias into the resulting index of need. In her work, Thomas reported discrepancies determined only from those individuals who had completed both scales.

The numbers of people who did not respond to either or both scales are very important pieces of information. Large numbers of nonrespondents to both suggest a lack of interest in or awareness of the topic. (With regard to awareness, we sometimes have included choices such as DK, don't know, or NA, not applicable, on our surveys.) Some respondents may not have completed the double-scaled items because they were unfamiliar with or intimidated by the format. If large numbers did not rate current status, it may signify that they have opinions about what should be, but they have limited knowledge about what is currently taking place. The missing data provide information and are significant for interpreting NA results.

Its value cannot be underestimated. In the Hamann (1997) study, return rates were somewhat lower for the double-scaled format when compared to the preference items, even for supposedly knowledgeable individuals. Consumers of mental health services in her sample were administered single-scaled and double-scaled surveys in group settings at conferences and statewide meetings. She obtained considerably lower completion rates for the double-scaled format. In addition, she noticed that respondents required a lot more time to complete that format, many did not do so, and numerous questions were asked about the nature of the double scaling. Given these observations, we recommend that formats be tested with different constituent groups before the use of a survey in NA. The double-scaled format may not be appropriate for some respondent groups.

In addition to Table 3.1, Witkin and Altschuld (1995) provided another way of portraying the data collected from surveys. Figure 3.3 is a grid in which the results of two groups are shown on a question-by-question basis. The right side of each bar on the grid represents the what should be status for the group, and the left side represents the current status. With this graphing approach, the discrepancies are

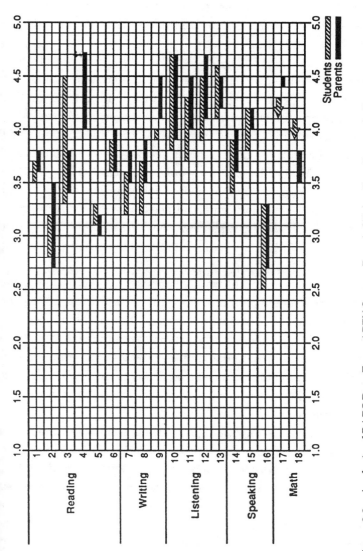

Figure 3.3. Analysis of BARS Data From APEX Survey, Part A, With a Two-Response Discrepancy Format
SOURCE: Witkin & Richardson (1983, pp. 22-23). Used by permission.
NOTE: Comparison of median scores from student and parent questionnaires.

immediately discernible. Bars with an arrow pointing to the left indicate that the current status is higher than the desired one.

Table 3.1 and Figure 3.3 are based on the direct subtraction of the current status mean from the desired status mean. They are related ways of portraying the same data.

The table has the advantage of displaying the rank orders of items, the size of the discrepancy, the current and desired mean values, and the size of the group doing both ratings. Its disadvantages are that tables must be done separately for each constituency, and it would be possible for a very large discrepancy to occur for an item rated somewhat low (3.5) on desired status and very low (1.5) on current status. This 2-point discrepancy would rank relatively high in the order of discrepancies, but the ranking violates a general rule of data analysis in NA—the most important needs would tend to be those with high *what should be* scores and with low *current status* scores. What should be is the "necessary" or essential condition for first looking at the size of a discrepancy.

Figure 3.3 is an excellent way of summarizing the data, but one could lose sight of the varying *n*s per item, and with a lot of items, the figure may be a little difficult for some members of committees who are not visually oriented. Both the table and the figure fail to take into account the nature of the underlying scale and the unique opportunity for analysis afforded by double-scaled, 5-point formats. Such formatting has led to two other indices of need—the means-difference analysis and weighted needs index (WNI).

Before leaving the simplest form of calculating the needs index, one additional and subtle problem merits attention. There is, as stated previously, a proclivity for respondents to rate what should be fairly high for most items. After all, the needs assessor has carefully chosen and prestructured the survey items based on prior study of the important aspects of the need area. As a result, what should be scores (means) from surveys usually cluster into a narrow range near the top of the scale, leading to leptokurtic, negatively skewed distributions. Discrepancies, therefore, are largely a function of the means from the what is status only. Such leptokurtic distributions were observed in the Hamann (1997) study.

One sophisticated way of handling this situation would be to perform log transformations for the what should be and current status scores and then calculate the discrepancies from transformed scores. This normalizes the distributions, thereby reducing leptokurtosis and skewness in obtained data. Yet even with the transformed scores, it is unlikely that major shifts in rank orders would occur from what is observed in straightforward, simple discrepancies.

MEANS-DIFFERENCE ANALYSIS

The use of means-difference analysis (MDA) is very similar to the concept of effect size in meta-analysis. The scores obtained from the what should be and what is questions are seen as representing two separate scales. They are summed, the averages are calculated, and the difference between the averages is then determined, leading to a simplified proxy for effect size. Then, for each item, the difference for the what should be and what is score is calculated and compared to the effect size. If it is larger, it is denoted with a plus (+) sign in an NA table (see Table 3.2). MDA employs a standard derived from the total data of the survey. In general, from the standpoint of effect size, the mean difference determined across all items from the two scales would have to be approaching one standard deviation to be meaningful.

A form of MDA was used in the aforementioned evaluation of administrative performance (Altschuld et al., 1985). To highlight what were the largest differences, standard errors of the means for the what should be and what is scales were determined. One standard error was added to the mean for what should be, and one standard error was subtracted from the mean of the what is scale—creating an even larger effect size that had to be achieved for each discrepancy. This more stringent criterion for the mean difference obtained for each individual item was justified in that falsely identifying an item as a need has a high amount of risk, especially in a personnel context. If an item exceeds such a criterion, the needs assessors were more certain

Table 3.2 Means-Difference Analysis

Item Number and Stem	Mean for the What Should Be Status	Number of Respondents	Mean for the What Is Status	Number of Respondents	Size of Discrepancy[a]	Exceeds Discrepancy Standard of 1.20 in Means (+)
1. _____	4.30	75	3.09	60	1.21	(+)
2. _____	3.90	69	3.23	61	.67	
3. _____	4.55	72	3.86	57	.69	
4. _____	4.68	70	3.20	65	1.48	(+)
12. _____	3.65	68	2.38	49	1.27	(+)
23. _____	2.90	56	3.79	40	-1.1	

a. Based on the subtraction of unweighted means.

66

that it truly represents a need. This was judged to be the appropriate strategy for looking at discrepancies in administrative performance.

The advantages of MDA are that tables are easy to construct, and the standard is derived from the entire set of the data. In addition, only items with a substantial difference will show enough strength to exceed the standard. The disadvantage is that mean difference for an item with a relatively lower score for the what should be status could still attain a plus (+) value (see item 12 in Table 3.2). The other disadvantage is that the analysis does not use all of the information produced by respondents.

THE WEIGHTED NEEDS INDEX AND PROPORTIONAL REDUCTION IN ERROR

The WNI, developed by Cummings (1985), is a derivation of an index proposed by Misanchuk in 1982, which, in turn, is based on a statistical approach known as proportionate reduction in error (PRE) (Hildebrand, Laing, & Rosenthal, 1977a, 1977b). To understand the thinking underlying WNI and PRE, issues affecting other indices of need must be explained. First, other indices were based on the assumption that the data were interval or nearly interval in nature and that means could be calculated. This may not be appropriate for the actual level of measurement. PRE makes few assumptions about the level of measurement.

Second, in using means (central tendencies), some information from the data set is lost. A PRE-based index uses all the information contained in the data from an item in arriving at a measure of need. Third, a PRE type of index can be compared to an absolute statistical standard. In other indices—the MDA, for example—the standard varies from one data set to another. To follow the concept behind PRE, examine the two matrices shown in Figures 3.4a and 3.4b.

The values above the columns represent the what should be scale, with 1 standing for very low on the dimension and 5 being the top value. The values for the rows go from 1 (the current status is very

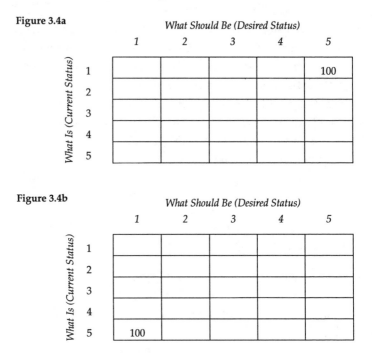

Figure 3.4. The What Should Be and What Is Matrices

low) to 5 (the current status is very high). In Figure 3.4a, let us assume that 100 people were rating an item on the two dimensions, and all of them gave the item a 5 for the what should be scale and a 1 for current status. The 100 in cell 5,1 is the frequency of respondents who have made the 5,1 choice when responding to the item. Similarly, a matrix display could then be created for every item contained in the survey.

If a decision was made regarding whether the data depicted in Figure 3.4a indicated a need, it would be virtually certain that a need was there. The decision makers would have total faith (100% certainty) in saying that the data from the item represented a need. That is, they would feel that there was zero chance (.00 probability) of making an error if they stated that this item was a high need.

The data shown in Figure 3.4b provide a striking contrast. The 100 respondents have chosen responses that fit cell 1,5. All of them felt that the item was lowest in terms of desired status and highest in terms of current status. By no stretch of the imagination could this response pattern be construed as representing a need. The decision makers would be 100% assured that if they chose this item as a need, they would have perfect probability (1.0) of being in error.

This is the rationale of PRE. For high needs, responses would have to fall in the cells in the upper right-hand corner of the 5 × 5 matrix. As the response pattern moves further and further away from that corner of the matrix, the support for an item as a need starts decreasing. As responses fall into the lower left-hand corner, the decision makers are able to rule out the item as indicating a need to which they should attend. Using PRE as the premise for analysis, Misanchuk (1982) developed an index (the del statistic) that can attain values ranging from 1.00 to minus infinity. Values high and close to 1 represent need, and as the values decrease from 1.0, the need becomes less. Low values, zero, and values below zero are not needs.

To calculate the del statistic, it is necessary to weight each cell using a linear progression of weights, starting with 0.0 for the upper right corner cell (5,1). This weight would represent the fact that there is total certainty of not making an error if all the responses fall into this cell. The weights progressively get larger as you move diagonally down the matrix toward the left-hand lower corner, where the assigned weight is 1.00 or total certainty (a probability of 1.00) of making an error. All cells in the matrix receive weights, which are used in subsequent calculations involving observed cell frequencies. Figure 3.5 is a matrix that shows the weights that are traditionally assigned to the cells.

Misanchuk (1982) calculated the del statistic for data collected regarding training in a business and industry setting. (Note: he made some additional assumptions about the marginal column and row totals, which were used in the specific numerical formulas for calculating a modified PRE index.) In his work, many of the del statistics never exceeded values of +.25. Misanchuk suggested that this was

What Should Be (Desired Status)

		1	2	3	4	5
	1	.7071	.5303	.3536	.1768	.0000
	2	.7289	.5590	.3953	.2500	.1768
What Is	3	.7906	.6374	.5000	.3953	.3536
	4	.8839	.7500	.6374	.5590	.5303
	5	1.0000	.8839	.7906	.7289	.7071

Figure 3.5. Error Weights for Use With the PRE Technique
SOURCE: Misanchuk (1982). Used by permission.

because his respondents were successful workers who would rate many job tasks as highly desirable, and because they were successful, the current status for job tasks would not be low.

The advantages of the del statistic are evident. First, although computational formulas have not been presented, they are easy to use and computer algorithms for the details exist. Second, the comparative metric (ranging from 1.0 to negative infinity) always stays the same irrespective of the specific data set. Third, the entire distribution of responses enters into the calculations, and few assumptions about the level of measurement are made. The disadvantage is that for decision-making audiences, values that go from 1.00 (very understandable) to minus infinity (seemingly unintelligible for some groups) may be daunting or even intimidating.

Cummings (1985) developed an alternative index that would alleviate the latter deficiency. He proposed that the only part of the matrix that is important for selecting needs is the upper right-hand corner—that is, the cells that hover around the cell 5,1 (i.e., those cells that represent high desired status and low realized or current status). Almost always, most of the attention focuses on this area anyway. Cummings also noticed that the cell weights employed in PRE computations affect the nature of the size and sign of the resulting index.

To provide a readily understandable index, Cummings (1985) focused attention on the cells in the upper right-hand corner and disre-

| | | | | *What Should Be* | | |
		1	2	3	4	5
What Is	1	0	0	.791	.884	1.000
	2	0	0	.637	.750	.884
	3	0	0	0	.637	.791
	4	0	0	0	0	0
	5	0	0	0	0	0

Figure 3.6. Error Weights for Calculation of the Weighted Needs Index (WNI)
SOURCE: Cummings (1984). Adapted with permission.

garded the rest of the cells in the matrix. In other words, he used only part of the data—but a critical part. Then, he simply reversed the weights so that the upper right-hand corner now had a cell weight of 1.0 and the other nearby cells had high weights that became progressively lower as they were more distant from the corner cell (see Figure 3.6). To analyze the data, he developed a WNI index computational formula, as shown below, and calculated the high and low limits of the statistic that ranged from 0 (no need) to 5 (highest need).

$$\text{Weighted needs index (WNI)} = \frac{\sum_{i=1}^{3} \sum_{j=3}^{5} f_{ij} \, v_{ij}}{N}$$

where f_{ij} = frequency of responses in a given cell (i = rows, j = columns), V_{ij} = the assigned for a given cell, and N = total number of people responding to an item (Cummings, 1984).

Lastly, Cummings (1985) compared the results from MDA, PRE (the del statistic), and WNI analyses based on data collected in a business and industry setting. If the list of needs was long, there was a high degree of correlation between the rank order of needs chosen, regardless of the technique used to compute the index. If a much smaller set of needs was to be considered as candidates for further action, then, as would be suspected, the agreement dropped somewhat. This suggests that where only a very small number of needs (less than five) could be attended to, perhaps all three ways of producing indices should be calculated and compared. Where resources for attending to needs are greater (i.e., with longer lists), the three methods yield about the same results.

Our general recommendation favors the use of the WNI. The computational procedure is easy to apply, the range of the index (0-5) is simple to explain to constituent and decision-making groups, the index is based on a reasonable statistical procedure, and it deals with only the key part of the data for each item. The disadvantages are that it does not use all of the data generated per item (thereby losing some information), and at times, decision makers may have to deal with items in which the current status exceeds that of the desired status. Lastly, Misanchuk (1985) noted that the WNI may produce somewhat of an erroneous index for some data distributions.

In 1994, Penta reported the results of a study that replicated the research of Cummings (1985) but with data generated by educators as opposed to workers and/or managers. She obtained high correlations of rank-ordered needs across the three methods (Spearman rank order correlation coefficients exceeding +.80), even though in some cases only a small number of subjects provided data. Thus, her findings generally supported Cummings's earlier work.

Penta (1994) observed that PRE worked better than the WNI approach, and the WNI was better than the means-difference analysis. On the basis of these results, Penta cautiously suggested that the PRE-based approach might be the best method to use.

CONCLUSIONS

There are subtle, almost hidden issues in collecting, analyzing, and interpreting NA data. The task of the needs assessor is difficult especially with regard to deriving meaning from information tha inherently has much embedded error and will become even more difficult when data generated from diverse methodological approaches are added to the mix. The problems described in the beginning of this chapter are testimony to the complexity of working in the NA field.

Furthermore, the most commonly used technique, the survey, has many variations and comes with its particular set of challenges. Designing NA surveys of high quality is a major endeavor for the needs assessor and the NAC. Although the survey is the most frequently observed method in NA studies, other sources of quantitative data and many qualitative methods are also used. A sampling of them and strategies for combining findings from multiple methods are addressed in the next chapter.

OBTAINING NEEDS
ASSESSMENT DATA IN OTHER
WAYS AND PUTTING THE
DATA PUZZLE TOGETHER

here is no denying that the survey is the major method of
needs assessment (NA). It is an excellent technique for
determining the importance of NA areas and for collecting
data that can be converted into indices of needs. Even though costs
can be high, the survey is a good way to obtain perspectives about
needs from concerned individuals and groups. As Witkin observed
in 1994, surveys have been the mainstay of praxis for many years. We
strongly support their continued use in NA.

But it would be a serious oversight if other sources of data were not
discussed. They are important for the field and produce valuable
quantitative and/or qualitative information about needs. Let us begin
by examining other quantitative methods.

NEED DERIVED FROM TESTS AND
OTHER SOURCES OF QUANTITATIVE DATA

Test results can easily lead to the development of indices of need by simply presenting test outcomes in a table with comparisons to norms or standards and then rank ordering the resulting discrepancies. A potentially better way to portray the data would be to examine discrepancies in terms of effect size, that is, a measure of effect in standard deviation units. (This concept was used by one of us in analyzing data from a survey that was part of a national evaluation. See Altschuld et al., 1997, chap. 8, for this application.)

Another alternative with regard to test results would be to collect data not only on achievement but also on a variety of school input factors (expenditures, socioeconomic status, etc.) over a number of years, as is done in educational accountability systems. When the resultant longitudinal database is used, stable prediction equations can be developed in which predicted achievement could be compared to observed test scores. If the expected scores are much greater than the obtained ones, a need would be indicated.

When test scores are looked at in terms of norms, it is also important for the needs assessors to examine the group on which the test was normed. To what extent is it similar to the one tested in the local NA situation? Comparability of groups is necessary for drawing conclusions from test data. If a test consists of many subtests, the relative importance of the subtests would have to be considered. In other words, it would be of value to have the needs assessment committee (NAC) or other concerned stakeholders rank the importance of the subtests. These ranks or weighting factors would be helpful in reviewing subtest results and discrepancies.

As with tests, standards often exist for other sources of numerical data. There are commonly accepted values for body temperature, white blood cell counts, electrical rhythms of the heart, the prevalence and incidence of diseases, appropriate amounts of daily exercise, caloric intake, amount of saturated fat in a diet, immunization rates for childhood diseases, and related aspects of physical well-being. Medical personnel, through appropriate tests, can determine whether we fall into acceptable ranges on such variables or whether treatment is needed. Similarly, standards exist for many types of variables—for example, sick leave (reasonable numbers of days out sick for teachers), time per mile and distance to be covered for yearly physicals for individuals in the armed forces or in law enforcement, caseloads for mental health counselors, and so forth.

Data for determining needs for the kinds of variables just mentioned often are found in already extant sources such as records, specialized databases, major studies that contain large amounts of data on populations (the National Educational Longitudinal Study), and the U.S. census. When archival types of sources are available and fit the focus of the NA (i.e., they are valid for the purpose of the NA study), they are valuable and definitely should be used. Utilization assumes that records can be accessed and that appropriate measures for safeguarding the privacy and anonymity of individuals have been established.

Such sources should be used only after seriously questioning their quality. To what extent is the information they contain reliably maintained? Is the information in-depth? How has it been collected? Could error have been introduced if different individuals have been responsible for providing the basic information (intake records used in the mental health system, counseling records compiled by different counselors)? When was the data collected?

The needs assessor(s) should raise additional questions about what has been included or excluded from records, why such decisions were made, and how variables have been defined. For example, records about public school students could be misleading in that teachers do not supply certain kinds of information for fear of legal suits. In other instances, perhaps successes are reported more often than failures. Furthermore, varied definitions for terms (e.g., recidivism, abuse) might be used in different locations. Lastly, in regard to needs assessment, data from records represent the current status of a situation, with discrepancies to be determined in comparison to standards.

Although the size of discrepancies is easily determined for some quantitative data, rank-ordering discrepancies in some other data sets may be somewhat difficult. Refer to the example in Chapter 3 in which students were asked about how much time should be spent on an activity and how much time currently is spent on the activity. Suppose this type of scale was used to collect data for mathematics, English, speech, science, social studies, physical education, foreign language, recreation, and so forth. Furthermore, suppose that data obtained from students indicated that there was an hour deficit between the what should and what is in mathematics, 1½ hours in foreign language, and a whole host of other hard-to-interpret discrepancies. What do we mean by *hard to interpret*? The concern is in regard to which of these discrepancies is larger than the other. Is a 1-hour gap in mathematics larger than a 2-hour discrepancy in social studies? The dilemma is apparent—how do we make the comparison? The discrepancies could be listed in rank order by size, but that does not help very much in terms of making comparisons and ultimately needs-based decisions. Possibly the areas (mathematics, science, etc.) could be rank ordered, and somehow that ranking could be factored into the ordering of the discrepancies, but this does not seem to fully resolve the interpretation problem.

The use of goal attainment scaling (GAS) provides a tentative solution here. GAS scaling is a method for comparing items and ideas on a common scale when one does not really exist (seems like a contradiction but it works).

Here is how it would be applied to the current situation. Form a panel of experts and ask them to rate the observed discrepancies across the academic areas from 1 to 5, with 1 representing a discrepancy of little or no value and 5 representing one of high value. Thus, each discrepancy would be rated on the same scale, even when the absolute size of the discrepancies is noticeably different. A common metric has been created. The ratings of the discrepancies using GAS could be rank ordered and, along with the actual discrepancies, displayed in a table.

There are more ways than those just presented for working with quantitative NA data. Within an NA context, D'Agostino (1997) suggested an interesting application of tree analysis diagrams for depicting and making data meaningful to decision-making bodies. D'Agostino noted that presenting complex statistical results in an understandable manner to stakeholders and the perception that statistics may seem to be impersonal are common problems faced by needs assessors. A tree analysis diagram is a pictorial method for illustrating relationships and helping individuals to understand possible causal linkages. Unlike causal analysis approaches in NA (fishboning, fault tree analysis, etc.), which rely on judgment, tree analysis diagrams are based on empirical data and generated by means of computer algorithms.

To produce the diagrams,

> the researcher first chooses a dependent variable of importance to the NA group and then predictor variables which are hypothesized to cause the outcome variable. The predictor and outcome variables can be either dichotomous, coded 0 or 1, or continuous, and they can be either categorical or quantitative. (D'Agostino, 1997, p. 3)

D'Agostino employed the approach to assist lay, stakeholding groups in using statistical data. The diagrams proved to be a good way of showing differences (i.e., potential needs) for different Level 1 groups in the NA he was conducting.

In a tree diagram, we might look at the achievement of a group of children in terms of its relationship to the educational level (completion vs. noncompletion of the general equivalency diploma [GED]) of the parents of the children. Rather than having the value of a correlation coefficient or frequency counts in cells of a table, students are color coded (in D'Agostino's 1997 work) or shown in black and white (in this text) based on their achievement levels and whether a parent had received a GED. Figure 4.1 is a representation of the diagram so produced.

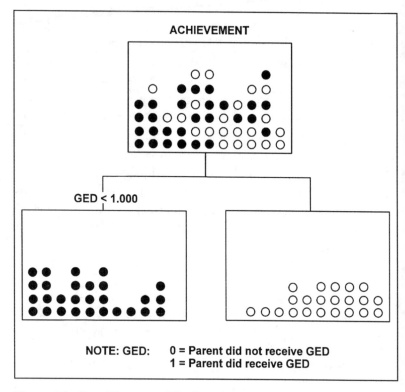

Figure 4.1. Tree Diagram of Student Achievement, Classified Based on Parent GED
SOURCE: D'Agostino (1997). Adapted with permission.

The top cell in the figure contains a histogram of student achievement with coded dots or entries for 50 students. The next row contains cells indicating that, for the most part, students with lower achievement scores came from a parent population that had not received the GED. D'Agostino's (1997) point about the visual impact of the tree was well taken, and his paper should be referred to for a more in-depth explication of tree diagrams as adapted to an NA context. (The paper also included a tree diagram with many more levels.)

Another way to deal with quantitative data comes from a recent advancement in regard to Trochim's (1989) concept mapping (CM) technique. In CM, key themes espoused by a group or groups are determined via a cluster analysis and then depicted in a maplike projection showing the clusters, their relationship to each other, and how strongly they are held in terms of group perceptions. In 1996, Trochim and Riggin created a ladderlike diagram comparing the importance ratings of clusters by different groups of respondents for an Internet study of accreditation standards for evaluation training programs. *Pattern matching* is the term applied to the ladder diagram. Ratings for one group were on the left side of the ladder and for the other group on the right. The ratings were connected by the "rungs." Obviously, if the ratings were similar, the rungs would tend to be parallel across the ladder.

Donnelly and Florio (1997) posited that pattern matching could also be used for discrepancy analysis in NA. Ratings of the current and desired status of clusters emerging from group CM exercises could be obtained. They would then be incorporated into the ladder diagram with desired and current status on the left and right sides of the ladder, respectively. If they were connected by rungs and if the rungs were parallel, the desired status and current status would be essentially equivalent, and there would not be any needs. This generally would not occur, and needs would, indeed, be identified (See Figure 4.2).

Witkin (1984) indicated that there are numerous options for constructing NA indices. Some are a bit more involved than those explained previously. The intent of the prior discussion was to portray basic ways to derive indices and present them in a form that is understandable and usable by decision-making groups. For other options, readers are referred to the 1984 source.

The process of determining needs from qualitative data is unique when compared to working with numerical data. The information gained from qualitative methods is important due to the fact that needs are seldom simple concepts. In reality, they are complex and multifaceted, and having more perspectives from which to view them helps in understanding their subtle dimensions. Deriving needs from qualitative data and fitting them into the overall NA picture are considered next.

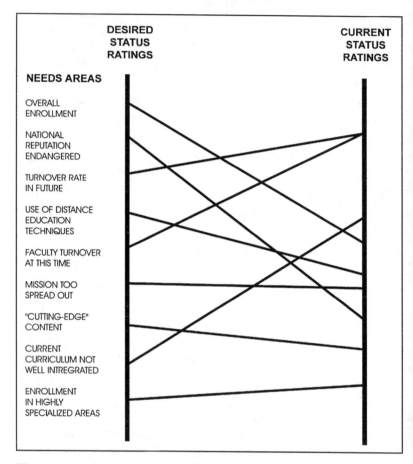

Figure 4.2. Adaptation of Pattern Matching for Needs Assessment

DERIVING NEEDS FROM QUALITATIVE DATA

A question asked earlier in the preceding chapter was, "How do I begin to understand needs obtained from qualitative data?" Here, discrepancies must be inferred rather than being directly measured as in double-scaled surveys or by comparing existing data to norms as with tests. This is the problem one faces when using qualitative techniques in NA. Even though the nominal group technique and community group forum may incorporate rating or voting in their procedures, they do not produce numerical data that directly target the concept of discrepancy—the very heart of NA. Qualitative techniques enable us to see how groups and individuals perceive an area of need. Many times they are used in conjunction with quantitative techniques to explain subtleties in quantitative data.

To illustrate this point, Demarest, Holey, and Leatherman (1984) studied the training needs of nurses in a hospital through the application of multiple (mixed) methods. Records and patient treatment charts were analyzed to identify problem areas that could be rectified through training. (Keep in mind that charts would be subject to the same types of problems found in records.) A randomly selected sample of staff was surveyed, and another randomly selected sample was interviewed. This is a form of a between-methods (completely different methods) NA. One method, the survey, was considered to be quantitative; another, records, may be viewed as partly quantitative and qualitative; and the third, individual interviews, would be qualitative. When results from the methods were compared, different needs and priorities of needs were apparent. These results led to questions such as the following: Which outcomes were really representative of the needs of the group, and how would we allocate resources based on disparate findings?

Demarest et al. (1984) noted that even though the data did not agree, the conclusions drawn from the NA were significantly affected by having used three methods and that the authors developed altered insights into the nature of the data, particularly the survey data. They recommended employing multiple methods and suggested that the gain in understanding offsets the problems encountered and the costs associated with their use.

Let us back up for a minute, lest we stray too far from the main point of this part of the discussion. Despite the fact that the majority of the literature indicates that qualitative methods have been implemented in conjunction with quantitative ones, qualitative techniques have been applied by themselves to determine needs. In 1995, Yoon,

Altschuld, and Hughes conducted an NA regarding the needs of international Asian students studying at a large university in the Midwest. Focus group interviews (FGIs) were the sole methodology. It was assumed that by engaging small groups of students in a somewhat informal setting, by choosing an appropriate group facilitator (an in-group member), and by asking thought-provoking questions, needs could be ascertained.

In general, the intent of each FGI was to get participants talking about problems they had encountered because they were international Asian students in this particular campus setting. The interviews started by having students think about concerns they had, difficulties that had confronted them, and so forth. From there, the facilitator probed into the responses offered by the participants. Needs were derived from an examination of the main themes emerging from the three FGIs conducted in the study. Thus they were inferred rather than being directly measured.

Other uses of FGIs in this manner were reported in a set of papers presented at the 1988 and 1992 annual meetings of the American Evaluation Association (AEA). Krueger (1988), Sadowske (1988), Casey (1988), and Nefstead (1988) described the use of FGIs for NA, community planning, and strategic planning. Indeed, one of the examples presented in 1988 was quite similar to the way Yoon and her colleagues (1995) had used the technique. FGIs were conducted with students from rural, small community backgrounds who had just entered a large Midwestern university (different from the one in Yoon's study) located in a major urban area. The purpose of the study was to develop an understanding of what the students were facing and the problems they were having in their new environment. In other words, what were their needs? In the same vein, Gamon and associates in 1992 used the FGI as a way of determining the needs of new members of AEA.

A major advantage of the FGI and indeed other qualitative techniques over quantitative ones, as well as the survey in particular, is their flexibility. They afford the needs assessor with an opportunity to modify and change the process as new insights and possibilities emerge. For example, in the Yoon et al. (1995) study, as the interviewing progressed, concerns were raised by an all-female group about sexual harassment. They reported that they were being harassed ("hit upon") by males within the international Asian community as well as by those external to it. Because these unanticipated comments were mentioned by a number of the women, the facilitator probed the issue in depth.

Looking more closely at the FGI, we see that there is another, almost hidden problem that affects it and that often may even affect surveys. In many cases, we are unable to determine whether there is more of an *expressed need* versus (what might be termed) a *real need*. Participants in the FGI discussed harassment, they complained about it, and it was bothersome to them. It is not acceptable behavior and in no way is it to be condoned. On the other hand, if the FGI had probed more deeply, we might have found that the females had learned how to deal with the problem. Furthermore, if they were asked about the funding of programs to reduce harassment or to help them to better cope with it in comparison to other problems dealing with academic, language, or housing needs, it might have ranked lower in priority. In other words, they were expressing their concerns, but when faced with making a hard needs-based decision, the area may have been a lesser need or did not represent a real need.

Before we move to the analysis of qualitative data, one final design consideration should be mentioned. Because qualitative procedures are most often combined with other techniques in a multiple-methods framework, a question could be raised as to how the overall NA is structured. Multiple methods could triangulate on a single aspect of NA, or they could complement each other so that one method would fill in the data that another does not provide. Furthermore, they could be sequenced so that one would be employed first, leading to a more well-developed second method (e.g., using an FGI to determine concerns of individuals and the way in which they refer to some aspect of an NA prior to constructing a mailed survey).

In our examination of the NA literature, we found very few examples of the use of multiple methods, and it was not always clear as to whether the use was for triangulation, complementariness (Greene et al., 1989), or for some other purpose. In a number of cases, it was evident that the function of interviewing was to provide guidance for constructing a survey (Mitra, 1994) or for gaining more insight regarding the interpretation of survey responses (Laffrey, Meleis, Lipson, Solomon, & Omidan, 1989). In other instances, the intent was vague and generally followed the notion that somehow greater understanding of the needs will emerge through these multiple sources of data. Indeed, as described in the case studies in Chapter 8, the data often neither were complementary nor did they triangulate, leaving the needs assessors with almost disparate data sets.

In regard to the analysis of qualitative data, the goal here is not to duplicate the vast and growing literature that treats such analysis but to provide general ideas for qualitative analysis observed from our years of work in NA. At a very generic level, qualitative data are first coded into categories (variables or similar ideas), a fairly exhaustive list of categories is developed, the data are examined in terms of how prominent each category is, and then the data are reviewed across categories for emerging, explanatory patterns or themes. The analysis can be accomplished through the constant-comparative method or by using available analysis packages such as Ethnograph (Seidel, Friese, & Leonard, 1995) and QSR NUD*IST (1995).

From the standpoint of NA, there are several important concerns here. In the Yoon et al. (1995) study, the needs assessors were unable to determine the extent to which harassment was occurring in the overall community of international female Asian students. It was not possible to develop prevalence estimates without some other source(s) of information. Besides that, it is difficult to generalize from qualitative sources, and need must be inferred rather than directly measured. Conversely, the study by Yoon et al. revealed a potential need or problem that would have been difficult to learn about through a survey, especially with the specific population that was sampled.

With these concerns in mind, a few suggestions for analyzing qualitative data as collected for NA purposes are given below. To reiterate, the intent is not to substitute for the plethora of well-accepted and extensive texts available on qualitative analysis but to provide some guidelines that have proved useful in our work.

1. Each qualitative aspect of the NA should be carried out independently of other parts of the study and by individuals who are independent from others involved in data collection, if at all possible. Although this suggestion will add to cost, it tends to reduce contamination in the data and its subsequent analysis.

2. The qualitative data should be collected and analyzed by needs assessors who are members of a team. It is highly desirable that the analysis be done initially by team members working alone. Then they should compare, discuss, and synthesize the separate analyses. In essence, this is a form of an independent verification of the analysis, and it has been used by Kumar and Altschuld (1995, 1999) quite successfully.

3. Use standard procedures for analyzing the data, initially looking for main categories, regularities in those categories, overarching or explanatory themes, and so forth.

4. Examine the data (the categories, the explanatory themes) in regard to the emphasis of the NA. Ask yourself questions such as the following: Are some needs clearly indicated? Are some needs being inferred? What information in the data set supports those needs and helps to explain the nature of the needs or problems?

5. Start a process of comparing the results from the qualitative and quantitative data sources in regard to the specific emphasis of the NA. An easy and effective way to do this was recently used by one of us to create meaning in an evaluation that employed three very different methods. This large-scale evaluation was conducted by a national evaluation board for a federally funded, major project. The first step was to carefully examine the results from each method. Next, starting with one method, key supportive data for each major finding were summarized and placed on a separate sheet of paper. Then the results produced by the next method were similarly perused to see if they corroborated the individual findings from the first method. If so, the

supportive data were entered on the same sheet, and the process was repeated for the third method. Unique findings from the second and third methods were similarly entered on separate sheets, and the process was repeated in regard to corroboration of results as well as identifying unique findings from each method. Lastly, the summaries were again reviewed to see if there were any other patterns that seemed to occur across the data. In a sense, this is a constant-comparative process conducted across methods rather than within one qualitative data set. It was straightforward to implement and proved to be invaluable to the national evaluation board for developing meaningful findings and recommendations for the final evaluation report.

6. Provide the opportunity for the needs assessor and the NAC to discuss the findings in a group session. This will allow all parties to question results, understand the reasoning underlying them, debate, and arrive at consensus.

7. If time is available, the needs assessor might conduct a peer debriefing or a form of a member check process. A peer debriefing entails that an uninvolved peer, especially one who is familiar with qualitative analysis in particular, be asked to review how the data were collected, analyzed, and interpreted, as well as the overall extent to which the findings seem reasonable and warranted. Analogous debriefings could be conducted with a few key stakeholders or other peers if feasible. Member checks are a related but somewhat different process. In a member check, for example, the needs assessor would share the transcript and even the interpretation of an interview with the interviewee and ask the individual to verify the accuracy of both. Cullen (1992) used member checks in a very interesting way in a study of teachers' perspectives of accountability. She not only shared transcripts with her sample but also invited them to attend a debriefing session (similar to an FGI) in which the results from the study would be summarized and discussed. The idea was for the sample to serve as a kind of review board, a partially external review board. Such an adaptation of member checks could be used in the NA context.

8. On the basis of the prior seven steps, compile the final report on needs and give all members of the NAC time to review it before distributing it to decision makers and concerned stakeholders.

PUTTING THE DATA PUZZLE TOGETHER

The fifth question posed in the prior chapter is critically important because it becomes the foundation for the process of bridging the gap from need to solution strategy—setting needs-based priorities. That question is the following:

> How is this jigsaw puzzle of results synthesized into a usable body of information for making needs-based decisions and for developing programs to resolve the identified needs?

The answer is not particularly difficult if the NA consists of quantitative data from which discrepancies can readily be generated (and in which the discrepancies are relatively similar if collected from multiple sources). Numerous options for analyzing and presenting NA results have been offered in this chapter as well as in the prior one. Numerical data, although not free from problems, can directly and easily be placed in tables or figures for use by the NAC and/or other decision-making groups. Similarly, the main themes from a qualitative NA could be summarized with the inclusion of inferred discrepancies and then provided to decision makers.

But difficulty arises when a multiple or mixed-methods NA approach is employed. So often, the resulting data, although not in conflict, may reflect quite different information—information that does not really fit together. One way to handle this situation was employed in the evaluation study completed by Altschuld et al. (1997). Reexamine the fifth step given above for how to analyze qualitative data. As implied in that step, the executive summary of the final report of the study included its main findings along with a very brief write-up of supportive data for each finding. Because the study was extensive, the national evaluation board first concentrated on looking for findings that were supported by all three methods or at least two of them. Findings that were felt to be important, although derived only from a single method, and recommendations for each finding were also included in the summary. Each method and the results from its use were described in detail in the body of the final report itself.

In a paper presented at the annual meeting of the American Evaluation Association, Wilson, Shayne, Lipsey, and Derzon (1996) described a unique way of presenting NA data from multiple methods, even in instances in which the obtained data were not in complete agreement. The data in this NA, which was conducted for the United Way organization of a metropolitan area, were complex and derived from numerous sources (see Chapter 8 for more details about the study). Among the methods were focus groups, phone surveys, mail surveys, service provider data regarding various aspects of agency capacities, financial data from the same providers, and other sources such as the U.S. census, local surveys, and so forth. Depending on the source, the data came from multiple constituencies: service recipients, service providers, community leaders, the general public, individuals with low income, and agency-based sources. Although the majority of the data was quantitative, part of it was not.

To pull this varied set of data together, Wilson et al. (1996) used a GAS approach. They created scales for each source, with larger scale scores representing a bigger gap between a need for a service and the degree to which it was available. Rather than providing tables with this information, a display such as Figure 4.3 was used. In the figure, data from three of the sources are provided in the second column. The data from all of the sources were equally strong for the child care and housing and assistance service areas. By the same token, in the financial and emergency assistance service area, the community perception data were stronger than that from the financial reserves data, which, in turn, were stronger than the service capacity data.

Visually, this presentation is easy to read and interpret. On one page, a great deal of information is summarized from what are almost

Service Areas	Private Nonprofit Community Services[a]	Public Community Services[a]
Child care	⊠⊠⊠⊠□□□□■■■■	⊠⊠⊠⊠■■■
Housing assistance & shelter	⊠⊠⊠⊠□□□□■■■	⊠⊠⊠⊠■■■
Adult day care & home care	⊠⊠⊠□□□□◧◧◧◧	⊠⊠⊠ ◧◧◧
Service for abuse, neglect & domestic violence	⊠⊠⊠⊠□□□□■■■	⊠⊠⊠■
Nutrition, food, meals	⊠⊠⊠□□□□□■■	⊠⊠⊠■■■
Transportation	⊠⊠⊠⊠□□□□■■	⊠⊠⊠■■
Employment services	⊠⊠⊠□□□□■■■	⊠⊠⊠■■
Mental health & counseling services	⊠⊠⊠□□□□■■■	⊠⊠⊠■
Parent support services	⊠⊠⊠⊠□□□■■	⊠⊠⊠⊠■■■
Legal assistance	⊠⊠□□□□□■■	⊠⊠■
Life skills and remedial education	⊠⊠⊠□□□■■■	◧◧◧■■■
Support services for disabilities	⊠⊠⊠□□□■■■	⊠⊠⊠■
Financial & emergency assistance	⊠⊠⊠⊠□□□■■	⊠⊠⊠⊠■■■■
Foster care & adoption	◧◧◧◧□□■■■	◧◧◧◧■
Substance abuse prevention & treatment	⊠⊠⊠⊠□□□■	⊠⊠⊠■■■
Health care support services	⊠⊠⊠⊠□□□■	⊠⊠⊠■■
Social & recreational activities	◧◧◧◧□□■■	◧◧◧◧■■
Pregnancy prevention & maternity	⊠⊠□□□■	⊠⊠■■
Immigration support services	⊠□□□◧	⊠ ◧◧

[a]Longer bars reflect larger need-service gaps
⊠ = Community Perceptions (same values used for both private nonprofit and public services)
□ = Financial resources (available only for private nonprofit services)
■ = Service Capacity (separate indicators for private nonprofit and public services)
◧ = Estimated from partial data

Figure 4.3 Indicators of Need-Service Gaps for Different Service Areas
SOURCE: Wilson et al. (1996). Used by permission.

orthogonal sources of data. Needs assessors and the NAC can readily see which sources are strong with regard to a particular area of emphasis in the NA and the extent to which the results are in agreement. On the other hand, the use of the scale represents a summary for a variable and does not contain the richness of the original data.

For example, a scale score could be a summary index derived from questions on a survey, records, census data, and so on. It is useful as a summary, but there is a loss of the full depth of information collected from the survey or whatever the other source(s) of data may be.

Is the loss critical? We don't think so! When it comes to making final decisions regarding needs-based priorities, the NAC or other decision makers generally are going to be faced with a mountainous amount of data and information. If they have to go through every source in detail, the task of arriving at priorities becomes not just daunting but potentially defeating.

The overall size of the effort such as in this United Way NA in itself would probably overwhelm the decision makers, let alone their having to carefully deal with so many results in their deliberations. The situation will become even more complicated if the data do not agree. Analogously, Altschuld et al. (1997) conducted a multiple-methods evaluation that contained some of these same elements of complexity. The text of their final report, along with the executive summary and appendixes, was nearly 200 single-spaced pages, with much of the material being in a highly compressed format. Reading and assimilating the report by a decision-making body would be staggering, especially if it has not been intimately involved in data collection and analysis.

Although many NA studies will not be as voluminous as these two, many others will be, based on a large amount of data generated from varied sources. Translating the NA data into a format that guides priority setting and bringing the NAC (or the decision makers) to a common level of understanding of what has transpired will be major and difficult steps in the NA process. Here are several general recommendations for easing the translation process:

1. Keep the decision makers informed during the first two phases of the NA process—Phase 1 (preassessment) and Phase 2 (assessment)—to the extent possible. Altschuld et al. (1993) observed a positive relationship between decision maker involvement (including communication) and the use of NA results. How to accomplish good

understanding of the NA process and end results (i.e., what mechanisms to use) depends on the judgment of the needs assessor, the nature of the local situation, and the importance ascribed to the NA. But it should be stressed that communication is important, and the needs assessor must be vigilant in attending to this aspect of the NA process.

2. Provide write-ups (summaries) of results and methods to the NAC prior to holding a formal meeting of the group. Request that NAC members review the materials supplied to them before coming to the meeting.

3. Hold a meeting that starts with a brief review of the methods used in the NA and any problems or issues in the quality of the obtained data and their interpretation. Follow this part of the meeting with presentations and discussions of summaries of the findings from each aspect of the NA followed by an overall summary across all of them. Although the NAC should have reviewed the write-ups in some depth before coming to the meeting (the ideal), it cannot be assumed that committee members have done so (the current situation). Nor can it be assumed that even if they have made the effort to stay on top of the NA process that they will have intimate familiarity with it. Like any meeting process designed to produce group decisions, this one will require extensive preparation, including having many materials available in advance as well as others to be handed out at the meeting. A fairly well-thought-out agenda is absolutely mandatory.

4. Conclude the meeting by seeking agreement on the overall summary of NA findings. By one means or another, this summary will be the focus (the key input to) of priority setting.

Note that it probably will require more than 1 day to review the NA process and resulting data as well as to reach agreement. If the data set is not unusually large and the NAC has done its homework, a day may be sufficient. In our experience, meetings lasting closer to 2 consecutive days were needed. For a moment, let us return to Figure 4.3. In some fashion or another, a one- or two-page summary of results is highly desirable for the group to consider when it sets needs-based priorities. Such a summary keeps the group on target rather than getting sidetracked when it moves to Phase 3 of NA.

At this point, the NAC would have not only the summary but also a common understanding of the methodology and the specific, detailed findings from the various methods employed in the assessment. At any time, if it wanted, the NAC could go back to those details that would be in the handouts and materials prepared for the meeting.

Good notes should be kept of what transpired in this meeting, particularly for documenting the final consensus in regard to the findings. The results then become the input for the needs-based priority-setting activity of the NAC. In Chapter 5, examples of rough summaries (perhaps more closely in line with what happens in real-world NA processes) are used to illustrate how the NAC might go about placing needs in priority order.

CONCLUSIONS

In the Program Evaluation Kit, Herman, Morris, and Fitz-Gibbon (1987) suggested a challenging and different approach to thinking about multiple sources of evaluation data in situations when they agreed and when they did not. Their approach is adapted here for NA situations. Consider the vignettes or sample cases 1, 2, and 3 shown below. In each instance, we have illustrated a different level of agreement for NA data and what actions might be taken to deal with the case. The second sample case is what probably results most often, with the first case being less common and the third case representing the rarest occurrence.

In our writings, we encourage the use of multiple sources and constituencies in NA. In the NA process, it is assumed that the collection of data from multiple sources and constituencies is intrinsically good and that the resulting information will clearly indicate needs. In practice and experience as well as in the literature, this often does not reflect reality, and the needs assessor will be faced with the complex problem of sorting through a mazelike set of data.

Sample Case 1

Multiple data sources that agree in regard to identified needs.

Discussion

This situation is ideal because the data all point toward the same needs as potential problems that should become the center of attention for the needs assessor(s) and the decision makers. In this instance, it would be important to indicate the level of agreement that was observed.

Actions to Be Taken

Consider the data to be highly corroborative of all major findings regarding needs. Recognize that even with flaws in individual methods, there is strength in collective evidence. Use the richness of the qualitative data to provide depth and meaning to the findings from surveys and quantitative sources. When numbers and indices of need are enhanced in this manner, decision makers are more likely to attend to the results and see them as being more credible.

Sample Case 2

Multiple data sources are in partial agreement with some independent findings, and a few major findings are in disagreement.

Discussion

This situation probably is the most frequently occurring one in NA in which multiple methods have been used and data have been collected from multiple constituencies. Three examples were given in the previous text (Altschuld et al., 1997; Demarest et al., 1984; Wilson et al., 1996) in which this type of result was apparent.

Actions to Be Taken

First, analyze the data by looking for needs on which all the methods have produced findings that are in agreement, strongly indicating the same need. If these areas are considered to be important, then they should be reported as needs supported by all sources of data.

Second, look for results in which there is some degree of agreement across most of the methods but not all of them. Are there any other sources of data that are in conflict with these findings? If not, report the results as a second tier of findings that have potential importance as needs (refer to Figure 4.3 for this type of data).

Third, if there are sources in conflict, then make efforts to understand and resolve the issue. For example, if two groups provide quite different answers on a survey in relation to a specific area of need, ask questions such as what is known about the respondents that might help in explaining the conflicting results. Is one group primarily service providers who might view the area one way, and is the other group service recipients with their own slant on the problem? With this information in hand, make the best interpretation of the data that you can (see Anderson et al., 1990, for a more detailed discussion of how to understand this situation). Other ways to handle this problem would be to consult the literature or seek the assistance of local, impartial experts (needs assessors at the United Way, at the university, etc.). Ask them to participate in a peer debriefing session, and use their input to arrive at a final interpretation.

Fourth, consider the quality of the data produced by each source. Were the survey questions well constructed, and was the survey process implemented according to plan? To what extent were the individual interviews conducted in a consistent and reliable manner? Based on questions such as these, make a judgment as to whether more faith should be placed on some results than others. Then draw conclusions in accord with the judgments about the quality of the methods.

Fifth, when results from different methods are not in agreement, but the methods were reasonable and conducted in appropriate ways, include the needs derived from each separate method in the report. Concede that different methods may simply not produce the same results.

Sample Case 3

Multiple data sources that are not in agreement with even conflicting data.

Discussion

This is the worst-possible situation in that it becomes difficult to draw any conclusions about needs, especially if the data are in conflict. Some of the data collected by Demarest et al. (1984) were of this nature. Depending on the data source, different recommendations would have been made in regard to needs.

Actions to Be Taken

First, look at the fourth action described for the second sample case. If one source or method is better, rely on it more in reporting needs.

Second, if some resources are still available, consider collecting some additional data that might help to clarify the results. Report how additional information was sought to explain the conflicting results that were observed. Suggest to the decision makers that they examine all sources closely and discuss how they would interpret the results and why they would interpret them in that way.

Third, if all resources have already been expended, simply describe the results with a direct discussion of the different needs that were found.

Whatever sample case represents your situation, after the data are analyzed and reported to the decision-making group, it will now be necessary to determine needs-based priorities. Prioritization is a highly value-laden step in the NA process and will reflect the diverse views (implicit as well as explicit) held by the decision makers. Decisions at this point lead to the expenditure of funds (often sizable in amount) and to the commitment of human resources to some course of action at the expense of not choosing or emphasizing other areas of need. Needs-based prioritization is at the very heart of a public and political process. In Chapter 5, a number of procedures for arriving at priorities are examined.

Before proceeding, one final observation is in order. A subtle pitfall that could occur in NA is that there would be objections to certain types of data or data collection procedures, especially when reports are made available to the general public. For example, some groups might perceive that arrest records, enrollment in special education programs, and other sources of data have cultural biases embedded in them. This is a serious concern for the needs assessor and the NAC, and we can only offer a few suggestions to help.

First, the careful selection of members of the NAC is underscored by the need for sensitivity to cultural issues. It is mandatory for the NAC to be well balanced in this regard. Second, the needs assessor should tactfully ask the NAC about how cultural concerns could affect the NA and ways to handle them. Third, the audit trail (an aspect of qualitative methodology) of NAC work assumes great importance here. We have continually stressed that the NA process should be well documented, with a strong historical record of what actually transpired and how key decisions were made. This record will facilitate describing the deliberations and actions of the NAC in the delicate area of culture. The audit trail will also help future needs assessors and NACs in working on subsequent NAs.

SETTING NEEDS-BASED
PRIORITIES

*O*nce data have been collected and analyzed, it is necessary to determine which needs are the most important (i.e., to set priorities). Four approaches for prioritizing needs will be described, including simple procedures, a technique developed by Sork (1982, 1995, 1998), disaggregated decision making, and risk assessment.

Deciding about priorities initially appears to be an easy proposition. If the numerical indices of need and information from qualitative sources point in the same direction, it is obvious that the largest discrepancies for the goals of greatest importance should be chosen. Another alternative is for the needs assessment committee (NAC) to discuss possible priorities and, by a vote or some other consensus-oriented procedure, arrive at a decision about priorities. After all, by this point, the group has been involved in all deliberations about needs and the actual implementation of the needs assessment (NA) process and is familiar with every aspect of the endeavor.

On the other hand, there are perils in relying on these approaches to prioritizing. They may not work well when needs are complex, the

choice of needs will have to be justified to major external constituencies, and a large commitment of resources will have to be directed
toward a priority area. The following points illustrate the difficulty in
prioritizing.

To begin, in organizations and in society, decisions related to needs
require that funds be allocated for their resolution. This occurs at the
expense of other needs, which will not be given attention or support.
The lives of individuals and groups will be affected.

Secondly, all decisions about needs ultimately are based on either
implicit or explicit criteria. Considerations that influence decisions
relate to how much we know about the general problem area; the
amount of risk we are willing to take in not attending to a need;
whether we are dealing with Level 1, 2, or 3 needs; the types of causes
that contribute to needs; the motivation of the organization to deal
with problems; the quality of information available about needs; the
degree to which the need is amenable to solution by the organization;
and so forth. Unfortunately, many times priority-related decisions are
made without the full examination of key factors that have an effect
on subsequent action.

Given these caveats, what generally takes place in NA is that
numerous important needs are identified. They often relate to multiple constituencies, come from multiple sources that may not agree or
triangulate, and may even be for different levels (1, 2, or 3). The NAC
when it goes about the process of prioritizing, has to work with a
multifaceted data set and one that may contain conflicting data. The
group could be confronted with a lot of data (from surveys, records,
observations, focus groups, external references, past deliberations,
and other sources of input) to review and synthesize into a coherent,
well-thought-out, and defensible set of priorities for action. Needs
and the subsequent allocation of resources must be justifiable to
stakeholders.

To prioritize, it will be necessary for each member of the NAC to
have studied all of the NA data. To facilitate this process, the need
assessor should prepare a summary (perhaps 2-5 pages in length) for
the NAC, which includes a description of how data were collected and

what the main findings were. A quick, general review might occur through a meeting led by the needs assessor in which the data are presented to and discussed by the NAC. Although more details of the NA are readily available elsewhere, the summary of highlights will help the NAC to establish priorities. Without it, the group would bog down in a myriad of details. The summary streamlines and focuses the work.

To give some sense of what committees might face in the prioritizing process, we have developed three short scenarios that are provided below (Altschuld, Cullen, Thomas, & Witkin, 1996). They have been employed in workshops as part of the application of a decision-making technique developed by Sork (1982, 1995, 1998). The scenarios, which come from the experiences of the authors, are rough rather than polished, thus representing the "messy" real world of NA (see also the SMART technique in Chapter 6 for another example of presenting NA data to a policy-oriented group).

Needs Assessment Scenario 1:
A Library System

A city of 65,000 people, near a major urban center, has a library system consisting of a large main facility in its downtown area and two fairly good-sized branches. The system serves an expanding population. Recently, the city annexed several outlying rural areas, and the population is expected to increase by 15% or more in the next 5 years.

The libraries serve patrons of all ages. Preschool children have special story hours, students from the local high schools and their feeder schools use the libraries for research, and seniors often spend hours reading the latest newspapers and magazines. Library buildings and facilities have been modified to permit easy access for people with disabilities. The system is also the repository of important materials relating to regional history. The catalog cards for all print materials have been transferred to computers, accessible by CD-ROM. Checking out materials is computerized. Books and articles not in the collection can be ordered through interlibrary loan. Audio and video materials are available but not completely catalogued. A section on computer technology has been added.

The library system conducted an NA using community surveys, focus groups, population data collected by regional planners, NAs completed by other similar library systems, and evaluation cards that patrons filled out when using the library facilities. The results of those efforts led to the following needs being identified: (a) more senior citizens than previously thought were in the community and could become potential users of the library, (b) the number of school-based users would also grow substantially, (c) rapid changes in technology require different skills for using the libraries than many patrons currently possess, (d) a number of seniors could not physically or electronically access the libraries, (e) emerging trends in what was being used (CDs, videos, audiotapes) did not correspond to the strengths of the present library collection, (f) there were radically different patterns of use of materials by age groups (e.g., health care, financial books, and golf magazines for seniors vs. fiction and technology for students in the schools), and (g) there were inadequate numbers of certified staff to handle needs at this time, let alone in the future.

Needs Assessment Scenario 2:
Reorganization, Early Retirements, and Downsizing—
Needs Everywhere in Higher Education

The field of education and colleges of education, in particular, are under severe pressure on a number of fronts. They include negative publicity about education, growing concerns about the quality of teachers being educated, reduced funding (or the potential for same) in higher education, early retirement incentives (ERIs), downsizing trends, shifting university priorities, the press for greater teaching loads from the state legislature, emerging stress on undergraduate teaching at the expense of graduate education, increasing demands to keep pace with rapid technological change, more requests to work collaboratively with the schools, and so forth. Based on pressures such as these, a major state college of education (with a top 10 ranking and a very large graduate enrollment) decided to identify and examine its needs and then develop needs-driven priorities.

Here are some of the data that guided the needs assessment and decision-making process: (a) faculty had decreased by about 31% over a 15-year period to about 110 faculty members; (b) graduate enrollment had remained stable at 1,200; (c) undergraduate enrollment was smaller, and its nature had shifted due to involvement in the Holmes Group, with its greater emphasis on postdegree programs primarily designed to train individuals who have degrees in fields other than education; (d) ERIs and normal faculty turnover had severely affected nationally recognized programs in counselor education, health education, vocational education, second language learning, and school psychology; (e) some stable programs were staffed almost entirely by aging faculties (mean age in the mid-50s) that probably would retire en masse if another ERI became available; (f) approximately 53% to 55% of the total college faculty were of the age that they would seriously consider another ERI; (g) the technological base of the college had seriously eroded; (h) some programs had high enrollments that were concentrated in service courses, and others had lower enrollments, but the job market for their graduates was strong; and (i) some programs with excellent reputations were still strong and could even become more prominent.

To identify and deal with its needs, the college conducted collegewide discussions, meetings, and smaller group meetings that produced summaries of their deliberations; formed a committee to guide the effort and create a plan for future directions and possible reorganization; and established a curriculum committee to facilitate the combination of programs and the movement of faculty within the college. The process had to contend with vested interests ("politics") and different views in the college regarding the importance of key programs.

Needs Assessment Scenario 3:
Be Well, HMO!

In the past 15 to 20 years, there has been unprecedented growth in the number and size (individuals covered, affiliated health care professionals) of health maintenance organizations (HMOs) in the United States. This growth has been predicated on pressures from the government and insurance companies to contain costs and on the view that collective medical practice creates a potent, critical mass for the delivery of high-quality care. As HMOs have increased in size and number, they have amassed the resources to fund departments of research and development (R&D) that, it is hoped, will assist them in best serving the needs of their members. One way that the new departments can help would be to identify needs by monitoring trends in both HMO medical practice and in statistics provided by national and regional health organizations.

The R&D department of a multicity HMO in the Northwest recently examined national data, completed an extensive study of 5 years of adult patient records kept by the HMO, and conducted personal interviews with a cross section of the professional staff. That study revealed many problems (read: needs) for adult patients ages 50 to 60. A sample of the problems were (a) males, in particular, and females to a lesser degree were on average not coming in for yearly physical examinations; (b) diets, to the extent it was possible to determine, were too high in fat content and too low in the intake of vegetables, fruits, and fiber; (c) reported levels of daily exercise were far below recommended aerobic and strength levels; (d) many patients were not following physicians' directions for medication; (e) patients were not very knowledge-able of the symptoms of cancer, heart disease, and other major afflictions of the age group; (f) the average patient was 15 to 20 pounds overweight; (g) there was an inability to monitor treatments or activities once patients were out of the office; (h) patient health histories were not in sufficient detail to be fully useful; and (i) patients in general did not seem to be following healthy lifestyles (regularly eating breakfast, taking vitamins, using short breaks to alleviate stress and tension, etc.).

The scenarios illustrate the complexity of NA data, how difficult those hard-to-make priority decisions can be, and what might be a good way of starting a group into the process of prioritization. Prioritization is tricky when the NAC is faced with juxtaposed, possibly competing needs that may not reveal (at least on first look) any issues or concerns that cut across target audiences or constituencies. In some cases, no matter how much the needs assessor has tried to keep the NA effort directed toward Level 1 needs, the resulting summary may be a mixture of needs across multiple levels (1, 2, and 3).

These scenarios were designed to train needs assessors about priority setting. During the workshops, the following observations were made about the process of prioritization:

individuals seem to get into a quiet, pensive, thoughtful set of individual deliberations about priorities;

the overall process of prioritization will slow down noticeably; and

most needs assessors have generally not used carefully delineated criteria to prioritize needs. (We drew this conclusion from discussions with workshop participants after they had worked with the scenarios and the priority-setting strategy.)

The last observation indicated that decisions about needs are not often made from an explicit or a thoughtfully reasoned position. Individuals and groups may cursorily review data and draw conclusions without looking at the data comprehensively, considering contextual factors, and dealing with the risks of not resolving a need. These aspects of decision making affect the quality of decisions.

Table 5.1 provides a summary of some techniques for setting needs-based priorities. The needs assessor would choose one based on the specific nature of the particular NA under consideration and the consequences of needs-based decisions. If the needs were relatively straightforward, if the group involved was small and had the wherewithal to resolve the needs, and if there was not much of a requirement to justify priorities to external constituencies, then the simplest and easiest of the techniques should be used. Examples of such situations

Table 5.1 Summary of Needs-Based Priority-Setting Techniques

		Techniques		
Features	Simple Approaches	Sork's Multiple-Criteria Approach	Disaggregated Prioritization	Risk Assessment
General structure	Procedures such as paired comparisons, rank ordering, zero-sum games, and so on (criteria not spelled out in any detail)	Needs judged against defined importance and feasibility criteria, and then criteria scores are combined for a total priority score (criteria may be weighted)	Criteria are placed in rank order; then a needs candidate is screened through each criteria, starting with the highest-ranked one first	Examining needs in terms of the risk associated with not attending to or resolving them
When to use	Situation regarding needs is not complex, and the NAC or organization can resolve the needs itself	Needs are complex, and needs-based priorities will have to be defended to external constituencies	When it is desirable to simplify the prioritizing process and work with the criteria one at a time	For situations in which the risk of not meeting a need has major import (health, child abuse, etc.)

Pluses	Easy to use and understand by the NAC; group will complete it in rapid order	Well-thought-out criteria are explicit, and can be weighted; approach recognizes interaction of criteria to some extent, and requires the NAC to more carefully consider its decisions	Ordered criteria, used one at a time, keep NAC focus on a single criterion rather than having to deal with multiple criteria simultaneously	Risk is often not considered in prioritizing (could be used with other priority-setting techniques)
Minuses	Criteria for priorities are not explicit, may not work well for more complex situations	More complex than some of the other techniques, requires a longer amount of time to set priorities; most needs assessors are unfamiliar with the technique	Does not fully deal with the fact that criteria generally will interact with each other, may fractionate the decision-making process too much	Difficult to assess risk for educational and social types of programs; most needs assessors have limited exposure to the concept

would be a small-sized, statewide professional group deciding on its priorities for the next year, a department in a college considering needs that demand immediate attention, and a medium-sized retire ment community that is considering the social needs of its residents When the situation is complex and decisions have to be explained and even defended to a much wider set of audiences, then other tech niques should be selected that fit better with the types of needs to be prioritized. In all instances, the process by which priorities were determined should be documented (i.e., via a paper trail).

SIMPLE APPROACHES TO SETTING
NEEDS-BASED PRIORITIES

As indicated in the table and preceding text, simple approaches are appropriate for many situations, especially for small decision-making groups. These well-known techniques are briefly described below (for a more in-depth discussion, see Witkin, 1984; Witkin & Altschuld 1995). For each approach, individual members of the NAC should work independently with a technique, with the results then summed across the group. This reduces somewhat the tendency toward "group-think."

Priority-setting techniques commonly used are the following:

- simple rank ordering of a list of needs;

- the use of the rule of three (thirds or some other variation) in which NAC members choose the top three or top third of the needs and the rank order them (the rule may also require that the bottom three or third also be identified to see if the members are viewing the overall list in similar way);

- paired comparisons (paired weighting procedure) in which each need is compared to each of the other needs in a pairwise manner;

- zero-sum games in which each person is given so many votes or dollar amounts (either in the form of chips, tokens representing votes or dollars, check marks, dots, etc.) that they can apportion to needs in any fashion they wish; and

- "Q" methodology or other similar techniques for sorting needs into groups of the most important to the least important ones.

A few aspects of these techniques should be emphasized. If chips, check marks, or even dots are part of the technique, color code them. By so doing, it is possible, in a small group, to see if several individuals are affecting the priorities by placing all of their votes on only one or two needs. This is not negative but probably an indication of different values held by some members of the group. If such a pattern occurs, it should be included in an open and informative discussion among group members about the reasons underlying their choices.

All of the simple approaches work well when certain conditions are met: the list of needs is not unusually long (perhaps less than 20), the area of the NA is not complex either from a programmatic or a conceptual point of view (short-term needs for a small unit in a research center vs. needs related to drug problems), and the consequences of directing resources and attention to the prioritized needs are not likely to be challenged to any major degree. The application of the techniques to contexts that fit such conditions is encouraged. Conversely, simple approaches mask the subtlety of the decision-making criteria on which judgments are made. Furthermore, it is likely that, without consistent decision-making criteria, each person is using his or her own.

NAs that are more complex and politically exposed should probably employ other mechanisms for setting priorities. To systematize the process (i.e., reduce the tendency to use fluctuating decision rules), Sork (1982, 1995, 1998) has identified two sets of criteria (importance and feasibility) for prioritizing needs. Both sets have a high degree of generalizability across settings. He has also devised a procedure for applying the criteria in a group environment.

SORK'S APPROACH TO SETTING
NEEDS-BASED PRIORITIES

Sork (1995) suggested that there are two basic criteria for prioritizing needs—importance and feasibility. Determining the *importance* of a need is not a singular judgment but one consisting of multiple components that, with minor adaptation by us, are shown below.

Importance Criteria

1. How many individuals are affected by this need, with the greater the number affected representing greater importance? (Number of individuals affected)

2. If we dealt with this need, to what extent would it contribute to organizational goals, with a larger contribution indicating a need of greater importance? (Contribution to organizational goals)

3. Does the need require immediate attention—that is, can attention be deferred for a period of time, or will the need tend to resolve itself with the passage of time? (For example, in 1990, Anderson et al. noted that some social needs are of this nature.) (Immediate attention)

4. How large is the discrepancy? The larger the discrepancy between the degree of the desired status for an area of concern and the current level of achievement in regard to it, the greater the importance. (Magnitude of discrepancy)

5. To what extent would resolving a need in this particular area have a positive effect on a need in another area? The more positive the effect, the greater the importance. A need that does not affect other needs would be given a value in the middle of the scale to be described shortly, and one that has a negative impact would be given a low value.[1] (Instrumental value)

Each need would have to be evaluated against each component of importance using a 1- to 5-point scale, with 5 representing greatest importance and 1 lowest importance. To understand how importance is assessed, refer to Scenario 1, which deals with a library system. Every need area would have to be rated in terms of every component of importance. Each person in the NAC would independently rate all aspects of importance, ratings would be summed across the NAC, individual and group ratings would be compared and discussed, and then the NAC would arrive at a final consensus.

A good illustration about the value of this process comes from an interesting situation that occurred in a large not-for-profit organization that deals with the needs of individuals who are from the late middle-aged years to elderly (Straw, Brown, Kutner, Marks, & Takeuchi, 1996). Based on an observation from national statistics that breast cancer was a problem of elderly women, the organization initiated a program to encourage regular examinations on the part of females in the appropriate age group. The program was extensive, was national in scope, and employed a variety of local groups as the delivery mechanism.

The need was there, but whose need was it? After the program had begun, the organization decided to conduct a *retrospective NA* of its female members. The data indicated that there was a large difference between the females belonging to the organization and female elderly in the general population. Females in the organization were somewhat more affluent and had a considerably higher rate of yearly breast cancer screenings than did the latter group. However, the decision to undertake the program had been based on overall population values rather than knowledge of the specific situation of the organization's members.

Using Sork's (1995) schema, the rating for importance (criterion 1) would have been low because not many female members of the organization (i.e., its clients) were in need. Therefore, the contribution to the organization's goal of serving its female members (criterion 2) would also have been low because few of them were in need. The ratings for all of the five components of importance would have probably averaged around 2 on the 5-point scale.

Consequently, even though the program had noble intentions, it probably should not have been started. The organization had established a priority in an area that simply did not fit its needs. The retrospective NA led to a discontinuation of the national effort. A good deal of money and effort would have been saved if the importance criteria had been applied prior to introducing the program.

In addition to importance, Sork (1995) developed three criteria for dealing with the *feasibility* of meeting a need. They are as follows:

Feasibility Criteria

1. The degree to which an educational intervention, particularly an adult education strategy, can contribute to reducing or even eliminating the need. (Educational efficacy)

2. The extent to which resources are or could become available for programs to reduce the need. (Availability of resources)

3. The commitment or willingness of the organization to change. (Commitment to change)

As in the case of the importance criteria, each component of feasibility is rated from 1 to 5, with 5 indicating the highest value and 1 being lowest on the 5-point scale. In essence, what happens is that each need is rated on two separate criteria: importance (five components) and feasibility (three components). A summed rating per person and then across the rating group is obtained for overall importance and overall feasibility. The higher the summed rating in each category, the higher the rank order or priority of the need.

Although the educational efficacy criteria fit most closely with the adult education context of Sork (1995), they pertain to others such as health, ecology, and safety. These fields rely on the involvement and training of adults—patients, service deliverers, and community members. Almost any program we can imagine takes place in communities or social situations that are subject to complex political and economic presses, and as such they connect in some fashion to adult education. The needs assessor and the NAC, depending on their situation, should feel free to substitute or add feasibility criteria that relate better to their specific setting.

Figures 5.1, 5.2, and 5.3 were developed by Sork (1995) to assist groups in understanding and using his process. The first figure is a funnel in which needs would be filtered through sets of criteria, and

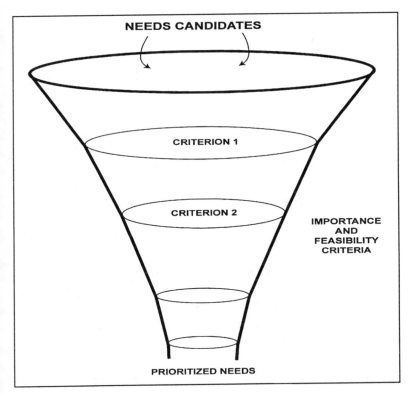

Figure 5.1. A Funnel for Prioritizing Needs
SOURCE: Sork (1995). Adapted with permission.

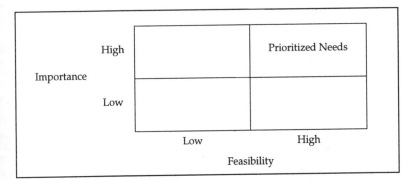

Figure 5.2. Two-Dimensional Graphing for Viewing Importance and
Feasibility Criteria
SOURCE: Sork (1995). Adapted with permission.

5.3a Importance Criterion and Final Importance Rank

Need	Number of People Affected Weight =	Contribution to Organization Weight =	Immediate Attention Weight =	Instrumental Value Weight =	Magnitude of Discrepancy Weight =	Sum of Weighted Importance Ratings	Final Importance Rank
1.							
2.							
3.							
4.							
5.							
6.							
7.							

5.3b Feasibility Criterion and Final Overall Rank

Need	Educational Efficacy Weight =	Availability of Resources Weight =	Commitment to Change Weight =	Sum of Weighted Feasibility Ratings	Final Feasibility Rank	Sum of All Weighted Importance and Feasibility Ratings	Final Overall Rank
1.							
2.							
3.							
4.							
5.							
6.							
7.							

Figure 5.3. Scoring for Sork's (1995) Prioritized Method

SOURCE: Adapted from Sork (1995). Used by permission.
NOTE: All components of a criterion would be given a 5 rating for highest value and a 1 rating for lowest value on a 5-point scale. Weights should be whole numbers.

only those with high-priority scores would be considered for further action or attention. The second figure is a 2-by-2 cross-break in which just the needs that fall into the high-importance and feasibility quadrant would warrant further consideration. The third figure is a scoring sheet for recording ratings. If the NAC decides that some components of importance or feasibility are of greater magnitude than others, it can weight them on the scoring sheet. The decision to weight must be determined by consensus of the NAC prior to the ratings of importance and feasibility. If weighting is desired, then the ratings for a particular component would be multiplied by the weights prior to summing. The process works best if whole-number weights (1, 2, 3) are used. The scoring sheet contains provisions for weighting.

Sork's (1995) procedure allows the NAC to see if it agrees in regard to importance and feasibility and therefore priorities of needs. If sharp differences in ratings occur, the needs assessor should have the group explore why this result has occurred. The consequences of not having an agreed-on and fully supported set of priorities are serious, and differences of opinion must openly and honestly be discussed. If they are not, they may arise in other forums and potentially lead to confrontation and conflict. The moral is, "NAC get your ducks in order."

In our judgment, Sork (1995) has provided an excellent means for prioritizing needs. He has provided explicit, clear, and utilitarian criteria for arriving at priorities. Sork correctly observed that because a lot is at risk, the prioritizing process should force deeper consideration of needs. It should lead to sound and well-reasoned judgments.

Other aspects of Sork's (1995) procedure merit further discussion. First, by using feasibility as a criterion, he has interjected preliminary thinking of solution strategies, at least at a general level, into the prioritizing process. Previously, we (Witkin, 1984; Witkin & Altschuld, 1995) have cautioned against this course of action. Our position was that when groups consider solutions too early, they begin to lose sight of the primary concern (i.e., prioritizing needs) and, in particular, Level 1 needs (those of the direct recipients of services). Premature focus on solutions diverts attention away from the job at hand, prioritizing based on the nature of the needs. But, in practice, it may not be possible to preclude some thought about solutions during prioritizing. Sork's approach is a reasonable compromise and probably is closer to how the NAC would function in its organizational context.

Second, the decision-making strategy is an example of what could be termed an *aggregated decision*. Components within a criterion are rated, and then the ratings are summed to create an overall score for the criterion. A different method for establishing priorities could be through a disaggregated procedure. Third, yet another way of prioritizing would be to look at needs in terms of the risks associated with not attending to them, an idea suggested by Kaufman and Stakenas (1981) and Witkin and Altschuld (1995). These alternatives for prioritizing will be briefly examined below.

A DISAGGREGATED DECISION-MAKING APPROACH TO SETTING NEEDS-BASED PRIORITIES

Many prioritizing decisions are made through summarizing ratings of various criteria. This process could be approached in an alternative manner.

In virtually all procedures, criteria for prioritizing have to be identified and defined. In disaggregated prioritizing, the components of an individual criterion such as importance or feasibility are first ordered from highest to lowest based on careful deliberation by the NAC. Next, each need is rated in terms of the ordered components, one component at a time.

For example, let us assume that Sork's (1995) first component of importance (number of persons affected by the need) was given the highest rank by the NAC. We might say that only those needs that had ratings averaging 4 or above on that component would be eligible for continuing in the prioritization process. Thus, some needs would be eliminated from further consideration at this time. Needs that passed this first test or through this screen would be examined in terms of the next highest-ranking component of importance. Those that were high on this component would continue in the process, and those that were not would be eliminated. Only the needs that remained at the end of the five screens (i.e., having successfully passed through them) would be considered to be of high importance.

This process was used by a major Midwestern school district for looking at its physical facility needs, particularly in relation to closing buildings to reduce costs (Edwards, 1997a). To determine which buildings to close, the district used four ordered screens:

Screen 1: "Is the school under capacity and/or a low-enrollment school?"

Screen 2: "Can nearby schools accommodate students and educational programs with minimal impact on the student-assignment plan?"

Screen 3: "Does consideration of board policy on safety, handicapped access, burden, diversity, future use, trends, location, or age and condition of building indicate that the school should be considered for closing?"

Screen 4: "Do circumstances indicate that the school be considered for closing?"

Because the decision to close a school tends to have traumatic effects on neighborhoods within a community, the school planning group needed to establish systematic procedures for judging schools. In this instance, the group looked at each school by means of the screens just described. Of the 12 high schools that entered into the screening process, 12 passed through Screen 1, 6 through Screen 2, 2 through Screen 3, and those same 2 through Screen 4.

The advantages of disaggregated decision making are obvious. The process is clear and well organized and consists of steps that are simplified and easy to explain to others. In the above example, the disaggregated process was explained to the community by means of extensive newspaper articles published over a number of months. A very clever way of summarizing the process in a table is shown in generic form in Figure 5.4. The format depicted in Figure 5.4 requires very little additional information.

Needs	Screen 1	Screen 2	Screen 3	Screen 4	Screen 5[a]
1. _____	Yes	Yes	No		
2. _____	Yes	Yes	Yes	Yes	Yes
3. _____	Yes	Yes	No		No
4. _____	Yes	Yes	Yes	Yes	
5. _____	No				
6. _____	No				
7. _____	Yes	Yes	Yes	Yes	Yes

Figure 5.4. Example of How Data From a Disaggregated Method for Setting Priorities Could Be Portrayed

SOURCE: Edwards (1997a). Adapted, with permission, from the *Columbus Dispatch*.

a. Only needs with a yes in the last column would be considered as high priority.

On the other hand, the disadvantage in disaggregating is also readily apparent. By fragmenting the decision, it is possible to lose sight of the interactions between what are often related components of the criteria for setting priorities. Decisions do not always consist of separate, orthogonal entities that are judged independently of each other.

What happened to the final priorities for closing schools resulting from the disaggregated procedure used by the school district? The procedure, which was sound, carefully executed by a districtwide committee, and extensively documented, led to the conclusion that a total of seven schools should be closed—two high schools, one middle school, and four elementary schools. Initially, the decision received the full support of the school board and excellent publicity in the local media.

But school closings are a highly charged undertaking that brings to the surface the feelings and, potentially, the ire of an affected community. Emotions began to rise. Pressure from the areas most affected by potential school closings became noticeable. Even before the prioritizing was completed, political pressure was being exerted on the school board, and the possibility of delaying a decision became a serious reality (Edwards, 1997b). Eventually, due to a tremendous outcry, the board backed away from a decision and established a timetable of approximately 1 year to reexamine the issue. This pleased some constituencies but angered others who argued that the board was abrogating its responsibilities.

The saga continues. Later in the year, the school board received new recommendations from a committee of administrators and volunteers from throughout the school district (Edwards, 1997b). These recommendations called for the replacement of 6 schools and the renovation of 10 others. The earlier school closing priorities were effectively discarded, based on additional data and the committee's taking more variables into account. Although more information would be helpful, in itself, it does not fully explain the radical shift in the latter committee's report. It is interesting to note that the struggle over this issue continued into 1999 (Alford, 1999). It undoubtedly will occupy much of the school board's time in the foreseeable future.

With the best of intentions and a good procedure for arriving at priorities, other forces can still come to bear and seriously have an impact on the process. As Burns (1785/1992) observed in days of yore, "The best laid plans of mice and men aftimes gang aglay."

A RISK ASSESSMENT APPROACH TO SETTING NEEDS-BASED PRIORITIES

Another way to view needs-based priorities is in terms of the risks associated with a need. Consider the following situation:

One of the coauthors recently had a yearly physical examination in which his overall cholesterol level was too high in comparison to the desired standard of 200. This was a bit discouraging because he had already reduced the amount of saturated fats in his diet and greatly increased the level of his daily exercise.

If we look more closely at the cholesterol level, the high-density lipids (HDLs) were at 72, a relatively positive sign, but the low-density ones (LDLs) were above the suggested standard (165 vs. 130). Other aspects of the physical examination were quite good for the individual's age and gender (blood pressure 126/70, pulse below 80, normal triglycerides, and so forth).

Let us further assume that many people will be in a similar situation with elevated cholesterol, and hence they have a need. Or do they? In almost any kind of NA procedure, we make comparisons between current status and ideal status. This is the basis of NA. Because ideal or desired conditions are the benchmark against which current conditions are compared, we will almost always observe discrepancies.

The question is, To what extent does a discrepancy constitute a problem? Or, stated alternatively, what is the risk in not meeting the need? In relation to the risk of heart disease or heart attack, how much greater risk is there if one is at an overall level of cholesterol of 225, 250, or 300? It all depends.

How do we begin to attack the question of risk? *Time* magazine has been carrying a questionnaire ("At Your Age," 1997) dealing with the risk of having a first heart attack. The questionnaire was produced as an educational service by Bristol-Myers Squibb Company and is endorsed by the American Heart Association. Points are assigned to an individual's answers to questions, such that the higher the point total, the higher the risk factor. The questions deal with age (with different scale values for men and women), family history of heart attack before a certain age, inactive lifestyle, weight (overweight in particular), smoking, diabetes, total cholesterol level, HDL level, and blood pressure. Any point total above 4 indicates that one could be at risk of a first heart attack.

Thus, risk is not a singular concept but instead consists of many subtle factors. Risk assessment is complex and, like other approaches to prioritization, necessitates considering the potential interplay of multiple factors in estimating the overall degree of risk. So how does the coauthor fare in terms of the likelihood of a first heart attack?

Not too badly! If one is a male and older than 54 years of age, then 4 points are added to the score. (It's tough getting older, and there is nothing one can change in this regard.) For the questions about family history, inactive lifestyle, weight, smoking, diabetes, HDL, and blood pressure, no points were added and indeed 1 point was subtracted for an HDL level above 60. One point was added for the total cholesterol level of between 240 and 315. The total point score on the risk assessment was 4.

This is certainly not a high score, but one that indicates that the coauthor should continue to maintain a healthy lifestyle and make efforts (diet and exercise) to reduce his cholesterol. His physician is taking a conservative approach to the situation due to the fact that most of the indicators of risk are not operative at this time. The cholesterol level will be monitored, and further action (drug therapy) will be taken, if warranted.

A point to note in the risk assessment questionnaire is that age is scored quite differently for women than for men. A woman would have to be older than 74 years of age to receive 4 points. As in the case of many aspects of need, risk assessment has to be tailored to the characteristics of the specific group to which it is being applied.

A word about research and its relationship to risk assessment in NA is in order here, especially in regard to the risk of heart attacks. The March 1997 issue of the *Cardiovascular Trial Review* (2nd edition) contains an abstract of the "WOSCOPS" study (Shepherd et al., 1995). This is a large-scale clinical trial that examined the effects of one of the new cholesterol-lowering drugs on males with health profiles similar to that of the coauthor of this text. A randomized control group design was used with a double-blind procedure, with the control group receiving a placebo. The results indicated that the drug reduced overall cholesterol levels by 20% and LDL levels by 26% with no apparent adverse or side effects. In terms of coronary events (medical euphemism for heart attacks and episodes), the group receiving the drug fared somewhat better than its control counterpart.

Based on studies such as this one, drug therapy, with reasonable costs taken into consideration, would be recommended for reducing the potential of a heart attack. In this instance, knowledge of research provided a critical insight into the nature of risk. It should be emphasized that WOSCOPS is a series of heart research studies that have been conducted over many years by many different individuals. For example, studies using large-scale databases have been carried out to examine the cost-benefit ratios of drug therapy and the association between the treatment of heart disease and social class. Collectively, the WOSCOPS[2] research has greatly enhanced understanding of the risk factors related to heart disease.

SOME ASPECTS OF RISK ASSESSMENT

Risk assessment has been used in areas such as rehabilitation and corrections, spousal abuse, at-risk students, epidemiological risks associated with the lack of immunization in children, substance abuse, and others. Sometimes, risk is viewed in terms of solutions more than in terms of needs. In this vein, Claire, Dinan, and Wade (1997), in the auditing and accountability context of state government, defined risk as "anything that could jeopardize achievement of an objective or expected result" (p. 1). For them risk consisted of two types—inherent and control. Inherent refers to risks derived from agency profiles based on level of funding, complexity of operations, changes in management, and so forth. Control risks are derived from audits and external reviews.

In other settings, risk assessment is predicated on the identification of factors that predict negative occurrences in the future. Risks are determined by two means—a synthesis of research studies related to negative outcomes or the experiences and understandings of individuals who have worked with the programs in consideration.

Van Voorhis and Brown (1996) examined risks in rehabilitation and corrections. They defined risk classification as "the prediction or identification of those individuals most likely to get into trouble during a period of criminal justice supervision" (p. 4).

They observed two methods for classifying risk—clinical (which corresponds to the experience method described above) and actuarial, which is more quantitative in nature. Actuarial classification is derived from the characteristics of individuals (demographic variables such as age, ethnicity, gender) and variables representing past behaviors, experiences, and so forth. Among the purposes for risk assessment in corrections cited by Van Voorhis and Brown are the following:

to allocate resources in an informed and rational manner;

to make decisions about the level of supervision, intervention, or security level in an efficient manner;

to reduce the risk of incidents occurring while under correctional supervision;

to help target our most intensive treatment efforts to high risk offenders; and

to provide a means for directing low risk offenders to less intensive interventions. (pp. 5-6)

A consistent theme underlying their discussion is that risk consists of multiple factors that, if looked at cumulatively, will predict those individuals at higher risk.

In essence, that means that risk will not be easily determined. Lyons, Doueck, and Wodarski (1996) reviewed the literature related to risk assessment for child protective services. They indicated (based on Wald & Woolverton, 1990) that three basic procedures are used: cases categorized on the basis of the severity of risk; NA, although NA will not necessarily lead to the prediction of risk; and likelihood or prediction of an individual harming a child in the future.

They identified five ways in which risk is assessed: matrix models (tables of risk factors), empirical prediction models, behaviorally anchored items or scales, ecologically structured scales (scales built around themes such as the child, the parent, the family, etc.), and expert systems that use computer modeling and the expertise of staff in child protective services. Variations of these approaches are used in 42 states. Lastly, they compared existing instruments and approaches to assessing risk in their field on a variety of dimensions. Clearly, risk in child abuse is neither a singular nor a simple concept.

Van Voorhis and Brown (1996) suggested that dynamic factors (factors that are changeable) should be included in the prediction of risk as opposed to focusing solely on static, demographic ones. These factors, they argued, will be critical when programs and methods to reduce risk are being considered. Furthermore, risk factors do not uniformly apply across groups and will have to be weighted when applied to different populations. (Recall the differential points assigned to age for males and females when calculating the risk of a first heart attack.) This concern about dynamic factors was echoed by Fitzhugh, Wang, Eddy, and Westerfield (1993) in the field of worksite health promotion. They noted that the NA surveys used to determine worksite health risks should contain not only questions about actual health behaviors but also questions regarding the willingness of employees to participate in programs designed to improve healthful behavior (i.e., to reduce the risk to health).

In reviewing the literature in rehabilitation and corrections, Van Voorhis and Brown (1996) identified numerous flaws in risk assessment, many of which generalize to any field. Below is an adaptation of some their observations:

1. Risk classification or assessment is not validated for the specific population or setting in which it is being used, and the accuracy of prediction will therefore decrease.

2. Data collected on individuals may not be accurate, and hence errors in the process of obtaining information affect prediction. Many data collection instruments require staff members to make judgments about subtle variables—judgments that could reduce the validity and reliability of the resulting risk scores. Consider the intake process in mental health that requires observation and specification of the nature of the presenting problem. Deciding on the entry to be made on an intake form is a vastly different proposition than measuring blood pressure or cholesterol level.

3. Is it clear what risk is being predicted? In other words, what is the predicted variable, and is it clear to all interested parties who have a stake in subsequent policy and action decisions? Prediction of heart disease may be considerably more predictable than the risk of not meeting needs in the foreign language or social studies programs of a school district. Risks may be simpler to assess in some areas as opposed to others. Here are some examples. In health, the immunization rates of preschool-age children in Ohio had fallen to approximately 70% to 75%, whereas from epidemiological studies an immunization rate of between 90% and 95% is considered to be necessary for preventing the spread of certain childhood diseases (V. Haller, personal communication, August 1996). The risk in this instance is apparent and direct. But in mental health, teenage suicide is a case in which risk is estimated for an event of relatively low prevalence.

White, Murdock, Richardson, Ellis, and Schmidt (1990) observed that developing a suicide risk assessment inventory is beset with numerous difficulties, particularly in terms of validity. They pertain to the level of occurrence, knowing only some of the potential predictors of suicide, and the differences in critical predictors across varied (cultural, racial) groups of individuals. In addition, these authors reported that their research work also suffered from the retrospective recall of subjects who were required to remember their specific state prior to attempting suicide.

4. What are the actual failure rates as compared to predicted failure rates, and do we have data in regard to this comparison for specific subgroups within the population? Related to this point, Lyons et al. (1996) found that there are false negative and false positive predictions in the field of child abuse. Two mathematical functions that come into play in this instance are *sensitivity*, correctly predicting individuals who will maltreat in the future, and *specificity*, correctly identifying individuals who will not maltreat in the future. (Serious consequences could result here from mislabeling based on incorrect identification.)

5. How is the classification or assessment of risk linked to programmatic changes, or how will it be linked?

We might add to this list a concern about the selection of variables to be used in predicting risk. If we refer back to the questionnaire dealing with the risk of a first heart attack, suppose a question had been added about occupation and, in particular, occupations with high levels of stress such as a fireman, a police officer, or, for that matter, the writer of a book under the pressure of a harsh deadline. This type of variable in conjunction with age, elevated LDL, and other factors may combine to reveal a high level of risk.

As described previously, the literature could play a major role in developing a risk assessment procedure. Its value is illustrated in the work of Beman (1995) in respect to the risks leading to adolescent substance abuse. Beman suggested that four main categories affect the risk (demographic, social, behavioral, and individual), with each category, in turn, consisting of subcomponents. The *demographic* factors of age and gender; the *social* factors of family, peers, and the environment; the *behavioral* factors of prior use of alcohol and marijuana; and *individual* factors such as poor academic achievement and self-esteem all seem to predict substance abuse. Furthermore, the author indicated that the risk factors tend to interact with each other, thereby increasing the probability of substance abuse. Thus, the literature underscored the complexity of the substance abuse construct.

Similarly, Menzies and Webster (1995) provided other evidence in support of the complexity of predicting risks. They attempted to predict the risk of violence on the part of mentally disordered, criminal defendants in Canada. Using an actuarial approach that incorporated clinical judgments into the prediction, they were able to account for less than 25% of the variance in the violence variable.

Another feature of risk assessment is sometimes observed in instrumentation. Instruments may employ scales with unequal or unbalanced measurement units. For example, instruments might not use equidistant scale points for items. The "yes" response to an item dealing with "conviction of juvenile adjudication for an assaultive offense within the past 5 years" might receive 15 points, and a "no" response would receive 0 points. Because the overall point total is the indicator of risk, the implications of such scaling are obvious. Conversely, in Ohio the recently revised risk assessment form for use in parole guidelines (Ohio Department of Rehabilitation and Corrections, 1998) employs more traditional equidistant scaling points. Decisions about scaling in risk assessment are important, as well as subtle, and should be based, where possible, on prior research efforts, clear support from institutional databases, and/or consistent expert judgment about which scaling is appropriate.

So far, the preceding discussion of risk has tangentially been tied into NA. The original proposition was which of the important needs poses the greatest risk to the organization or community if it goes unattended. Do the descriptions about risk assessment given above tell us how to conduct this type of analysis? To a high degree, the answer is no.

In searching the literature, we crossed the terms *risk, risk assessment,* and *NA* and were able to locate only a few references directly focusing on the issue. Researchers and social scientists are interested in risk but more on the level of which members of a group would tend to have this or that type of problem as described in many of the previous references. For the most part, the determination of risk has looked at individuals, not programmatic needs within organizations.

Certainly, identifying individuals at risk, whether in health, education, mental health, rehabilitation, or other fields, is important and does have implications for the risks associated with programs designed to resolve needs. Yet the NAC will require other approaches beyond those found in the literature.

AN APPROACH TO RISK ASSESSMENT IN NA

The NAC might take its list of prioritized needs and subject them to risk assessment. Estimates of risks could be determined by using a 5-point scale, with 5 representing high risk and 1 standing for low risk. Risk criteria (questions) could be as follows:

1. Is this need really worth the effort? Will clients suffer that much if we do not attend to it? (Worthwhile effort risk) (see Guba & Lincoln, 1982, for a discussion of this risk)
2. What are the short-term negative economic consequences for the organization of not attending to the need? (Short-term economic risk)
3. What are the long-term negative economic consequences for the organization of not attending to the need? (Long-term economic risk)
4. Will the risk increase with the passage of time? (Greater time risk)

Health risks are good examples of this type of idea. Contaminated food produced under unsanitary conditions at food facilities could, if not located in the distribution chain, lead to high levels of risk for the general population. Another illustration would be in relation to AIDS.

Epidemiologists warned us of the increase in the incidence of AIDS once they began to understand the disease.

5. What is the likelihood of new developments or programs decreasing the level of risk? (New development risk reduction)

Again, using health as the example, what is the likelihood of developments, such as antibiotic cocktails or new drugs, in reducing the rate of mortality due to AIDS? Are we likely to see an actual cure for AIDS in the near future?

6. What are the short-term negative political consequences of not attending to the need? Will our organization lose political support in the short term by not attending to the need? (Short-term political risk)

7. What are the long-term negative political consequences of not attending to the need? Will we be able to maintain political support? (Long-term political risk)

8. Will our competitors be in a stronger position if we do not attend to the need? (Competitive risk)

9. Will attending to the need be disruptive to the internal operations (processes, communication channels, structure) of the organization? (Internal disruption risk)

10. Will the culture of the organization be unable to adjust and buy into the need and changes necessary within the organization to meet it? (Internal morale risk)

The list of criteria is intended not to cover all kinds of risk but to sensitize needs assessors and NACs in regard to how risk might come into play prior to establishing final priorities for needs. Also note that dealing with risks might require that they be split into categories—internal and external would be one such possibility. There may be advantages to examining risks through these two distinct lenses.

Another way of thinking about risk assessment in NA comes from an observation made in the previous discussion of risks in child abuse. There, NA itself was viewed as form of risk assessment. Risk assessment is at least partially and subtlety interwoven into the process of prioritizing needs. If the size of the discrepancy, the number of people affected by the need, and the perception that the need is not immediate or will disappear with the passage of time are factored into the decision, we are dealing with risk to some degree. Causal analyses, which are sometimes employed in NA, will tend to reveal potential risks in resolving a need. Strategic planning, which is closely related to NA, necessitates that threats external to the organization be delineated. It is not much of an extension to think of threats as risks that have to be assessed.

Despite our previous discourse regarding risk, the social science literature did not contain many examples in which the levels of programmatic risk (especially of not meeting a need) were factored into the prioritizing decision. Why is this the case? One reason may be that incorporating risk into the long chain of NA events may make the whole endeavor appear to be too complicated and involved.

Another reason is that the idea of risk may have negative undertones that NACs, needs assessors, and other stakeholders would prefer not to consider or discuss. We, as human beings, have an inclination to think positively in planning programs and new directions. Formally adding risk into the equation may dampen and possibly even douse the "creative fires" (Scriven, 1967) of a group. It may dissipate energy, and the NAC, the needs assessor, and others associated with the process could become frustrated. Risk assessment in NA could be a very important way of prioritizing, but its promise lies more in the future than in current practice.

A RECAP: WHAT METHOD OF SETTING PRIORITIES SHOULD BE USED?

The answer depends on your situation. We have presented four ways for prioritizing needs, with one admittedly not seeing much current use. Does that mean we would not recommend it to others or incorporate some portion of it in the process? Of course not! If an NAC had information about health risks (e.g., the lack of appropriate prenatal care and its effects on low-birthweight infants and subsequent health

care problems and associated costs), that information should enter
into decisions about needs-based priorities. Similarly, if an NAC has
information about children at risk from the literature, it should in
clude that knowledge into its deliberations. At the present time
however, risk assessment will seem to be more of an adjunct to the
setting of priorities based on simple approaches, Sork's (1995) proce
dure, disaggregation, or even other techniques.

The simple approaches have merit for many NA situations. I
regard to Sork (1995) and the disaggregation method, we like both
strategies, and they have their strengths. Sork has given us good idea
about criteria that an NAC committee could use to establish prioritie
The criteria and process are generalizable, and we encourage nee
assessors to consider his ideas when prioritizing. Disaggregation is
very reasonable way to set priorities, especially when the decision
amenable to separation into clearly distinct, ordered criteria that ca
be analyzed one at a time. The choice is yours because you know th
local situation best.

As a final note, let us return to the idea of levels of need. As w
discussed the various strategies for prioritizing, only a few reference
were made to the three levels. Level 1, the service recipients
beneficiaries of services (e.g., students, children, patients, customer
still remains prime in our perspective. The simple approaches, Sork
(1995) procedure, disaggregation, and risk assessment all could
used to establish priorities for Level 1 needs. Analogously, the met
ods strike us as being suitable for establishing priorities for Levels
and 3, the providers of services and the overall system level, respe
tively. Indeed, the example we provided for disaggregation was at th
system level. Put simply, the methods are sound and can be flexib
adopted to different prioritizing situations.

NOTES

1. The idea that resolving one need will have impact on another one
similar to a feature of quality function deployment discussed in Chapter

2. WOSCOPS, the West of Scotland Coronary Prevention Study, as mentioned in the text, is based on an extensive database regarding heart disease that has been amassed over a long period of time with data still being collected. Various risk factors that potentially predict heart problems and ways to prevent or reduce the incidence of heart disease have been studied. Some of the many published articles from WOSCOPS come from an analysis of the existing data, whereas others are experimental in nature. The authorship of WOSCOPS reports is generally very long due to the involvement of different types of health professionals and the complex requirements of the data analysis. The published studies are excellent sources of information about risks in this area, and we encourage needs assessors to review them. Two that we used in generating the discussion in the text were *Economic Benefit Analysis of Primary Prevention With Pravastatin* (Caro et al., 1997) and *Identification of High-Risk Groups and Comparison With Other Cardiovascular Intervention Trials* (West of Scotland Coronary Prevention Group, 1996).

FROM NEEDS TO
SOLUTION STRATEGIES

 olutions now must be located or developed to alleviate the problems represented by high-priority needs. Needs assessment (NA) has clearly moved into Phase 3 activities. Many end somewhere in Phase 2 and seldom progress to the selection of solution strategies. The goal, however, is to enhance the ability of the organization to provide services to Level 1 target groups. Not dealing with solutions is to leave the NA in a crude, unfinished state. Delivering a list of prioritized needs to decision makers will not suffice. If the needs are complex, finding solutions will be a demanding and involved activity.

A number of considerations should be kept in mind as the needs assessment committee (NAC) begins to move into this facet of NA. They are the following:

- Do not become frustrated because selecting a solution strategy requires group deliberations and, in some instances, a serious investment of time and resources (it is worth the cost if the need is serious and major).

- Avoid getting so enamored with looking for a solution strategy that prioritized needs seem to get lost in the process (solutions must always be defined in terms of the needs for which they are intended).

- Do not fixate on one solution; try to identify multiple strategies or design features that have the potential to affect a prioritized need.

- Develop and/or identify criteria against which potential solution strategies can be assessed.

Five approaches for identifying and selecting solution strategies have relevance here: reviewing the literature; benchmarking; multi-attribute utility theory (MAUT), a well-established but perhaps underused technique; simple multi-attribute rating technique (SMART); and quality function deployment (QFD), a relatively recent arrival on the NA scene. Their main features and examples of their application to NA will be described below.

HOW DO THE FIVE APPROACHES COMPARE?

Table 6.1 contains a brief summary of the approaches. All are predicated on a group of individuals working together to come up with a solution strategy or a set of solution strategies. Generally, the group should be small, ranging in size from 8 to 10 on the low side to perhaps 20 on the high side. The group must have a fairly open decision making style with the ability to debate the pros and cons of solution from a variety of perspectives. Continuation of the original NAC is one option because there is an established decision-making environment. As discussed in Chapter 2, it may be desirable to alter the composition of the group in accord with the requirements of Phase activities, particularly the identification and selection of solution strategies as well as the development of action plans.

There are many points of overlap across the five approaches. For example, in benchmarking, criteria are used when looking at the efforts of other organizations, even though those criteria may not be as explicitly developed and prioritized as in MAUT. Similarly, QFD could be applied for the identification of critical design features that then are the criteria used for benchmarking.

Another area of overlap is communication. Taking QFD as an illustration, communication is mandated across pertinent groups within an organization. This is an important principle to follow, whether the needs call for new or improved "hard" products such as consumer goods or for better social programs. Communication lays the groundwork for making the difficult decisions related to solutions and the allocation of funds for their subsequent development and implementation. The need for extensive communication is common across the entries of Table 6.1.

All of the approaches take place after Phase 2 of the NA has been completed. Getting into solution strategies earlier is premature and would interfere with a full analysis of the problem area.

REVIEWING THE LITERATURE AND BENCHMARKING

REVIEWING THE LITERATURE

Certainly, consulting the literature is a good activity. Take this book as an example. We had a need (how to bridge the gap from NA to the development of action plans) that required attention. Despite more than 45 years of collective experience, there were major deficiencies in our NA knowledge. It was not reasonable to expect that we would have used and have intimate understanding of all aspects of NA. Without the literature, the richness of text that we attained would not have been realized.

The literature provided the basis for including SMART and QFD, two techniques with which we had only some familiarity, in this chapter. Again, if the literature had not been available, there would have been limited discussions of multiple-methods data and risk assessment in previous chapters.

Table 6.1 An Examination of Approaches to Selecting Solutions for Prioritized Needs

Features		Approaches			
	Reviewing the Literature	*Benchmarking*	*Multi-attribute Utility Technique (MAUT)*	*Simple Multi-Attribute Rating Technique (SMART)*	*Quality Function Deployment (QFD)*
Description	Use of literature to identify potential solution strategies and possible exemplary sites	Looking at how other similar groups and organizations have handled needs comparable to those of your organization	Develop criteria against which to rate solution strategies	Modified version of MAUT designed to simplify the process, especially the first few steps of MAUT	Identify key program design features and assess their likelihood of resolving the needs
Major outcome	Identification of solution strategies used successfully as reported in the literature or in similar organizations	Identification and observation of solution strategies used in similar organizations	Summarized rating of solution strategy with the highest potential utility for resolving the need	See MAUT	Determination of which design features to emphasize via a one-page chart or figure

Pluses	Focus on scouring the literature for solutions; excitement in looking at other organizations; may get NAC out to the field	There are no substitutes for direct observation of solution strategies and discussion with those who have experience implementing them	Forces the NAC to identify criteria and their importance; relatively short group process	Same as MAUT except that the process has been modified for large group use	A large amount of needs-based information is summarized on a one-page chart; recognizes the potential of positive and negative interactions of design features
Minuses	Criteria for solutions may not be fully specified; generalizing solution strategies to contexts with subtle differences	Could be costly due to the need to visit similar sites, and sometimes subtle variations in context will limit the ability to generalize a solution	Groups may struggle in defining and agreeing on criteria and their weights; different groups may have different values for criteria	Process may appear simpler than it actually is; groups may not be familiar with some of the criteria	Adapted from manufacturing contexts and may not fit some other NA situations well; limited application to social problems; may appear to be complex on first inspection

As we return to the emphasis on programmatic NA, much has already transpired. At this point in the NA, there have been meetings, most of the NA process has been completed, and causal analyses have shown where organizational action could be taken. With these activities behind it, the NAC now looks for possible solutions based on what is known about high-priority needs. There is a lot of information available to guide the NAC in searching for references about solutions. One thing the committee might first do is to locate experts and ask for their input regarding ways to resolve problems and fruitful avenues to explore in existing sources. The literature is also a vast repository of information about solutions.

If the problem area is complicated and the task large, the NAC should be divided into subcommittees, each with the charge of reviewing a portion of the literature and reporting it back to the needs assessor for synthesis and later presentation to the entire group. To aid in the final selection of promising approaches, a format such as the one shown in Table 6.2 might be employed.

When filled in, the table and supporting documentation provide the NAC with a basis for an in-depth discussion of solution strategies. In many cases, members of the NAC and the needs assessor(s) will be familiar with the library. Virtually all libraries now have access to an extensive array of electronic databases that provide a means for locating solutions. Seek the help of the local librarian, if necessary. In reviewing sources, keep in mind the suggested criteria that constitute the rows of Table 6.2.

Once the group focuses on several key strategies that would seem to fit best and work in the local situation, pay special attention to the row labeled "Exemplars." Exemplary sites could be visited by NAC members or other key stakeholders. This entails expenditure of funds, but for major areas of need, it is a wise outlay. There is no substitute for direct observation and on-site discussion with personnel who have the responsibility for delivering and administering services to those in need.

Table 6.2 Example of Format for Summarizing Possible Solution Strategies Located by the NAC

Key Criteria of Solution Strategies	Possible Solutions				
	Solution 1	Solution 2	Solution 3	Solution 4	Solution 5
Characteristics of the strategy					
Populations served					
Staff training required					
Evaluation data supporting effectiveness					
Space and equipment needs					
Start-up costs					
Continuing costs					
Advantages					
Disadvantages					
Fit with our situation					
Exemplars (successful sites)					
Other observations					

BENCHMARKING

In the mid-1980s, one Midwestern, suburban school district undergoing rapid growth (from 6,000 students to upwards of 11,000) identified other school districts that had recently seen similar changes in their schools. The other districts had comparable populations and were mainly in the Midwestern and Eastern parts of the country. Teams from the planning committee then visited the districts for several days to see how they coped with the need for space and how they viewed the challenge for new academic programs. The district looked for benchmarking situations in which this type of change was seen as an opportunity not only in regard to physical space but for moving into innovative educational delivery systems. The visiting teams asked probing questions that would help them to see beneath the surface of the benchmarking organization. Overall, the expenditure of funds was justified, given the magnitude of the needs the district was facing.

Many times, other organizations would be flattered to be chosen for benchmarking purposes (i.e., examining their programs for adoption in another location). They would enjoy interacting with outsiders and participating in the give-and-take of the discussion and the questions raised. In general, social service organizations are not in competition with each other and should be willing to share what they are doing. In instances where there is a good deal of competition, the willingness to share may be reduced. (Thomas and Altschuld observed this occurrence in a Delphi study conducted in 1986 in a very competitive business setting.)

Let us now examine the concept of benchmarking more closely. Benchmarking is defined as a process whereby organizations identify other organizations similar to themselves that are doing better jobs of producing a product, serving a specific set of constituent needs, creating a more positive internal environment, and so forth. Seeking another organization for benchmarking is an open and honest admission that we must do better. Improvement is predicated on defining the needs of those being served (Level 1 target groups), establishing goals and objectives, having measures of outcomes, being competitive, and basing efforts on best practices (Camp, 1989, as adapted by Siegel, 1997; see also Alstete, 1995).

The organization then begins to locate other groups or agencies that have demonstrated that they are more capable than others at achieving the same or similar results. The ultimate objective would be the improvement of services offered to meet needs.

Six overarching or basic steps are required for benchmarking. First, the organization in which you are located must carefully define and prioritize its needs. Where and in what ways is it deficient? How is it failing to serve its constituents? Could it lose its market in the future? How will the needs of those it serves change over time, and is it prepared to meet those needs? What must it do to maintain its current viability or grow over time? The leadership and staff of the organization should be in agreement about needs and should be committed to and supportive of benchmarking as a procedure for learning better ways of meeting needs.

Second, the organization must search by whatever means are at its disposal for information about solution strategies and organizations that have managed to succeed in identical or highly parallel contexts. These are the "Exemplars" in Table 6.2. Third, if the organization perceives that benchmarking would be a good investment of monetary and human resources, it must contact the exemplars to see if they would be willing to be benchmarked.

Fourth, it would be important for the organization to develop a list of probing questions to ask of the assisting organization(s). Samples are provided below. (Note: they are just that, samples. Questions would have to be prioritized so that the major decision-making concerns of the adopting organization are well represented.)

How did they get into the process of change?

How did they go about identifying their needs?

What kinds of information did they collect?

How did they determine the direction for change, and how did they build organizational commitment and buy-in?

How was the process of change facilitated?

What major barriers or problems did they encounter, and how did they resolve them?

How much time does it require to get new efforts off the ground?

How much start-up cost was there, and what are the current maintenance costs?

If more money were available, what would you do and why would you pursue this action?

If less money were available, what would you cut and why?

What advice would you give to another group starting out in this direction? What specifically would you do, and what would you not do?

What were the biggest mistakes that were made?

The questions do not have to be formulated to the nth degree. They are semistructured and reflect areas of greatest importance to the adopting organization, those that are most closely related to its local situation. The questions are used during the site visits as part of the discussion with staff members and administrators. Avoid grilling respondents; rather, think of a rich interaction that would transpire between a group of old and close friends, where everyone would feel free to express their opinions and perceptions. (Also keep in mind that it is desirable to stay in contact with the benchmarked group after returning to your organization. They could become a good sounding board for the solution strategies eventually chosen for the local situation.)

Tape-record key comments where applicable, and the visiting team should allot time each day for individually summarizing their perceptions and group debriefing. Collect materials that the benchmarked organization has available and is willing to share.

The fifth step would be to analyze the data. In general, the procedures given in Chapter 4 for working with qualitative data should be followed. Perhaps a table such as Table 6.2 or modified along the lines of that table could be used to portray the information in a way that would help the NAC and other decision-making bodies to select a solution or a combination of solutions.

The sixth step would be to make decisions based on the information that was collected. Materials should be supplied to the decision makers for their review in advance of a group meeting. It would be wise to include a brief synopsis of the entire NA process up to this point with prioritized needs highlighted so that everyone has the same frame in mind when they examine the results of the benchmarking activity.

MULTI-ATTRIBUTE UTILITY THEORY (MAUT)

Multi-Attribute Utility Theory (MAUT) and the related procedure of SMART represent another set of techniques that have been used to select solution strategies. Benjamin Franklin employed a version of MAUT to make personal decisions (Posavac & Carey, 1989). Posavac and Carey provided an in-depth explanation of MAUT in which they noted that it would be applicable to the selection of solution strategies for prioritized needs. These authors—as well as Pitz, Heerboth, and Sachs (1980); Pitz and McKillip (1984); McKillip (1987); and Camasso and Dick (1993)—have described the nature of MAUT or SMART and their utility for NA.

What is MAUT? MAUT is a procedure for making virtually any type of decision for selecting solutions by defining and judging the extent to which different solutions satisfy key criteria of importance to the decision-making group. MAUT looks a bit similar to some of the prioritizing techniques in Chapter 5 but focuses on a comparative analysis of solution strategies, not on a rank ordering of needs. One of its best uses is in juxtaposing and rating alternative solutions for resolving problems or for meeting needs.

Posavac and Carey (1989) described a 10-step process for implementing MAUT. Eight modified steps (we have combined some of them and added discussion of the steps in relation to their fit to NA) are presented below.

Step 1. Identify the organizational context, the needs for which solutions are to be selected, and the issues inherent in making decisions about needs. The context for decision making has to be clear and understood by the needs assessor and the NAC. Have needs been identified and prioritized? Have the priorities been established, taking into account issues of the size of the discrepancy, the number of people being affected, and the will of the system or organization to deal with its needs? Is it apparent as to how decisions will be made? What is the power structure? Are there provisions to include concerned stakeholders in the decision-making process? In other words, has the importance and the feasibility of attacking the needs been analyzed?

Step 2. Identify alternative solution strategies or options for high-priority needs. To use MAUT, it is necessary to identify alternative solution strategies. This aspect of MAUT is very desirable. It forces the NAC out of thinking only of a single approach to resolving a problem or need. It puts pressure on the thought processes. It challenges the NAC to go beyond the normal boundaries of thought.

What are other ways that we could solve this problem? What does this solution do for us that another does not? How do the solutions compare to one another on various criteria?

Step 3. Identify criteria or dimensions of value for judging alternative solution strategies. Potential criteria at this point in an NA would be somewhat obvious. If the NA has been based on multiple methods and sources of data, if the literature has been studied, and if a causal analysis has been conducted, then the NAC should be able to establish multiple criteria for judging solution options. They might consist of immediate cost, staff skills necessary to implement the option, time necessary for design, costs of long-term maintenance of the option, likelihood of affecting the problem, acceptance of the solution by Level 1 target groups, and so forth. The criteria should be stated clearly and in measurable terms. It is wise to limit the number of criteria—less than 15 and preferably less than 10. The reason behind this recommendation becomes clearer when Step 5 is explained.

Step 4. Rank the criteria in order of importance. It should be stressed that many of the steps in MAUT require that group consensus be reached in ranking the criteria in terms of their relative importance. Other steps in the MAUT process also require consensus of the group. An experienced leader encourages the voicing of different views by members of the group, allots adequate time for discussion of varied perspectives, and helps the group to arrive at agreement.

Step 5. Rate the criteria in terms of importance, "preserving ratios," and normalize the ratios or resulting weights (Posavac & Carey, 1989, p. 102). The title of this step is more imposing than what is actually required to put it into operation. First, start with the lowest-ranked criterion from Step 4 and give it a value such as 10. Then look at the next lowest criterion and give it a value of 20 if it is perceived as being twice as important as the lowest criterion, 30 if it is three times as great, 15 if it is one and a half times as great, or 10 if the group feels that it is of the same magnitude of importance. This is done for each criterion in relation to the value for the lowest-ranked criterion. (This is the preserving of ratios idea.)

Next, the values or ratio scores for importance are summed, and the importance value for each individual criterion is divided by that sum and multiplied by 100. The results of this procedure are what are called *importance weights.* They add to 100 and play a role in the subsequent calculations. (This is normalizing the ratios or weights.)

This procedure clarifies the relative strength or emphasis of each criterion. If the NAC started with many criteria, a lot of them would receive relatively low normalized weights and would be viewed as potentially trivial. A Pareto principle is in operation here (i.e., only a small subset of the criteria will be important), and only five to eight will be used in judging options. The smaller set simplifies the decision-making process, hence the earlier suggestion to limit the number of criteria in Step 3.

Step 6. Estimate the probability that the option will maximize the criterion. Now that a relative weight for each criterion has been specified, what impact does a given option or solution have on that criterion? To obtain this measure, members of the NAC individually examine each solution and give a probability estimate of the degree to which the solution would affect a criterion.

The scale used for this purpose has values of 0, representing the probability of no effect on a criterion (the use of 0 in such estimates is discouraged), to 1.00, representing maximum impact on the criterion. Generally, values of around .20 are recommended for a low probability of impact and around .70 for a high probability.

The final probabilities are termed *utilities*. They are the average of the estimates of individual NAC members who, at this time in the overall NA process, will probably agree to a large extent. The committee has worked together to identify options, criteria, the rank order of the criteria, and the relative weight assigned to each criterion. NAC members now share common understandings, and it is unlikely that radical differences in probability estimates would appear. If they do, the needs assessor should have the group discuss and reconcile any disparities in probabilities.

Step 7. Calculate the final utilities for each option. For each option there is now an average (or utility score) of the probability estimates for each criterion. To calculate the final utility for each option, take the utility score and multiply by the importance weight for a criterion. Do the same for all criteria for that particular solution. Sum them, and the higher the sum, the more likely it is that the solution should be selected over others (i.e., it has higher likelihood over others in its ability to satisfy the important criteria).

Step 8. Make a decision. The MAUT procedure has given the committee a pretty good idea of which solution to choose. The solutions have essentially been sorted by weighted importance factors and probability estimates.

Still, decisions remain for the NAC. If cost has not been included in the criteria, which cost parameters are necessary to implement an

Table 6.3   General Table Shell for MAUT Applications

		Solution Strategies		
Importance Criteria	*Weight*	*Normalized Weight*	*Build New Roads*	*Encourage Development in Satellite Communities*
————				
————				
————				
————				
————				
		$\Sigma W = 100^a$	Total[b]	Total[b]

a. All weights are added together; then the sum is divided into each weight, and the resulting quotient is multiplied by 100.
b. See Table 6.4 for an explanation and examples of totals.

option? What kinds of human resources will it take to initiate and maintain the option? Although one option may be better in the short term, would the probability estimates change if the long-term perspective were taken? The NAC must think about these considerations along with the results from the MAUT procedure before arriving at its final decision.

Okay, how do we put all these steps together? Table 6.3 is a generic example of how MAUT data could be displayed. Criteria and their importance weights are listed at the left, thus forming the rows of the table. Options or solutions are the column headings. The entries in a cell are the probability estimates or utilities. The sums at the bottom of each column represent the final utilities or likelihood estimates for each option. They are sums of the cell entries (probabilities) times the row normalized weights. The larger the sum, the greater the potential of the option to satisfy the criteria that the group established at the start of the MAUT process. Although MAUT at first glance may appear to be complex, it results in an easily interpreted decision-oriented process.

Let us now apply MAUT to an area of need. Consider the following example we have created to show the perniciousness of traffic problems affecting all major cities. After the example, we will demonstrate how MAUT helps us in looking at potential solution strategies.

Traffic, Traffic Everywhere and Nothing
to Do but Contemplate One's Navel

We live in very large cities, Columbus and Seattle. Like the vast majority of others who work or live in major urban centers, we are amazed at their growth and disheartened at the unbelievable traffic problems that are emerging everywhere. At rush hour, sections of the superhighway around Columbus grind to a standstill and are in virtual gridlock. Seattle and the shoreline corridor of which it is part are in a period of unprecedented expansion. The traffic in and around the city is incredible, and visitors to the area seem to comment about it under their collective breath. The loss of productive endeavor by individuals stuck in traffic runs into the billions of dollars, gasoline is wasted, and frustration can rise to Himalayan levels. It makes one long for the bucolic life!

Traffic in our cities will become worse unless something is done. One unlikely approach to the problem is to try to reduce the population growth by restricting migration to the cities and surrounding areas. This has led one Seattle writer (Watson, 1997) to comment (tongue in cheek) about what he titled the "KBO" movement. He noted that in accord with "Keeping the Bastards Out," he had even gone so far as to have advertised about the lousy weather and mudslides in the Seattle area, but he was losing his leadership of KBO. He had been unable to stem the rising tide of population. In a democratic society characterized by a high degree of choice, other solutions to the problem will have to be sought.

Another approach to studying and potentially resolving this problem was described by Chuang (1997). He cited research done by scientists at the Los Alamos National Laboratory in New Mexico regarding what are termed *critical density functions*. A density function for a road would deal with how many cars would have to be on it at a certain time to lead to a serious slowdown of traffic. Or what would happen if several slow drivers were on at the same time and traffic began to back up? Computer simulation models are used to determine density functions and the effects on them if key variables were to change (closing times at large employers, rainstorms that slow traffic, a major accident blocking one lane, etc.). Although computer simulations are helpful for examining the traffic problem, they may not fully reflect alternative solutions to it.

In addition, it would be important to recognize that traffic is further complicated by the topography of an area, the location of current and future highways, the location of businesses in relation to transportation systems, economic trends, and tourist and leisure attractions—admittedly a larger consideration for Seattle than Columbus. (In 1997, Turnbull reported that traffic gridlock grew faster in Columbus than all other cities in the United States except for Salt Lake City in the period from 1988 to 1994. So the bragging rights in this dubious category seem to belong to the Midwest.)

Whatever the solution chosen, something must be done about traffic to enrich the quality of urban living.

Assume that a group of knowledgeable planners is looking for ways to improve the traffic patterns of a major metropolitan area and they know that limiting growth is not an option. They have been considering solution strategies such as the following:

- building major new inner and outer belts;

- encouraging business and housing developments in satellite communities so that traffic would be localized to the satellites, which are connected by lightweight rail to the major center;

- working with businesses to set up "virtual" offices so that many employees could work at home several days a week and communicate electronically;

- encourage businesses and industries to restructure the workday to enable employees to report on a staggered schedule basis, thereby spreading the traffic out evenly through the day;

- provide tax abatements to development groups to encourage them to build new communities within the city for senior citizens and busy urban young professionals who are tired of the hassle of commuting; and

- other options, including the possibility of combining any of the above solution strategies.

MAUT is an excellent procedure, tailor-made for the situation in the example. The need is of high priority and will increase unless action is taken. Assume that options have been generated by a knowledge-able planning group with a great deal of experience in working with such problems. The only step missing before MAUT can be applied is the delineation, rank ordering, and normalizing of importance criteria or dimensions. For the sake of argument, let us postulate a small set of ordered criteria of importance. (Note: we are not experts in this type of urban planning, so just go along with the criteria shown below.)

Importance criteria in rank order from highest to lowest with their respective importance and normalized importance weights might consist of the following:

Rank	Solution	Weight	Normalized Weight
1	Cost of the solution strategy	60	40
2	Short-term effect on the problem	50	33
3	Long-term effect on the problem	30	20
4	Political acceptance of the solution strategy	10	7
	Sum of weights	150	100

Again for the sake of argument, let us look at just two solution strategies—building new roads and encouraging development in satellite communities. An illustrative MAUT decision table is provided in Table 6.4. Each solution has been examined in relation to each weighted criterion, the probability of that solution affecting the criterion has been estimated, and the resulting sum of utilities has been calculated.

Building new roads was the solution of choice in the hypothetical example. In the short term, it had good viability, and even in the longer term, it did not seem to be an unfavored solution. It might also be interesting to try out the MAUT procedure with other concerned and knowledgeable decision-making groups to see if their results would be similar.

Table 6.4 A MAUT Application to Resolving the Problem of Too Much Traffic

Importance Criteria	Normalized Weight	Building New Roads	Encouraging Development in Satellite Communities
		Solution Strategies	
Cost	40	.40	.80[a]
Short-term effects	33	.80	.15
Long-term effects	20	.60	.40
Political acceptance	7	.50	.30
	$\Sigma W = 100$	Total = 58[b,c]	Total = 47[b]

a. Encouraging development in satellite communities received a high probability in this case due to the fact that it was perceived as keeping costs down.
b. The totals were obtained by multiplying each row entry in a column by the normalized weight for the row and then summing the resulting products for each column.
c. Building new roads would be the solution of choice based on MAUT.

SIMPLE MULTI-ATTRIBUTE RATING TECHNIQUE (SMART)

SMART, as its name implies, is a shortened version of MAUT that has potential application with large decision-making groups. Camasso and Dick (1993) observed that MAUT may not work well in situations in which there are many alternatives, different constituent groups, and values that the needs assessor hopes to maximize. SMART is a technique that may be better suited to the complex environment of highly varied social services delivered to a wide cross section of groups within a community. It eliminates the need for a planning group to go through the rank ordering and normalizing steps of MAUT.

Camasso and Dick (1993) described how SMART was used in human services planning in New Jersey. Fifty-one advisory council members from a variety of agencies or programs were involved in a day-long process. They were divided into small groups of six to eight people who were provided with summarized NA data collected from surveys of the community, professional staff, and clients as well as from analyses of social indicators. They were also given a table with the top

20 problems in order from each of the three groups surveyed. Two hours were allotted for studying the results. (This is similar to the approach proposed for initiating the prioritization of needs in Chapter 5.)

When the 2 hours were over, a scoring sheet was distributed to participants that contained five highlighted clusters of problems or issues—economic opportunity, health, education, family/children development, and crime and delinquency. The participants were required to allot 100 points among the five clusters, assigning a higher number of points to those clusters that they felt were more important and smaller amounts to those that were less important. Participants were also allowed to place subproblems associated with each cluster from the top 20 list (see above) on the scoring sheet. For the subproblems within a cluster, they could assign a maximum of 5 points to a subproblem. The maximum score that could be obtained was 500 (5 points per each individual problem in a cluster × 100 points divided up and then assigned to the five main clusters).

At this point, while the group was at lunch, the staff calculated total weights (products) for each participant for each highlighted problem area and/or cluster. The total weights are the product of the points assigned to a cluster times the points assigned to a problem within it. They are the importance weights to be used with probabilities that are estimated in the next step of the SMART process. (Remember, the weights for a cluster and subproblems within it are analogous to the rank-ordered and normalized weights of MAUT.) When participants returned, they were given a second scoring sheet onto which they transferred their importance weights as column entries. The column entries also contained labeling indicating clusters and subproblems within them.

The rows of the new sheet showed the major social services (or solutions) offered by county agencies. What the participants then had to do was estimate the probability that each service was meeting the weighted importance criterion represented by a column. To do so, they used a scale with values from 1 (almost totally not meeting the criterion) to 100 (totally meeting the criterion). Again, this rating is akin to similar steps in MAUT.

The authors indicated that this activity was time-consuming and arduous, taking nearly 2¾ hours to complete. Fatigue and carelessness in assigning probabilities probably affected the validity and reliability of the process. In any case, the staff then determined the final results for each service by multiplying the probabilities supplied by the participants by the importance weights.

In other words, to what extent was a particular service (solution) satisfying the weighted criteria (problem areas)? Were some services achieving higher summed scores than others? These scores, which reflected the degree to which specific services were maximizing important criteria, were presented to state and county planning officials. The results were seen as being important for looking at the extent to which needs were being met.

Based on this experience, Camasso and Dick (1993) offered a number of insights into the use of SMART. One was that although it was easy to administer, a few people did not participate in their study and seemed to be confused or constrained by the process. A second observation was that a certain amount of "razzle-dazzle" in applying the technique could become a source of concern for some parties involved in an NA (they cite Chambers, Wedel, & Rodwell, 1992, on this point). They noted that SMART is just one method for arriving at choices, and as good as it may be, it is impossible for one method to incorporate all relevant variables and to carry the full weight of decision making. Lastly, we would reiterate that because SMART streamlined the process for arriving at importance weights, it would seem to work better in larger group situations similar to the circumstances of Camasso and Dick.

QUALITY FUNCTION DEPLOYMENT (QFD)

Throughout this chapter, we have hinted at the difficulty in translating prioritized needs into plans for action, especially when the needs relate to complex, major problems. Much energy has been expended in Phases 1 and 2, and often the effort has been so draining that few material and spiritual (commitment) resources remain for dealing with solution strategies. Moreover, planning with regard to solutions sometimes appears to be a separate entity, with a life of its own almost divorced from the earlier assessment work. Needs assessors and NAC members begin to lose the connection between the needs they painstakingly determined (at what now feels like a distant time in the past) and the current planning they are undertaking.

We have been there and know how real this state of affairs is. Needs assessors must guard against this disconnect, this potential dysfunctional fit between needs and program plans.

One way of translating needs into plans for action and for reducing the level of disconnectedness is Quality Function Deployment (QFD). QFD, which was originated in Japan in 1972 for developing products of high quality, makes needs visually and intellectually paramount in the planning process. Since crossing the Pacific to the United States in the early 1980s, it has enjoyed widespread and increasing acceptance here as well as elsewhere.

This discussion of QFD is derived primarily from the writings of Shillito (1994) and Hauser and Clausing (1988). Although their work is in business and industry, it has value for educators, social workers, mental health planners, evaluators, and others in the social sciences. The principles of QFD generalize to many different settings.

To understand QFD, the general purposes and nature of it will be explained followed by examination of a figure (the house of quality) that is at the core of the process. The house of quality (HOQ) shows the relationship between needs and features of programs that help to reduce or resolve them. The HOQ is a quickly understood visual summary of the QFD process and a procedure for quantifying solution strategies based on the needs of the client or consumer. The QFD process helps the NAC to determine and select solutions with a high potential for resolving problems.

After presentation of the HOQ from the business and industry perspective, examples from education will illustrate QFD applications in an area for which it was not originally intended. Lastly, a list of suggestions for how to implement QFD is provided.

QFD relies on strong communication across different areas within companies and organizations (Shillito, 1994). It entails that companies, school systems, community agencies, and government bureaus develop programs based on Level 1 needs—customer and client needs. Need is the cornerstone of the process and remains prominent throughout all QFD work. In QFD, need is referred to as the "voice of the customer or client." In QFD, solutions must constantly be compared to customer needs.

Shillito (1994) stressed that QFD is an interdisciplinary team process with five overarching features:

1. Focusing on the customer and the needs of the customer

2. Including competitive marketplace forces in the deliberations regarding the design of solution strategies (although social, educational, and public agencies are not generally in competitive environments, thinking about competition and benchmarking against actual or potential competitors tend to strengthen solutions that are generated)

3. Using and enhancing existing teams or collaborative groups within organizations as well as promoting the development of teams. QFD requires in-depth communication across many individuals and groups that have a stake in the programs that are eventually implemented. The impact of QFD in regard to organizational communication should be positive.

4. Documenting the process from initial examination of needs through the development of the means to resolve them

5. Translating somewhat nebulous customer needs and perspectives into goals with measurable outcomes and programs and products that are likely to meet those goals on the first try

QFD starts with the collection of information about customer needs or Level 1 needs. This information could be in regard to the use of a product, aspects of products that consumers find undesirable, or why consumers are not purchasing a company's products or services. The data are obtained from surveys, focus group interviews, individual interviews, observations, prototype tests, and existing databases. The QFD process also includes determining the priority of needs.

In QFD, the data are first analyzed with the goal of producing a tree diagram—a simple clustering into common categories or themes arising from the customers' point of view. The following is a practical example of how the QFD process might be started.

How to Start the QFD Process

A large Midwestern university began an extensive academic reorganization with a view toward devolving many responsibilities from the university level down to specific colleges (see Chapter 7 for a more extensive discussion of this example). As the reorganization proceeded, a number of key issues and problems relating to staff (support, clerical, and administrative) were uncovered. For each college, procedures for evaluating staff and enhancing their development were reviewed. It soon became apparent that the procedures were in disarray and unevenly administered. (Some staff members were evaluated yearly, whereas others had not ever been formally evaluated.) In time, new guidelines would be written for evaluation and supervision, and it was hoped that they would help staff to proactively engage in training to enhance their skills.

The human resources (HR) office of the university was charged with assisting colleges in their study of existing staff policies and in the subsequent development of new ones. HR provided consultants to assist performance management committees (PMCs) appointed within each college for carrying out this work. Each committee consisted of 6 to 10 individuals representing staff, faculty, and administration.

One college collected five kinds of data: (a) written policies used in departments of the college; (b) informal interviews with department chairs; (c) a survey of all staff members; (d) focus group interviews with supervisors, administrators, and other groups in the college; and (e) a brief review of the literature on personnel practices. The committee then devoted several of its meetings to brainstorming activities. The HR consultants compiled and organized the information to help the committee in its deliberations.

Through these endeavors, the committee began to categorize the variables or problems that were identified into common themes or needs. Examples were characteristics of successful employee-supervisor relationships, what a performance review should or should not include, employee input into the performance review, recognition for excellent performance, time problems associated with evaluating performance, training needs for those conducting performance reviews, and the relationship of job performance to pay and compensation (Performance Management Committee, 1997).

The information in the last part of the example could be placed into a tree diagram (see Figure 6.1) that depicts the main categories for an area of concern and the variables comprising the categories. Constructing the diagram requires relatively little time and is a visual summary of key variables. The figure becomes input for the next step of QFD and is a handy reference throughout the QFD process.

The main categories on the left side of the tree diagram can be one way of obtaining a sense of customer requirements or needs. They are important for the HOQ and are entered on an HOQ diagram or matrix (see Figure 6.2). In the above example, the needs would be the criteria against which any new performance management system would be judged. Only prioritized needs would be considered for further analysis.

(Note: the HOQ works for either services or products. Murgatroyd [1993] and Schauerman, Manno, and Peachy [1994] provided examples of its application to instructional services and course development. For products, Shillito [1994] used it in regard to manufacturing candles and pencils, and Hauser and Clausing [1988] described its application to the production of car doors—a product from one perspective and a component in a larger product from another.)

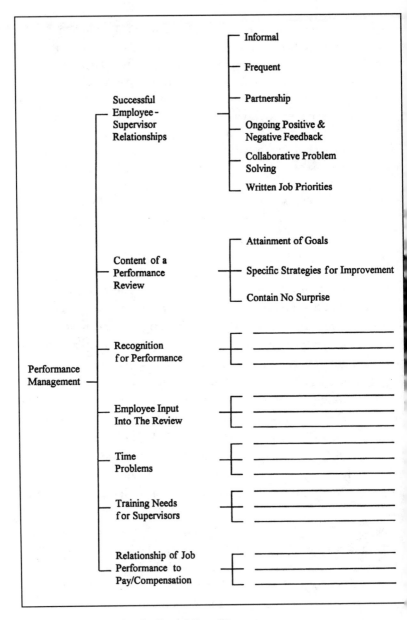

Figure 6.1. Example of a Partial Tree Diagram

After completing the tree diagram, the next step is to place the needs onto an HOQ matrix. A generic HOQ matrix, modified for use in the social sciences, is illustrated in Figure 6.2.

Needs are on the left side of the house. They could be unordered or placed in highest-priority order, but in either case they represent the most important needs resulting from an earlier phase of an NA process. In the fully configured HOQ, the right side of the house consists of the following set of scores for each need:

1. importance (priority) of a need (as determined in a variety of ways);
2. extent to which the organization is currently meeting the need (rated from 1 to 10, with 10 being the highest rating and 1 being the lowest);
3. extent to which others (competitors/benchmarking organizations) are meeting the need (rated using the 1-10 scale);
4. extent to which the organization would like to meet or truly has a desire to resolve the need (rated from 1 to 10);
5. an improvement ratio that is arrived at by dividing the extent to which the organization would like to meet the need (item 4) by the extent to which the organization is currently meeting the need (item 2);
6. a final score, which is the product of the importance score (item 1) and the improvement ratio (item 5); and
7. a percentage score obtained by simply dividing the final score for each need (given in item 6) by the total obtained from adding all the scores from item 6 and then multiplying by 100. The percentage scores sum to 100%, and scores are used in subsequent HOQ calculations.

Several scores on the right side or the planning part of the house contain information about the degree to which competitors satisfy client needs. Although benchmarking information is not used in the subsequent quantification of the HOQ, it is valuable for planning purposes. If the priority of a need is high, if the current status of your organization is low in regard to it, if a much higher level is desired, and if a competitor or benchmarking group has a high level of achievement, then a number of questions arise:

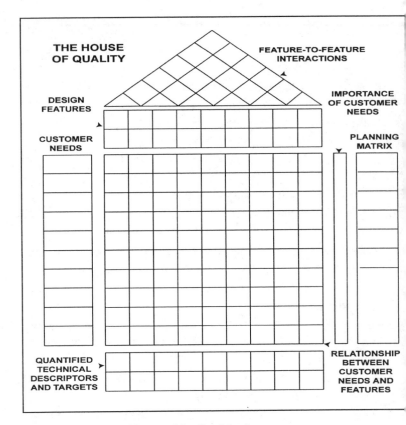

Figure 6.2. Generic House of Quality Matrix
SOURCE: Shillito (1994). Used by permission.

What are they doing right to achieve that level?

What are you doing wrong?

What are you not doing that perhaps you should?

These are pertinent concerns in the NA context. Processes used by the benchmarked group could become design features to be included in the ceiling in the HOQ.

The ceiling consists of design features that could possibly resolve the needs and that the organization has the ability to change or modify

Design features come from the literature, experience, benchmarked organizations, and cross-disciplinary teams with rich understandings of what might or might not work. Undoubtedly, the NAC will meet several times to determine the most important design features for the HOQ. Because the HOQ figure has its greatest visual impact when it fits on one page, care must be exercised in selecting design features. Generally, they are limited to 10 or fewer.

In the performance management example, the group might decide that the yearly evaluation process should be altered. Multiple sources of feedback should be sought for evaluation and review, more opportunities for training staff members should be made available, job expectations should be spelled out more clearly, and a series of other actions should be considered as candidates for the ceiling of the house, the column headings. Each design feature is compared to each need (left side of the house) to determine the potential effect of that feature on the need. If, in the judgment of NAC members, a design feature would have a high impact on the need, then a 9 would be placed in the appropriate cell. In turn, 3 and 1 represent medium and low impact, respectively.

To complete the HOQ, the roof and basement are added. (In the real world, you start with the foundation, but this is the world of NA, so allow us some latitude!) The roof reflects the fact that changing one design feature could affect other design features. The roof is a visual form of shorthand for capturing these interactions.

In a sense, as Shillito (1994) noted, the roof is a cross-impact analysis of design features. Each cell in the roof represents the intersection of two features acting on each other with values of 9, 3, or 1 for strong, moderate, or low impact of one feature on another. Other rating systems could be used that take into account the direction of the interaction (positive or negative) as well as its strength.

The cross-impact analysis is not used in the quantification of the HOQ, but it helps program planners see another dimension of the solution. It would be ideal to identify a design feature with high impact on needs and high, positive impact on other design features. Certainly, that feature would be of major importance for a solution strategy. Such interactions sometimes get lost in other solution selection processes.

Think about design features in regard to the performance management example. If more sources of information were desired for the yearly review process, they would have a major and, most likely, negative impact on the complexity of the review, the time required for the review, and so forth. (Despite these negative interactions with other design features, more sources may still be emphasized in the solution strategy due to its impact on high-priority needs.) Conversely, providing more extensive training for conducting yearly reviews may affect other design features extensively, and those effects would probably be positive. The basement of the house is where the quantitative foundation is developed. Recall that for every cell in the main body of the house, we have entered a 9, 3, or 1, depending on the effect of the design feature on each need. (Note: these are sometimes depicted by a shorthand set of symbols used in QFD. See Figures 6.3 and 6.4.) Also recall that on the far right, we have a column that contains the percentage score for that particular need. The percentage score is a function of the importance of a need and the degree to which the organization feels it should improve its current status regarding that need. Higher percentage scores indicate higher importance and higher demands for improvement.

To obtain values for the foundation of the house (values that guide the planning effort), each cell entry (9, 3, or 1) is multiplied by the corresponding percentage score from the far right side. This is done for every cell in the main part of the house. Then, for each design feature (or column), the products are summed to produce a total shown at the bottom of the column. The column totals are summed, that sum is divided into each individual column total, and the results are multiplied by 100 to produce a percentage score for each column. In this manner, design features with higher column percentages would be identified as those to be stressed in improvement efforts.

Thus, this one diagram contains an extensive amount of information about needs and solutions. Much of this information is in other approaches to planning, but it generally has not been pulled together as well as it has in the HOQ. To reiterate, the HOQ contains a listing of high-priority needs, benchmarking data, an improvement ratio for each need, key design features, the degree to which a design feature might affect a need, the interactions of design features with each other, and the design features of most importance for improvement. Beyond that, the entire HOQ has been generated through an interactive process.

A completed HOQ for the development of a quality pencil is shown in Figure 6.3 (Shillito, 1994). Traditionally, for products in manufacturing, other data such as sales point (amount that changes in a product are expected to affect sales), costs, outcome measures, and targeted levels of change may be included.

How might QFD and HOQ relate to education, mental health, health care delivery, state and government agencies, and other settings more pertinent to this text (i.e., social and educational programs)? In 1993 and 1994, QFD was adopted for use in developing programs in postsecondary (community college) education and for designing a distance education program.

Schauerman, Manno, and Peachy (1993, 1994) described the use of a modified QFD process in a community college. First, they stressed that it is essential to understand who the consumers are, understand what needs they have, and express those needs in the language of that customer. (This latter theme is consistently emphasized in QFD because the original nature of customer needs often loses its meaning when translated into the internal jargon of an organization.) In addition, the authors separated the customers into those who were internal and external to organization. They noted that it is helpful to clarify which group is the focus of the QFD effort. Separate HOQs tend to be required for different customers.

Then they briefly summarized the three main steps of their QFD analysis. Information was collected from various constituencies (Step 1), followed by a delineation of the delivery systems that were currently in place in their college (Step 2). The key aspects of those

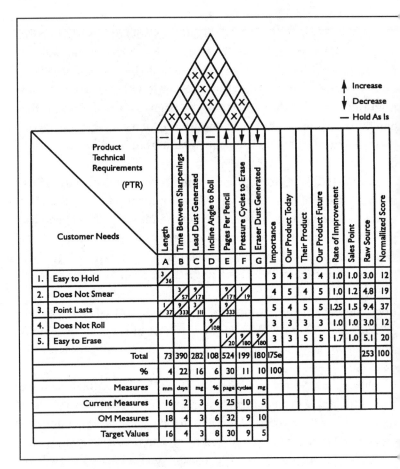

Figure 6.3. Matrix 1: The House of Quality for Pencil
SOURCE: Shillito (1994). Used by permission.

systems were the design features for their HOQ. These two sets of data
became input for the construction (Step 3) of two separate HOQ
matrices—one for education and instruction and the other for support
services at the college. In accord with the demands of QFD, the design
features were examined in terms of their impact on each specific need
identified from the key constituencies.

Instead of a traditional HOQ matrix, the authors provided tables for the highest needs for each of three constituencies (two external and one internal). In the tables, the needs were compared to 14 different design features (learning support, student growth outside of the classroom, research, etc.) in terms of how each design feature affected them. From these tables and a full QFD analysis, the community college decided to focus its efforts on 4 design features. By doing so it felt that it would improve its ability to meet its customers' needs, maintain appeal and market share, and enhance the quality of its services. It is now planning to use QFD on a yearly basis to study the delivery of services to external and internal constituencies.

The potential for distance education and for "virtual universities" has become apparent with the emergence of the Internet. Along this line, Murgatroyd (1993) discussed how QFD could be used to develop a distance education course titled "Organizational Change." On the basis of data collected from students who were representative of the target population for the course, Murgatroyd created an HOQ matrix that included the following:

- needs (*what* should be accomplished from the perspective of the consumer or student in this case);

- design features (*how* the needs might be resolved);

- the extent to which the needs are currently being met (based on student ratings of the extent to which the *whats* were being accomplished on a traditional 5-point scale);

- *whats* versus *hows*, which used a simple 3-point scale, with 3 representing a strong effect of the how on the what and 1 equaling a weak effect (these are the cell entries in the main part of the house);

- the difficulty of the organization to achieve or work on the *hows*, as rated by individuals within the organization using a 9-point scale;

- design targets for each of the *hows* that are measurable (e.g., so many case studies included in the course, the number of assignments, etc.);

- an assessment rating that is an estimate of how much value will be added to a learner's experience by virtue of incorporating aspects of the *how* into the course;

- an importance rating given to each *how*, ranging from 1 (unimportant) to 5 (very important);

- an overall measure of design difficulty, which is the sum of the ratings for organizational difficulty and importance;

- the interaction of design features on each other (the roof of the HOQ); and

- direction of improvement, which indicates the potential direction of change for a specific *how*.

Murgatroyd's (1993) HOQ is shown in Figure 6.4. Even though the author did not provide the QFD calculations that led to the final direction-of-improvement arrows and other aspects of the HOQ, a great deal of information has been captured in one coherent picture. Such a figure is helpful in developing programs to ameliorate needs. Murgatroyd concluded his article by suggesting that QFD is valuable for the design of training and the improvement of service quality in distance education.

Both Murgatroyd (1993) and Shillito (1994) offered pointers to assist NACs and planning groups in using QFD. Among them were the following:

1. *Avoid mixing whats and hows (Murgatroyd).* This is a theme that has also been emphasized by Witkin (1984) and Witkin and Altschuld (1995). Groups tend to jump rapidly into solution strategies without first carefully identifying and clarifying needs. Remember that a need is the discrepancy between current status and desired or "what ought to be" status. A need is not a solution strategy. The needs assessor must be vigilant and keep the NAC on task in regard to identifying and prioritizing needs before getting into the "hows."

2. *Develop a glossary of terms for needs (Shillito).* As deliberations move forward, it is easy to lose sight of the actual nature of customer or client needs. There is limited space on an HOQ matrix, and hence only a few words can be used to highlight or summarize a need. It would be easy, based on the tree diagram, to establish a list of needs

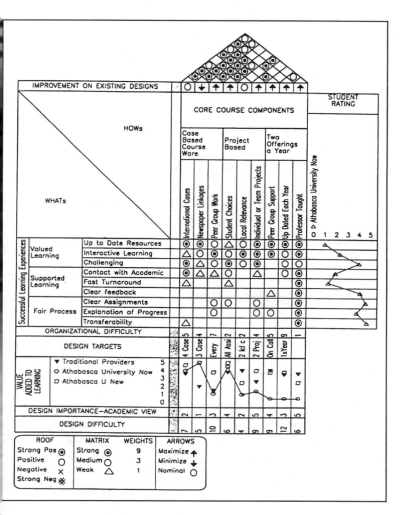

Figure 6.4. An Application of the House of Quality Model of QFD
SOURCE: Murgatroyd (1993). Used by permission.

defined in the words of the customers that would be available for referral. This list should keep the meaning of needs in the forefront of group thinking.

3. *Involve real customers and clients in the development of the HOQ matrix (Shillito).* Shillito (1994), in the business and industry context,

noted that it may be beneficial to include consumers (the Level 1 targets) in the process of constructing the house. This might be different in the social sciences and human services when compared to the design of products. If there are highly varied constituencies with disparate needs, as in the community college example, it would be necessary to construct separate HOQs and involve the constituencies accordingly.

4. *Consider using a difference rather than a ratio score for comparing the organization's current versus desired status in meeting a customer need (Shillito).* The right side of the house requires the specification of an improvement ratio. This is the degree to which the organization is currently meeting the need in the relationship to the degree that it would like to meet the need. In some situations, the ratio score can be misleading. Shillito (1994) noted that a 9:3 ratio is given the same weight in subsequent HOQ calculations as is a 3:1 ratio. If the difference score had been used, the first difference would be a 6 and the second a 2, resulting in vastly altered subsequent calculations. Shillito suggested that the choice of multiplier rests with the NAC or planning group. Perhaps the calculations could be done both ways and the results compared.

5. *Specify the hows as clearly as possible and carefully select which hows will be included in the HOQ (Murgatroyd and Shillito).* Murgatroyd (1993) observed that hows are often described at different levels of specificity, and Shillito (1994) proposed that it would be useful to have a glossary of descriptions for the hows (design features). The hows should be defined in enough detail so that they have common meaning across team members working on the HOQ and subsequent action plans. Shillito cautioned against overdesign by noting that only a small number of needs and key design features should be stressed. Similarly Murgatroyd indicated that a matrix consisting of 15 needs and 15 design features would lead to dealing with 225 cells. What is occurring here is an admonition to adhere to the Pareto principle for both the whats and the hows. The message is to keep it simple and focus only on the high-priority needs and major design features.

A final note is in order about QFD. Murgatroyd (1993) warned about unrealistic expectations in regard to the QFD process. We concur. As you get familiar with QFD and its promise as an NA and planning procedure, you may become enamored with its deceptive simplicity. Don't!

The HOQ matrix is not that difficult to understand once one has been exposed to the principles underlying its construction. Much needs-related information is consolidated into a highly compressed format. Just as our own houses appear, at first glance, as simple, single units, so too does the HOQ. But our views change as we see our homes as consisting of complex electrical, mechanical, water, and air/heat conduction systems. They are made of many materials and erected in accord with certain principles of structural design. Analyzing a house in this way shows a much more complicated picture.

If the analogy is carried further, QFD takes a fair amount of time, it requires in-depth discussion, ideas have to be clearly communicated to make it meaningful, and people (particularly administrators and planning group members) could and will get impatient (even frustrated) with the process. In sum, it is paradoxically both simple and complex. Perhaps the key question then is, "Is it worth the effort for NA?"

In relatively small projects it may not be, given the time and effort needed to develop the HOQ. The direct use of other planning procedures in these instances would probably work well. Relevance trees or traditional types of approaches starting with goals and then the construction of success maps, program review and evaluation technique (PERT) charts, and so on would be quite sufficient.

In other instances, we will be dealing with critical needs in social, educational, health, mental health, and other areas. Major expenditures of funds will be required to resolve problems. Intensive programs will be planned and implemented. QFD, as a strategy for selecting design features, could be of major value here. Its application in such situations is encouraged, and, over time, more adaptations of QFD to social programs are anticipated.

GOING BEYOND THE IDENTIFICATION
OF SOLUTION STRATEGIES

Reviewing the literature, benchmarking, MAUT, SMART, and QFD are all good ways to determine the best solutions for high-priority needs. They offer concrete procedures for selecting solutions and for making the criteria for that selection explicit. They provide excellent guidance for the dimensions to be included in the solution strategy. In other words, they are the foundation for the next activity in Phase 3.

Now the process must move forward into planning for action. Such things as organizational willingness to go ahead with changes; timelines for designing and implementing solutions; staff to accomplish the work, costs, and administrative responsibilities; and other related factors must become the center of our attention. Now, it is necessary to consider how to turn *proposed* solutions into *realized* solutions.

DESIGNING NEEDS-BASED
ACTION PLANS

REVIEW THE INFORMATION
THAT IS AVAILABLE TO YOU

Tremendous progress has been made to this point in needs assessment (NA) with only part of Phase 3, albeit a very important part, remaining to be done. The needs assessment committee (NAC), through its efforts, has set an elegant table for designing action plans. Now is the time to capitalize on the prior work. In Figure 7.1, key elements from the NA that are available for use in action planning are shown.

The NAC or a reconstituted NAC (see Chapter 2) has collected and synthesized a great deal of data and synthesized them into a strong information base, used the results of the assessment phase to establish priorities against specified criteria, identified solution strategies that have been compared to carefully defined criteria, developed growing understandings of what it will take to implement solutions, and

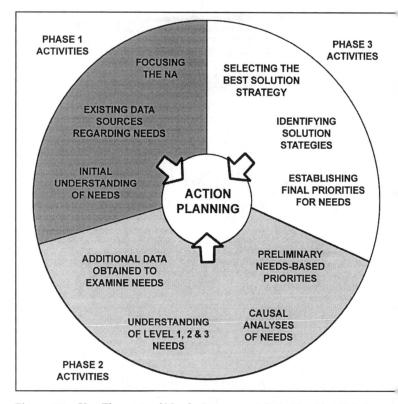

Figure 7.1. Key Elements of Needs Assessment Activities That Relate to Action Planning

interacted and communicated with decision makers and staff. The NAC also may have (through the literature, observations of bench-marked organizations, special studies, or causal analysis) learned about what is causing the need, especially factors that are under the aegis of the organization and could be affected by its actions.

Given the investment that has been made of time, money, and effort, the first activity in designing action plans is to examine everything that the NAC has done in Phases 1 and 2 and in the initial activities of Phase 3. Of special importance would be the nature of solution strategies that were identified and how they measure up to the standards established for them.

SOME SPECIFIC ASPECTS OF REVIEWING

CAREFULLY TAKE A SECOND LOOK
AT POTENTIAL SOLUTION STRATEGIES

Revisit the most likely solution strategy and compare it to its strongest competitors. Ask a number of key questions:

- What are the features of the top solution strategy that are its strongest assets?

- What are some of its less strong and even weak features?

- Were some of the competing strategies stronger in these areas?

- Would it be possible to combine features of solution strategies without compromising the integrity of the top solution?

- What is the scope of the solution in terms of location within the organization (i.e., will it reside in one unit or subsystem, or will it cut across many units)?

- How much time will the solution require—that is, from a relatively short time frame to develop and implement (less than 6 months) to intermediate and long-range time frames (2-5 years or even longer)?

- What is the scope of the solution in terms of focus—from narrow and fairly easy to implement to broad and complex to implement?

- Is it possible to divide a large solution strategy into smaller increments for implementation?

After several meetings in which these types of questions are discussed, the NAC will make a preliminary decision about the nature of the solution that it feels would be best for the organization.

THINK ABOUT HOW MANAGEMENT AND
STAFF WILL WORK WITH THE SOLUTION

The NAC should now proceed into thinking about how the solution would work within the organizational context. Initial considerations might include the nature of management involvement in the NA, management style, and staff involvement in the NA. Several things should be kept in mind when looking at these considerations.

First, management has been involved from the very start of the NA process. It has provided funds and staff for NA activities. It, like others in the organization, has sensed problems and recognized that business probably cannot proceed as usual. Why else would it have felt that an NA was necessary?

Management has clarified (especially if pushed by an external needs assessor) its stance in regard to the entire effort and to the fact that the NA could result in organizational change. It could even lead to management having to relinquish some aspects of control. Members of management have been invited and, it is hoped, have participated in supportive roles in meetings where critical parts of the NA process and results have been discussed. In other words, if the NA has been handled in the manner that we advocated earlier in this text, then the basis for commitment to change from management has been established.

But beyond involvement, the nature of the style of management and the support of individual managers is crucial for the ultimate success of a solution. The NAC, based on observations throughout the NA process, must answer the following question: Will the management of this organization accept and back this change related to needs?

What is its management style? Is the management collectively behind the change? If not, who is supporting it and who is not? What is the relative status of supporters and nonsupporters in the hierarchy? How are decisions made? Can the management tolerate a long-term innovation, or is its demeanor such that immediate gratification and results would be necessary? Is the management characterized by the patience so often required for implementing change? Is it a controlling environment or one that can adjust to and work with a lot less of "top-down" mandates? Has "lip service" been paid to spreading responsibility, or is there real commitment to this proposition? In other words, the NAC must assess the management climate for the solution.

Second, it is assumed that important staff members and outsiders also have been involved throughout the NA. Members of the NAC come from the ranks of the staff and are often the informal power brokers or sources of influence within the organization. Moreover, data and information have been collected from other staff members during the NA. Meetings have been held where the staff has been informed of progress and results. If the NA has been conducted appropriately, a positive climate should be in place. A sense of interest and the potential for change should have been fostered. Consider the following example.

Staff Involvement Is Worth the Time It Takes

As briefly mentioned in Chapter 2, Thomas and Altschuld (1985) led an NA effort for a nationwide consortium of businesses in a specialized technical industry. The consortium consisted of approximately 100 businesses and a major, public university. Monetary support was provided by the state in which the university was located, membership dues from the businesses, the university, and funds raised through services offered by the central staff of the consortium. The NA had been commissioned by the top leadership of the organization, and an important middle-level manager was designated to work with the external needs assessors. A two-wave mailed Delphi technique on current and future training needs was used with the respondents coming from the businesses in the consortium. Management interest and desire for change were clear at the start.

Staff commitment was another story. The staff primarily consisted of metallurgical and welding engineers, many of whom had advanced degrees. They had not been involved at the beginning of the endeavor. The needs assessors observed that they were somewhat hostile and viewed the NA as an intrusion on their turf by social scientists, a waste of time, a top-down mandate, and a needless expenditure of funds. Recognizing the negative dimensions of this situation, the needs assessors decided to seek the help of the engineering staff in analyzing the first Delphi questionnaire (the one with open-ended comments and ideas). Soliciting their involvement was not just for the purpose of gaining support for the NA, but it was necessary due to the technical nature of some responses. The input of the engineers also would have value for the design of the second scaled Delphi survey.

The engineers were trained to analyze the data; they then individually analyzed open-ended responses, and finally group meetings were conducted to discuss their interpretations and the categories produced from the answers to the first survey. Management agreed to underwrite all costs for the involvement of the engineers.

Thomas and Altschuld (1985) originally planned for half-day group meetings but had to expand the sessions to a full day. The meetings were lively. The engineers were not in agreement with each other. Analyzing the data provided an opportunity for professional growth and a way to understand the specialized expertise of other engineers. The meetings became a forum for lively, enriching discussions not available before. (This was an unintended benefit of the NA.) The engineers became very interested in the data and the outcomes of the NA project. Indeed, a cadre of individuals emerged who keenly awaited the final results of the NA and began to think of new directions for the consortium. Unfortunately, near the end of the NA, there was a massive reorganization, top leadership was replaced, and the NA no longer received the level of management endorsement it had previously enjoyed. Staff support, although highly positive, was unable to overcome the change in climate, and a unique opportunity was lost.

The example demonstrates the importance of communication and staff "buy-in." Once a new direction for an organization is chosen, the responsibility for the ultimate success of innovation rests on the commitment, energy, and enthusiasm of staff members. A well-implemented NA will create a broad base of ownership in its outcomes and in any new programs or procedures that are implemented. If the NA does not promote involvement, change will become more difficult.

NEXT, EXAMINE THE STRUCTURE
OF THE ORGANIZATION

Organizational structure affects the design of action plans. Organizations consist of systems and subsystems. NAs can be conducted at either the system or subsystem level. The choice will depend on the nature and severity of problems and issues confronting the organization as well as its size. A small agency or company may be able to look at needs across the entire organization, whereas a bigger one may find it easier to focus on the needs of a somewhat independent subsystem (or subsystems). At times, the nature of the problems confronting an organization determines the focus of the NA. In the consortium example described earlier, training needs were seen as cutting across all units of the consortium.

In Figure 1.3 in Chapter 1, a flowchart was given for a subsystem NA undertaken in a high school. Although the emphasis was on one department, the assessment produced findings relevant to other subsystems within the school. Therein lies the rub in NA. It is frequently difficult to confine the boundaries of an NA to only the subsystem. Often NAs uncover information related to other parts of the larger context.

Such findings have value, as indicated in Figure 1.3 by the notation "hold for systemwide NA." This kind of data may point toward critical interfaces or connections within the overall system that represent subsystem interdependencies. Subsystems are only somewhat autonomous, and there are constant trade-offs between autonomy and dependence. The data may also reveal a problem affecting the whole organization.

One consideration for the NAC would be the relationship between subsystems in the organization. How well do they work together? If a need is resolved in one subsystem, what effect would it have on others, and what help would it require from them? What resources do the other subsystems have that could be devoted to assisting another unit in regard to its needs? Is there a cooperative atmosphere that fosters such support? Is it possible to simply transfer resources without encountering political and psychological problems?

A practical illustration that highlights the complexity of the relationships between subsystems recently took place in a heavily populated Midwestern state. The situation is depicted below.

Subsystems! Subsystems! Subsystems!

The state department of education revised its teacher education requirements with the result that all colleges or schools of education in the state will have to provide certain courses and preparation experiences, some of which are not currently available for preservice teachers.

A large and diverse college of education in a comprehensive state university is organized into fairly independent units, one of which has the major responsibility for teacher training. Its resources would be stretched very thin to meet the impending need; indeed, they may not be sufficient to fully meet it.

Options for the unit include seeing whether additional faculty positions for teacher training could be funded (limited possibilities in this regard), redirecting resources by curtailing some courses and programs now offered, and/or seeking the assistance of the other units in the college. But there are problems with the last option. The other departments have different missions and staffing patterns. Their emphasis is not in teacher training but in areas such as educational administration, rehabilitation services, training and development in business and government, counselor education, higher education, exercise physiology, research and evaluation methodology, and so forth. Some of their faculty members may have education certificates, but they are involved only on the periphery of teacher training and certification. Given this context, the motivation of the other departments to help would not be high, and the ability to shift energy and resources across subsystems would be very limited and probably resisted.

The subsystems in this case are very independent and are, at best, a loosely coupled system at the college level. Forcing cooperation across them to resolve the specific need of one subsystem would be somewhat counterproductive and most likely resented. A better option for the department in question would be to reorient its priorities and use its resources to meet them. Another possibility would be to see if some of the existing courses in the college and elsewhere in the university could be used in lieu of new courses to satisfy the certification requirements. Whatever the solution chosen, the illustration is a clear example of how the structure (overall system and subsystems) influences the perception of needs and their resolution. Therefore, it is recommended that NACs carefully examine solution strategies in light of the structure of the organization.

CONSIDER THE ABILITY OF THE ORGANIZATION TO HANDLE DISRUPTION AND CHANGE

The life of an organization and the work of people within it can be seriously disrupted by attending to a need. The level of disruption is obviously dependent on the dimensions of a need (e.g., size of the discrepancy, number of people affected, susceptibility of the need to rectification, amount of resources required, etc.).

On the other hand, people are habitual creatures inured to patterns and ways of approaching their jobs and daily endeavors. We seek to guard our turf and protect it from an invasion. It takes time and effort for us to change. We have to develop a sense of ownership in the change, and, in addition to learning new skills and ways of operating, we need time to psychologically adjust to it. So change and stability will always be in a subtle tug-of-war, with needs being the focus of the struggle. But change we must; change is inevitable for social, educational, and health institutions as well as for businesses. Electronic technologies, communication techniques, ways of delivering health care, approaches to teaching, and financial investing are just a few examples of areas that have recently undergone rapid advances and transformations. They have challenged the status quo way of doing business.

Because resolving a need will result in varying degrees of disruption to the organization, the NAC must ask about the amount and level of upset that might occur. What is the ability of the staff to handle a specific change? To what extent will training be needed? Who will be hurt by the change? Who might benefit from it? Where will the resources come from? What types of reinforcement and support will be necessary to facilitate the solution? What incentives should be made available? How long will the disruption last? Will the enthusiasm of staff wane with the passage of time? Is it possible to divide a large, complex innovation into smaller discrete parts that could be implemented incrementally, thereby reducing disorder and the potential disenchantment that could arise from the longer, more involved total change package? (This latter issue, which was also raised near the beginning of this chapter, is based on an in-depth analysis of a failed NA by Witkin in 1984.)

The questions point toward the importance of context in supporting change. A number of researchers have recently been investigating the nature of variables in the context that facilitate change (see Altschuld & Kumar, 1995; Altschuld, Kumar, Smith, & Goodway, 1999; Goodway-Shiebler, 1994; Kumar & Altschuld, 1999; Smith, Steckler, McCormick, & McLeroy, 1993). Findings from these studies indicated that the implementation of innovations required awareness on the part of and strong support from administrators, a dedicated and critical mass of staff working with the change, communication channels that were frequently used by that staff to promote change, and a climate that makes nonadopters feel as though they are "out of it" unless they begin to adopt or move forward. It is noteworthy that mandates were not necessary in many situations to move forward. Rather, sometimes a press develops in the social environment, and it becomes the driving force, the impetus for change.

To summarize, the NAC must analyze the ability of the organization as represented by its staff and management to tolerate change. The context will make or break the implementation of the innovation, and there is no group better equipped than the NAC to make assessments about the environment. The NAC is on intimate terms with the needs, solutions, and the social subtleties of the organization.

FORCE FIELD ANALYSIS AS A TOOL TO PULL IDEAS TOGETHER

Force field analysis (FFA) is useful for synthesizing NAC deliberations about the organization and how it might handle the solution strategy. From the earlier questions, a long laundry list of concerns has been identified. Very quickly, the NAC should examine the concerns in regard to categories such as those in the preceding section, cluster ones that are similar together, and by a simple vote (or some other procedure) identify those that seem to be important to a category. FFA seems to work best when the number of items (concerns in this case) is kept relatively small in number (20 or less).

The concerns should then be rated in terms of their strength or importance to the success of the solution strategy. This might be done by each member of the NAC independently, with the individual ratings subsequently pulled together across the group. If there are major differences in ratings, then they are discussed and reconciled before going further (another reason for not having a very large NAC).

Once ratings are completed, the NAC should consider whether a concern is a factor that would impede the likelihood of a solution being successful or whether it would drive the solution to success. Then a force field diagram can be constructed as shown in Figure 7.2. Although FFA comparisons can be made by other means (e.g., calculating the total weights of driving and impeding forces and seeing which is larger), the diagram (with a weighted scale as shown) is an easily developed and understood visual device that helps the NAC in its work. It facilitates group discussion of which set of forces is stronger.

From the FFA, what forces are working for or against us? How strong are the driving and impeding forces? How amenable to change

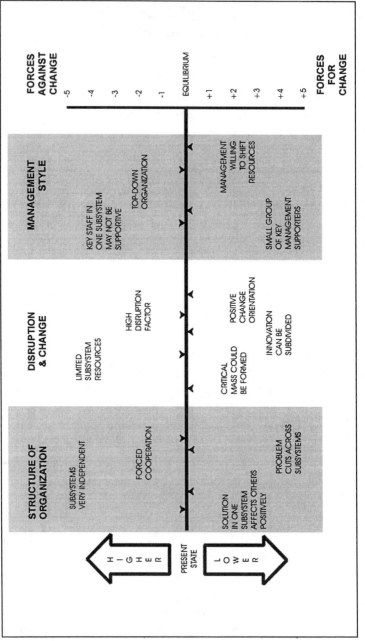

Figure 7.2. Force Field Analysis of Organizational Factors That Could Affect the Success or Failure of a Solution Strategy

are they? Will impeding forces be likely to change in a positive direction with the passage of time during implementation of the solution? Most important, action plans must take into account the impeding forces and build in strategies for reducing their impact.

ACTION PLANNING

PERSPECTIVES

Planning of social, health, training, and educational programs in our judgment has some major differences when compared to the planning for new products such as cars, computers, or telephone systems. Social, educational, and health programs are subject to variation in interpretation, implementation, and acceptance by staff within organizations. Those for whom they are intended (Level 1 needs) may perceive their benefits to be quite discrepant from the ones envisioned by planners and implementors. As an illustration, consider what happened with the swine flu epidemic in the 1980s. There was concern about the disease in regard to its impact on elderly senior citizens. Vaccine was made available at reasonable cost for the purpose of protecting the public. Unfortunately, vaccination was not widely accepted and used because some seniors became ill due to the shots, and a perception emerged (fueled by the media and most likely incorrect) that the treatment was worse than the disease. (Other well-intentioned programs for vaccinations may also not be accepted well by their target audiences because of religious beliefs or the misperception that some childhood diseases have been eliminated so there is really no need for the vaccinations.)

In addition, within organizations there are a substantial number of potential problems. Subsystems may or may not work well together. Staff members, who deal with a change, will have to feel its texture and grow with it before they implement activities. Undoubtedly, the implementation will have to be fine-tuned, shaped, and adapted to the skills and interpretations of the staff. If they are not ready for the change or if inadequate support is provided, haphazard implementation may result, and outcomes will fall short of expectations. Note the following case.

Implementation—The Critical Need for Staff Training

Consider how schools deal with computers. Some set up computer labs where computer skills are taught essentially as a new topic and one that is not highly tied into discipline-based content and instruction. Others use computer applications primarily for routinized drill, practice, or tutorial activities. Neither the training nor the time has been provided for teachers to use the full capability of the technology beyond its more mundane uses.

Efforts in some states are geared to providing schools with hardware, software, and wiring upgrades for networking. This support is necessary but grossly insufficient for moving to the more educationally exciting and promising uses of computer-assisted or computer-facilitated instruction. The funds available for training teachers and for providing them with the time to learn how to integrate computer technology into varied modes of instruction and content areas are far below what is needed now or will be needed in the future. Based on the current skills and understandings of teachers and other school staff members, it is clear that new initiatives will be less successful than would be desired (see Calnin, 1998, for an interesting study of how a school adapted to a major change in the use of computer-based technology).

From the above discussion, we are suggesting that action plans be very flexible. They serve as general guidelines and structures for change rather than straitjackets that will constrain staff and not allow for the emergence of the precious commodities of buy-in, initiative, and commitment. We are not opposed to the use of PERT (Program Evaluation and Review Technique), Gantt charts, or other detailed objectives-driven planning techniques (number of steps, step-by-step activity descriptions, timelines and schedules, and even determination of critical paths).

Program logic models could also be applied to developing action plans. By looking at the ultimate and along-the-way outcomes of a new program or project, valuable insights are gained about activities that must take place for the program to be successful and indicators that could be used to measure progress and results. In programs such as the implementation of revised procedures to guide mental health boards in their work with licensed providers or the implementation of new staff evaluation procedures at a very large institution, detail in planning is warranted, has value, and is appropriate.

The issue is not that such detail is bad but rather that a balance has to be achieved between the planning that occurs at the large system level and the need for flexibility and adaptability at the implementation level. Rigid mandates in a lot of the settings in which we have conducted NAs simply would not have worked.

INPUT FOR A SUCCESS MAP

An excellent approach for action planning is represented by a success map. The map depicts the major activities and events that must occur for the solution strategy to become a reality. The map is not overburdened with a huge number of specifics, but at the same time, there are enough to provide for a good understanding of the endeavor to be undertaken. Moreover, by having a general map, recognition is given to the subtlety of developing and delivering programs within complex social milieus. The plan must be able to adjust and take into account the specific nature of individual situations. This is analogous to the way in which houses are designed but then built to fit the contours and shapes of particular lots and in accord with the desires and needs of those who will live in them.

The NAC already has a lot of information for producing the action plan (success map). In addition to organizational factors, the techniques for selecting solution strategies (Chapter 6) provide insights into key design features to be stressed in the solution.

The example of the university that is revising its procedures for staff development and evaluation that was mentioned previously will now serve as the basis for the rest of this chapter. Within general guidelines, each college in the university was responsible for developing its own unique procedures. An oversight committee (a version of an NAC) decided to study the issue through numerous activities such as surveying staff members; conducting an extensive set of focus group interviews; examining procedures used in the college, university, and elsewhere; interviewing a small number of administrators; reviewing the literature; and meeting frequently to review information as it was collected and to deliberate about emerging understandings and directions. By these means, the nature of the need as well as the features that should be included in the new personnel procedures became clear.

Data collected from the staff indicated that there were many problems such as the following: Staff were not always evaluated, the staff evaluations that were done were characterized as being highly variable, multiple sources of input into the evaluation were seldom sought or used, evaluators (supervisors) were not trained in how to conduct the evaluations or versed in how to provide feedback (both positive and negative), the relationship of yearly evaluations to salary decisions was not apparent, feedback other than that on the yearly evaluations was rarely offered, and there were no provisions for staff to evaluate the quality of supervision and whether they felt a positive work environment was being maintained.

Support for updating skills (attendance at workshops, purchase of new software) was highly desired by staff, especially in light of the rapidity of technological change. In some instances, however, they literally had to fight to participate in training, and they had to deal with the attitude that somehow they were not doing their jobs when they were at workshops or training sessions. In other words, the climate was neither positive nor encouraging.

From interviews with administrators and supervisors, examination of current procedures and documents, and review of the literature, considerably more information was obtained. According to the administrators (department heads), the evaluation of staff was inconsistently implemented. The administrators were aware of many problems, and their responses indicated a receptivity to change. Supervisors noted that they had not been trained to be evaluators, they felt uncomfortable evaluating others, and they stated that they needed training and better ways of operating. From document analysis, the committee concluded that written policies governing personnel procedures in the college and its units were neither adequate nor up-to-date. Similarly, position descriptions were generally not up-to-date.

Review of the literature was also informative. A four-phase model of staff development and evaluation (planning, coaching, multiple sources of feedback, and outcomes) was identified and examined by the committee. Instruments and procedures used for staff guidance and evaluation in other parts of the university and from institutions in the metropolitan vicinity were obtained and studied. The literature also helped with regard to considerations about the storage and confidentiality of yearly review forms and the protection of employee rights.

Lastly, the committee spent a great deal of time discussing the environment of the college (the system) and the departments and units (the subsystems) within it. How much change would they or could they tolerate? Was the college willing to fund the training that was going to be needed? Who should be trained, and when should the new system be initiated? Because major disruptions would occur with a new and, it was hoped, improved performance management system, would it be possible to develop a system that could be divided into smaller, more palatable "stand-alone" pieces for implementation on an incremental basis? Would the new system have enough flexibility to be useful across the varied units of the college? How would it be received by all those involved? The information obtained by the committee in conjunction with its deliberations produced most of the ingredients needed to build the success map.

The committee was chosen well. It consisted of four respected representatives of the staff with extensive experience in the college. An administrator (not a faculty member) was asked by the dean to lead and facilitate the work of the committee. Two faculty members, one a department chair and the other a professor with a long historical view of the college, were asked to participate and agreed to do so. Two representatives from the human resource (HR) office of the university and a graduate student were full voting members of the committee. The graduate student handled many of the administrative tasks of the committee (minutes, meeting agendas, etc.), and the HR staff developed instruments and written procedures. Occasionally, one other staff member from human resources attended the meetings.

The charge to the committee and the work it represented were enormous. The college is quite large with major undergraduate, post-degree, and graduate programs and is consistently ranked in the top 10 education colleges in the country. Students come from throughout the university and the country, and many international students participate in the programs of the college. An average of 270 staff members, clerical and administrative and professional (A&P), are employed by the college. (Graduate students working on projects or teaching in the college are not included in the average.) Staff jobs are highly divergent, making it mandatory that performance management policies and procedures be flexible rather than rigid. Not much was in place, and hardly anyone in the college had been trained for the demands of a new performance management system.

To manage its work, the committee met approximately every 2 weeks or so during the full calendar year, including holiday periods. Meeting reminders were sent out via e-mail and by memo. All committee decisions were made by consensus and only after reasonable amounts of time were allocated to discussion and debate. The climate was open, and different points of view were encouraged. The atmosphere was challenging but not negative or confrontational.

Aside from the bimonthly meetings, there were subcommittee meetings, and materials were reviewed prior to the main meetings. In other words, committee members had to do their homework if progress was to be made. The committee maintained communication with the staff of the college via mechanisms such as collecting their perceptions, regular updates, and briefings of key staff advisory groups. The chair of the committee met with the dean and the dean's staff on several occasions to describe efforts and achievements as well as to clarify issues inherent in the emergent solution strategy (e.g., how will yearly evaluations relate to salary increments, and what is the college commitment to training and staff development?).

The pace and nature of the work were intense, and the committee would not have been successful without a keen sense of involvement and belief in the importance of the endeavor on the part of its members. The committee carried out many of the NAC functions described previously in this book.

Indeed, the committee really was an NAC! It cannot be stressed enough that the NA process is dependent on the quality of such a group and its work ethic. It was the cornerstone of the NA process.

The performance management system was viewed by both the college administrators and the committee as requiring 3 years to design, implement, evaluate, and modify with the sense that the committee would remain intact for that time period.

As the committee moved to the design of a solution strategy and a plan for action, it met as an entire group with key staff advisory boards for discussion and input. These meetings always started with a statement of what the committee had done, its next steps, and the frank admission that any proposed system should be viewed as a work in progress. The committee was open to comments and input as evidenced by the names, phone numbers, and e-mail addresses of its members being provided to all staff in the college. Staff members were encouraged to raise any concerns they had that, in turn, would be used in an anonymous fashion to refine and improve the system. The fact that the committee would stay intact and evaluate the system and problems associated with its use was conveyed in public communications. Many staff members took advantage of this option, which was an indication that the committee had achieved the openness it desired.

The committee, via its data collection procedures, was able to create a meaningful picture of current practices and needs. Although numerical discrepancies in a formal NA sense were not derived, the nature of the problems in the college was clear. What essentially had transpired was that the committee had completed Phases 1 and 2 of an NA process and concluded that action should be taken. There was strong basis for developing a solution strategy and planning for its implementation.

The committee was the ideal group to handle planning as well as implementation. By Phase 3 time, it was knowledgeable about the topic and had developed a good working climate with members understanding and valuing the perspectives of others. The group was neither too small nor so large that it became unwieldy. Although its members were unanimously behind the new system that would be developed, they were not casting a blind eye to the complexities of performance management. They were not zealots, and their commitment was a tempered one.

DEVELOPING THE SUCCESS MAP

The committee generated criteria for the solution and its implementation. The solution had to be systematic and yet, at the same time, had to accommodate the variability of work positions in the college. It had to have a way for staff to appeal ratings in year-end performance reviews, provisions for multiple input into the yearly evaluations, a formal mechanism for frequently revisiting and revising position descriptions, and an emphasis that went beyond performance review to the broader focus on planning and coaching activities. The new system would require that written materials be in place prior to staff training.

Any new system such as this one represents a huge amount of change and disruption to the social environment. Therefore, the committee felt that the system should be implemented incrementally over a 3-year period with sufficient time allotted for phase-in and modifications as needed. Extensive and ongoing staff training would be necessary to acquaint all staff with the system and to train the supervisors for the planning, coaching, feedback, and evaluating aspects of it. Because the system was expected to be modified over time, training would have to be updated and offered on a yearly basis for a number of years. The committee recognized that performance management systems are dynamic and subtle entities. Their development and

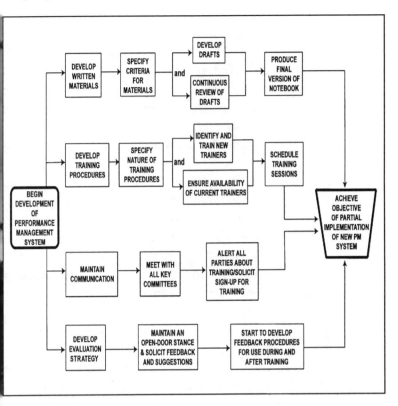

Figure 7.3. Success Map for First Tryout of Performance Management
System

subsequent improvement are predicated on open lines of communication, a willingness to evaluate how well they are working, and an
appraisal of whether they are worth the effort and cost.

With these parameters in mind, the success map shown in Figure
7.3 characterizes the action plan for implementing the solution. (Because the committee did not actually produce a success map, Figure
7.3 is a form of reconstructed logic of what happened in the situation.)

The action plan is divided into four basic parts—developing written
materials to guide all facets of the system, training for staff and
supervisors, maintaining communication with all involved parties in

the college, and evaluating the system. It was assumed that during first year of operation, the system would not be fully implemented. It was a major undertaking to develop training and, in turn, train all staff; install the new system; keep staff informed throughout the year; and evaluate the total endeavor. One year would be insufficient for full adoption of a new system that could be highly disruptive. Intuitively, the committee decided that the system should be introduced in a gradual manner.

The map represents the first phase of action necessary to develop and initiate the use of the performance management procedures. Although the four parts of the map are basically self-explanatory, some additional detail will be provided, followed by suggestions for altering the plan in the second and third years of system implementation.

Responsibilities for plan-related tasks were quickly decided on by the performance management committee. It had been a working committee during its entire existence, and specialized staff (human resource consultants) were assigned to it. The staff did the majority of the basic work on all tasks with review, commentary, and some direct input from the rest of the committee. (In other circumstances, it was necessary to use a more formal designation of responsibilities and duties to individuals and groups.)

Developing materials, in some respects, was the easiest aspect of the action plan. The committee had an impressive array of existing information and materials that had been obtained from its previous work on Phases 1 and 2 of the NA. Criteria established for development were quite simple—(a) written materials for the system had to be straightforward, and (b) they needed to fit closely with their use in staff training. The committee started by producing an outline of what would be the main sections of a looseleaf notebook to be given out during the training sessions. The system would have to be modified quite frequently in the first several years and less frequently later. Looseleaf pages and sections would accommodate the inclusion of such modifications in the notebook.

With the outline as a guide, the HR specialists generated the specific sections of the notebook. Examples included a brief discussion of why the system was required and key principles underlying it, working with staff in regard to planning for high-quality performance, forms for planning and setting objectives, approaches to coaching staff, a yearly performance review form, and the like. The system also called for the collection of multiple sources of input for the yearly performance review from a variety of individuals who had worked with the staff member and 360 degree evaluation (ratings of the supervisors by those they supervise that are conducted in such a way as to mask the identity of the latter individuals). Again, as noted above, committee members helped in the development and reviewed drafts of all materials. The notebook was assembled and examined for overall flow and design.

What seemed like an insurmountable task initially was completed in about 3 to 5 months, including numerous revisions. Five factors contributed to the relatively short time frame. Adequate staff resources, especially in terms of the HR consultants, were allocated to the work. Second, the consultants were knowledgeable and experienced, and that background came to the fore in producing the notebook. The discussion in Chapter 2 regarding the choice of committee members and its leadership is underscored. Third, the other members of the committee were willing to do some of the development, and thus it truly was a working committee. Fourth, the committee was able to capitalize on its earlier accomplishments rather than starting Phase 3 NA activities from scratch. This is essential for the process to proceed smoothly. Fifth, everyone believed in the effort and adhered to schedule as much as possible.

Training is the second part of the action plan. Virtually all new programs depend on some kind of adult education or training component (Sork, 1995). Training is an expensive and time-consuming proposition but is absolutely necessary. Training helps those individuals who would be responsible for implementing change to start learning about what is expected of them. In this case, training consisted of one 4-hour session in which the new system, expectations for staff and supervisors, timelines, the nature of the notebook content, what portions of the system might be implemented in its first year, and the evaluation of the system were explained. Trainees were expected to read and review the notebook after being initially trained. The notebook contained the names of the committee members with their phone and fax numbers as well as e-mail addresses.

The committee stressed that training should be provided in a small group environment. Performance management can become an emotionally charged issue, and small group settings are more conducive to raising questions and stating feelings. The committee wanted the same openness that characterized its work to carry over to training. This necessitated that many sessions be scheduled over approximately 2 months and that several external trainers (perhaps increasing the likelihood of slippage in the transfer of information) become involved due to the number of sessions required for all staff members and supervisors. The new trainers, in addition to the specialists, were assigned to the committee. Training had become even more costly.

We, the authors, agree with the committee's approach, even though it increased costs in this instance and will have the same effect in other situations. The approach represents money well spent.

Another aspect of the training focused on the performance management system as being in development and that feedback was actively being sought for modification and improvement purposes. The fact that the system was new and that not all of its features were expected to be used in a first-time tryout were also emphasized. For example, different review forms could be substituted for the ones in the notebook, particularly if they fit better with the parameters of specific jobs.

Timing of implementation will always be a matter of concern for all action plans. The committee had been diligently at its task for a year at the end of the calendar year. If implementation was delayed, the opportunity to test the system would be lost for a good portion of the second year. The committee felt that this was too long to wait.

Due to a collective sense of alacrity, the training sessions started right after the beginning of the new calendar year (midway into the academic year). A partial implementation would be accomplished by the end of the spring, so that the system would be synchronized with the regular cycle of staff evaluations at the university. It was anticipated that there would be a normal set of initial problems encountered, and some additional ones would arise from the press of the early beginning date. Furthermore, it was unlikely that components such as coaching or the reviewing and updating of position descriptions would be accomplished under the harsh constraints imposed by the starting date.

Communication could have been incorporated under other parts of the action plan but was separated for obvious reasons. Without frequent communication to staff and administrators, the efforts could have gone for naught. There were serious problems in performance management and evaluation uncovered during almost all of the data-gathering efforts. Some staff had never been evaluated, and a few units (including a major one) did not have a strategy for improving performance, providing feedback to staff, and conducting yearly evaluations. A climate had to be established that would help to support the system.

Given this situation, the committee maintained its proactive stance in communicating with staff, administrators, and the college community at large. More than 50% of all college staff had already provided data via surveys and focus group interviews during the early phases of committee work. Summarized results from these activities were sent to all staff. Regular updates were provided to the dean and the executive staff of the college. Areas that were problematic were immediately called to the attention of key administrators. The goal was to be credible to the college community and to develop a sense of ownership in a system that, it was hoped, would improve performance management practices in the college.

Evaluation, the final part of the plan, is closely related to communication. It should be remembered that the committee was carefully selected from respected peers throughout the college. It was anticipated that staff would contact committee members. Indeed, virtually every member of the committee was contacted informally about strengths and weaknesses of the new system as it was being developed and implemented. The strategy worked quite well here and would be successful in other situations depending on the quality of individuals serving on the committee. Are they perceived as being fair, open to communication, willing to take concerns back to the committee for consideration, and able to keep confidences? If the answers are yes, informal channels can be an effective mechanism for collecting evaluative data. Given the nature of the committee membership, it proved to be easy for the staff to contact members and express their concerns.

The evaluation also called for a small number (from 10 to 20) of individual interviews to be conducted toward the completion of the first tryout of the system. The interviews would be semistructured (with open-ended probes) in the hope that staff members and supervisors would freely discuss what had or had not worked and what their perceptions of the performance management system were. The committee assumed that it had established the appropriate atmosphere—one of trust, in which such evaluation procedures would work.

In conjunction, with the interviews the committee decided that a survey should be sent to all staff members to collect additional information about the system. Of particular importance would be the perceptions of those who are supervised of how the partial system was implemented, whether they were given sufficient time to review their yearly evaluations, how the supervisor helped them to plan for the next year, and so forth.

The last provision for evaluation was perhaps its most interesting one. During committee deliberations, it was observed that if the system was set up well, there would be many useful indicators of progress embedded in yearly performance reviews. How are the points on the evaluative scales being used? (Note: a new scaling approach, considerably different from ones on prior forms, was now being used.) Are there any completed yearly performance reviews in which multiple sources of feedback have been sought? Are different ratings being given to new employees as compared to individuals with more experience? Have supervisors stated what they are willing to do to support the development of the staff member in the coming year?

To collect such information, it is relatively easy to take archived yearly performance reviews and simply transfer the appropriate data to a summary form. Of course, safeguards for the privacy and anonymity of individual staff members and supervisors would have to be carefully maintained. In coming years, as the implementation of the system continues, more evaluative questions could be asked of the emergent database. In essence, what happened here was that evaluation was a direct outgrowth of the Phase 1 and 2 deliberations. Without that input, the conceptualization of the evaluation would have been more difficult.

As of this writing, the evaluation of the system is in process. Committee members have received some informal feedback from staff and their supervisors. The system appears to be a step forward, but concerns have been raised about the new scale and its interpretation, the structure and content of some of the forms, inadequate collection of multiple sources of feedback, the difficulty of delineating what such sources might be for a complex position serving many diverse publics, and the fact that the training was insufficient, particularly for units of the college that had not much of a prior performance management history. In the latter instances, implementing a performance management system was calling for a major shift in the culture.

To date, the committee has engaged in a preliminary discussion of the initial feedback. The discussion focused on the variability of units in the college, with some being able to rapidly adopt a more formal version of what they routinely had been doing and others having to adjust to a completely new way of operating. Discussion and analysis will continue as the implementation of the system moves forward and as more evaluation data are obtained. The goal of the committee is to modify and improve the system and its associated training for use in the succeeding years.

THE ACTION PLAN IN YEARS 2 AND 3

The action plan for the second and third year of implementation would be slightly different from the one in Figure 7.3. First, the materials in the notebook would have to be modified in accord with changes in the performance management system. Old materials in the notebooks would have to be replaced. Second, the training function would shift somewhat to issues of *planning* for quality performance and *coaching* activities, particularly for supervisors. More training will probably have to occur, potentially with multiple sessions spaced out over the year. Third, the communication strategy will be maintained as before, with the inclusion of information regarding how the system is working, changes in it, and newer perceptions of the staff.

Fourth, although some parts of the evaluation (interviews with staff and a staff survey) should be continued, the content might shift to staff satisfaction with the performance management system and perhaps more probing about the utility of the system as perceived by administrators and supervisors. In year 2 and even more so in year 3, the evaluation of the system could be based on the achievement of specified standards, such as 25% of supervisors engage in coaching and planning activities, supervisors formally meet with staff more than just when the yearly evaluation is to take place, the number of forms with multiple sources of input has risen to such and such a level, and there is a greater degree of support for staff development activities.

In year 3, as is obvious, the database will contain more information relevant to trends in the system. Key variables could be tracked over time to see the extent to which the system was being institutionalized. The committee will grow in its wisdom about the system and, it is hoped, will raise other questions about it.

OTHER IMPORTANT ACTIVITIES

The work of the performance management committee is not yet complete. Two other activities remain. The committee should make sure that it has documented all of its NA efforts to date. The committee has been doing this all along, and now it should double-check what has been archived and what else may be valuable to add to the formal record of efforts and achievements. Lastly, the committee should strive to evaluate its own performance in the introspective manner described in Chapter 2.

CONCLUSION

The endeavors of the performance management committee, which served as the main illustration in this chapter, did not include all of the activities in the three phases of NA. Although the initial charge to the committee narrowed the scope and focus of the work, the committee still did not go through a full and formal process of identifying and prioritizing needs. Causal analyses were not conducted, and multiple-solution strategies were neither sought nor compared. Is this situation so deviant from the processes described for NA that we would hesitate to classify it as one?

We would not propose viewing it in this way. The three phases were presented as an ideal set of activities to guide the NA process, not as "hard-and-fast" procedures to which an NAC must rigidly adhere. NAs will always be adapted to fit the features and texture of the local environment and the nature of the decisions to be made. The performance management example is a good illustration not only of adaptation but also of the success that an NAC can achieve.

The example could easily be generalized to other problems confronting organizations. Many educational and health organizations are currently dealing with issues related to distance education, using electronic means to facilitate group processes, providing diagnostic or specialized information to decentralized sites, and so on. Many needs require attention, priorities will have to be set, and many potential solutions will have to be considered. By looking at an effort such as that of the performance management committee and by examining the three phases of NA, other organizations should be able to develop reasonable strategies for conducting an NA within their own environment.

MULTIPLE- (MIXED-) METHODS
NEEDS ASSESSMENTS

n earlier portions of this book, frequent reference was
made to the use of multiple (mixed) methods in needs
assessment (NA) and the problems encountered in conducting a multiple-methods NA. With the issues and difficulties
brought out previously, why should a needs assessor consider a
multiple-methods approach for NA?

Let us begin by noting that in some instances, it would not be wise
to engage in or even consider a multiple-methods effort. First, the NA
may be funded at such a low level that only one approach to collecting
data is feasible. Second, the needs assessor may sense that the funder
has a focus solely on one method, is very attached to it, and therefore
would be reluctant to use an alternative method or multiple methods.
Third, the needs assessors may not have the skills required to implement some of the multiple methods. Fourth, the logistics necessary to
set up and use multiple methods may not be justified in terms of the
extra hassle needed to conduct the assessment.

Conversely, in our judgment, needs tend to be complex (not sim-
plistic) constructs based on highly varied values and perspectives.

Subtle factors enter into a decision that one need is more important than another and that funds and efforts should be directed toward a particular concern. A needs assessment committee (NAC) must be willing to justify and defend its choice of prioritized needs. In addition, the group must show that it is committed and willing to support programs designed to reduce needs. When looked at in this way, it is unlikely that a single method or strategy will reveal the full subtlety of needs in many situations.

Multiple (mixed) methods, however, come with obvious cost implications and a host of problems. Multiple-methods NAs require more time and money than most single-method approaches, and they tax the patience and methodological skills of many needs assessors. Even teams consisting of individuals with different methodological strengths may encounter difficulties working as a group and with the sheer volume of data that is often collected. Beyond these difficulties, deriving meaning from multiple sources is not a straightforward task when several individuals are involved, let alone when it becomes the focus of a larger group. Thus, the coordination required for a multiple-methods assessment will increase dramatically.

The final NA report will be complicated for the needs assessor(s) to produce and probably more difficult to read and understand, especially for the NAC and other involved stakeholders. It will take longer to generate. It will be lengthier, with the mandatory explanations and descriptions of individual methods and results as well as collective results across methods. If the results are not in agreement, the difficulty of writing escalates.

When choosing methods, needs assessors and NACs must take into account budgets, decision timeliness, organizational history, past studies conducted for the organization, the pattern of decision making, local politics, available sources of information, and other factors. Concerns such as these and the nature of the actual methods themselves influence final choices related to methodology. To illustrate what is involved, some advantages and disadvantages of single and multiple methods and other considerations regarding their implementation are provided in Table 8.1. The table is designed to depict the types of deliberations facing needs assessors when they select methods rather than being an exhaustive comparison of single and multiple methods.

Given our endorsement for multiple methods, the next logical question is, "How have they been used in NA studies?" Sources located through a search of the ERIC system, presentations made at the American Evaluation Association (AEA is the home organization for a large NA interest group), and reports and articles provided to the authors by other needs assessors were reviewed. In this manner, five multiple-methods NAs were identified. They are briefly summarized and analyzed in this chapter. All of them show the amount of effort required for a multiple-methods NA and the practical issues that arise in interpreting and combining different types of data to arrive at a common set of needs. After presentation of the *case studies,* a cross-case analysis will be provided.

The NAs were conducted in settings such as education, mental health, health, and community service (United Way). They were chosen based on the degree to which they met three criteria: the use of multiple methods (preferably three or more), the collection of an extensive amount of data, and/or the involvement of a team in data collection and interpretation.

It should be noted that not many multiple-methods NAs were found. There probably are more than those included in the ERIC system and the vast array of journals and reports that it indexes. (This is the traditional problem of many useful sources being located only in the file drawers of their authors.) Multiple-methods studies possibly do not show up in the literature due to the following reasons. One is that NAs are almost always conducted with the sole purpose of identifying needs and directions for a specific organization. They are internally funded for organizational use and are not intended for widespread dissemination. The interest is in relation to organizational policy and effort, not for publication or entry into a database accessible by others. Such NAs are not easily located.

Table 8.1 A Comparison of Some Aspects of Single- and Multiple-Methods Needs Assessments

Type of Approach	Advantages	Disadvantages	Some Considerations for Implementation
Single methods	Results are usually easier to interpret and understand	Will frequently not provide for in-depth understanding of needs	If budget is limited, only one method can be used; look for a method that is cost-effective in terms of information yield
	Needs assessor(s) are usually very familiar with the method	Information from one data source can be misleading; corroboration of needs is desirable	Consider the nature of the decision-making group, select a method to which they would attend
	Will take less time	If the single method is quantitative or qualitative, there are numerous embedded problems (see Chapters 3 and 4)	If possible, think of splitting even a small amount of funds to support "mini" multiple-methods approaches
	Does not require skills in multiple methods		
	Generally will be cheaper to implement	If the single method is qualitative there is no way to come up with an index of need	
	Will not require as many needs assessors		

Multiple methods	Tends to enhance understanding of needs, especially with regard to gaining an in-depth perspective of complex needs	Costs are higher than the single-methods case	Carefully examine the skills of the needs-assessing groups to determine how feasible a multiple-methods approach would be
		Requires skills in different methods and in the interpretation of results	Allot some money in the budget for following up the NA in the event that the data do not agree
	Corroboration across methods makes a stronger case for needs	Takes more time	Allot considerably more time and resources for final report generation than for single-method approaches
	May enable needs assessors to compensate for weaknesses in one method with the strengths of another	More needs assessors may have to be involved	
		Data may not agree	
	Challenges the needs assessors and decision-making group	Combining and interpreting data across methods is difficult	
		A final report is longer and more difficult to write	

A second reason for the lack of multiple-methods NAs is that they are difficult to implement, cost more, and require more time. Therefore, they may not be undertaken to any great degree. A third reason particularly pertinent to business and industry settings is that NAs may get into the realm of proprietary information that would not ordinarily be made available to others, especially competitors. A fourth reason may be that needs assessors in organizations perceive their roles as providing service, which would be quite different from how researchers or writers in NA would view the enterprise.

Lastly, there are some published multiple-methods studies that used multiple methods but do not quite fit the inclusion criteria. For example, Mitra (1994) used a focus group interview to determine how to design a survey. This type of situation, which is seen frequently in the literature, is valuable for needs assessors but does not reflect the use of multiple methods that are employed to better understand needs. In instances such as these, one method was implemented to improve the ensuing development and implementation of another.

In another interesting example, Laffrey et al. (1989) studied the health needs of Arab Americans by means of four methods (community forums, key informants, the U.S. census, and a small-scale survey). The study was conducted in a sound manner, with one finding being that understanding survey responses was immeasurably enhanced by learning about the nature of the specific culture in question. This study could have been included in the case studies, and we would certainly recommend it for review by readers of this text. Lastly, Iutcovich (1993) provided an excellent discussion of the use of multiple methods and the subtlety of interpreting the resultant data. Her article is also recommended for review. It is not part of this chapter because of its primary emphasis on the empowerment and buy-in of various stakeholding groups as opposed to multiple methods.

In Table 8.2, an overview of the five NA cases is provided. The table contains the name of the study, the authors and date, the content focus of the NA, the types of methods used, the nature of existing data sets included in the NA, a judgment about the degree to which the use of multiple methods was planned in advance, and a few comments

Table 8.2 Overview of Five Multiple-Methods Needs Assessments

		Case Studies			
Features	1	2	3	4	5
Authors and year	Demarest et al. (1984)	Lipsey et al. (1996)	Goering and Lin (1996)	Gutsche, Martin, Rumel, and Seaborn (1996)	Altschuld et al. (1997, Part 1); Cullen et al. (1997, Part 2)
NA focus	Continuing education needs of nurses in a large hospital	Community needs of large urban area in regard to social services	Determining the needs for mental health services in a highly populated province	Health care needs for a large province	Evaluation of a new, national educational information service that included a retrospective NA
Types of methods	Surveys, data from sources regarding quality assurance (records, patient charts, etc.), interviews	Numerous methods, including analysis of existing databases, focus group interviews, and a variety of survey procedures	Analysis of existing data from various databases, one of which consisted of survey data	Analysis of existing databases, focus group interviews, and information supplied by key informants	National survey, case studies of change-oriented sites, expert panel review of products

(continued)

Table 8.2 Continued

Features	Case Studies				
	1	2	3	4	5
Use of prior, existing sources	Yes	Yes	Yes	Yes	No (see detailed discussion)
Planned multiple-methods use	Yes	Yes	Yes	Yes (see detailed discussion)	No (see detailed discussion)
Comment	Quite different continuing education needs and priorities of needs identified from the multiple methods	Interesting way of depicting different information	Differing assumptions in regard to data kept on records, leading to complex problems in analysis and interpretation	Very large quantitative and qualitative data sets generated, making it somewhat difficult to summarize the data and define needs	Although the studies were not planned to corroborate each other, some very similar findings were observed

about the assessment. Each case will then be briefly described and analyzed in the text immediately following Table 8.2.

CASE STUDY 1—CONTINUING EDUCATION NEEDS OF NURSES

Background of the Study

In 1984, Demarest et al. observed that different methods used in an NA may yield different results and understandings of needs. They noted that in the health professions, surveys were the most prominent way of determining continuing education needs for health professionals. In contrast, limited continuing education needs were identified via examining quality assurance data in combination with data obtained from other sources (for examples of NA surveys in health and health-related fields, see Brunner, 1987; Hale, Altschuld, Gerald, & Reuning, 1989, 1991). Demarest and his coworkers cited the fact that although quality assurance sources (records, patient charts) could provide valuable information in this regard, it would be difficult to translate data from charts into educational needs. They then proceeded to identify the continuing education needs of nurses in a hospital setting by means of three distinct methods. The questions in their study were the following:

- Will the different methods yield different or similar data about the needs?

- Is it possible to use quality assurance data to identify educational needs?

An Overview of the Methodology

Three methods for collecting NA data were implemented independently by the three researchers. The NA was conducted at a midsized Veterans Administration medical center. The methods were individual interviews, a survey, and existing quality assurance sources (minutes from various committee meetings, an accreditation report, nursing quality assurance chart reviews, patient incidence reports, an annual study of patient incidents in terms of aggregated data, and others).

The interviews consisted of a small set of open-ended questions that allowed for probing or moving into new directions as the interviews progressed. The questions focused on problems encountered by nurses in the past year in performing their jobs, education that they felt they needed, and their thoughts about improving the quality of patient care. Forty-eight nurses were interviewed in this manner.

Another 100 nurses were surveyed by means of a short two-page questionnaire. The instrument contained two open-ended questions dealing with problems the nurses had encountered that they felt affected the quality of care delivered and their perceptions of further education needed to perform their work in a better manner. In addition, the survey contained a predetermined list of areas of care with the request that respondents supply specific examples of problems that they had in the area. The nurses could add other areas to the list, and they were also asked to rank order the items on the list.

The interviews were analyzed in a standard fashion (constant comparative method), and the number of responses per category was seen as an indicator of the relative importance or rank order of the category. For the surveys (60% completion rate), the rank order of needs was derived from the ranks provided by the nurses for the list of the areas of care. From the quality assurance data, five major themes were identified but not rank ordered. Then the findings from the three methods were compared.

Findings

This comparison of results from the three separate methods proved to be a difficult undertaking in this NA. Although there were similarities and points of overlap, in general, the needs identified or inferred were different. As the authors noted, "No distinct need was singled out as a priority via all three methods" (Demarest et al.,

1984, p. 10). They pointed out that although 12 needs were in common across two of the three methods, only 9 needs were uncovered by a specific, individual method. Even when needs were in common across two methods, the rank order of them often was not.

The needs assessors commented on how, at times, the findings from one method added meaning to those from another one. For example, in the interviews, the nurses expressed the opinion that the center was understaffed, which obviously would be a factor in the amount and quality of care delivered to patients—a problem uncovered from the quality assurance sources.

In their conclusions, the authors suggested that different methods led to different results, thus greatly complicating the issue of assigning priorities to needs. Indeed, the techniques, if used only by themselves, would have led to radically different decisions about the allocation of resources. Given these observations, Demarest et al. (1984) encouraged the use of multiple methods despite the lack of agreement across the three methods that were the essence of their study. They referred to combining multiple methods in assessing needs as a way to obtain a "more holistic or multifaceted approach to NA" (Demarest et al., 1984, p. 10). Another observation was that the data were not nearly as comprehensive as had been anticipated when the study was begun. Their final conclusion was that more research about NA methods and multiple-methods NAs was needed. (Their view in this regard completely coincides with that of the authors of this book.)

Analysis of the Case

First, the kind of situation that resulted in the above case is a typical result in multiple-methods NAs in which there is some concurrence as well as lack of agreement across methods. Second, it is clear that if programmatic choices were made and resources were allocated according to the results from a single method, they would not be as valid as those arising from a comparison of results from multiple sources, even if there is only partial agreement. The multiple methods forced the authors to more closely examine the continuing education needs of nurses. In most NA studies, we suspect that it is necessary to carefully scrutinize resulting needs in terms of how the data were obtained and the meaning ascribed to the overall data set. Third, the study depicts how difficult it will be to obtain discrepancy data from interviews, records, and even surveys that do not directly elicit discrepancy responses. In most of the data analysis in this study, need was inferred rather than directly measured. Fourth, by having different needs assessors independently conduct the three methods, the possibility of contamination in the study was probably reduced.

CASE STUDY 2—A COMMUNITY NA

Background of the Study

In 1996, Lipsey et al. conducted an NA for a regional United Way (UW) organization. Its purpose was to provide guidance for a new allocation process that was "designed to be responsive to identified community needs rather than follow the traditional model of annual grants to a designated set of United Way agencies" (Lipsey, Wilson, Shayne, Derzon, & Newbrough, 1997, p. 1). Within this general charge, two critical issues had to be addressed—classification of needs into categories or groups and how to measure or compare needs across a diversity of categories and types of data. Working with such issues is complicated because UW serves many different Level 1 target groups and funds numerous agencies that provide an extensive array of services.

An Overview of the Methodology

To accomplish the NA, it was necessary to collect data from quite varied sources. Among them were the following:

- demographic and epidemiological data from the census, local and regional health departments, and other groups that regularly keep and maintain databases on the population in the area;

- focus group interviews conducted with leaders in the community (those individuals who provide service) and Level 1 target groups (service recipients);

- telephone and mail surveys of agency directors, community residents, and residents of low-income neighborhoods; and

- an existing database that contained information on local service agencies (including financial profiles of the agencies).

Using information from the many sources of data, the project staff developed a categorization scheme to guide the NA. The scheme consisted of three dimensions, including major problem areas, major service areas, and population groups. They were depicted as the three axes of a cube and were then used to identify needs and as a way to organize the data from the different sources.

Of further importance to a multiple-methods emphasis is the concern of how to deal with and portray the data from multiple sources. To make sense of the data, the authors created a construct called the "need-service" gap, which is defined as a discrepancy between a need for a service and the actual services available to help with the problem. Although in this case it was neither easy nor possible to always have reliable and valid measures of needs and available services, the general construct made sense and would be utilitarian for looking at the UW situation.

Using the construct, project staff developed indices of the need-service gap. For example, via interview questions, they determined that if there were high demand for a service and limited ability to provide the service or to expand current services, then there was a high need. In their 5-point scale, a 5 represented high demand, but low expandability or ability to offer the service and a lower score might represent low demand and high expandability or ability to offer the service. A rating of 1 was the lowest point on the scale.

In a like manner, scales were developed from other variables such as financial reserves, community perceptions, and so forth. In all, scaled indicators of need-service gaps were developed in the areas of service capacity, financial reserves, provider's direct ratings of the gaps, perceptions of the general public regarding needs or problems, and the perceptions of residents of low-income areas about problems they or others had experienced in the prior 6 months.

Then, the reporting format depicted in Figure 4.3 (Chapter 4) was generated and used to provide information to UW for components of the three categories or dimensions of needs described above. Essentially, the procedure allows for the portrayal of sophisticated data in a style that can be quickly grasped by decision makers. To a degree, this is a clever adaptation of goal attainment scaling (GAS), with some loss of information as noted in Chapter 4. The loss seems to be within tolerable limits.

Findings

Lipsey et al. (1997) observed that nearly all the service areas achieved overall high scores across indices such as those shown in Figure 4.3. They also used this approach to analyze and present data for comparing need-service gaps for public and private or nonprofit agencies. Three of the main conclusions of this NA were the following:

- For the most part, the gap between needs and services was wide.

- The pattern of gaps was similar for the private or nonprofit as well as for the public agencies.

- Large gaps for the two types of providers were observed for seven common areas of need (child care, housing assistance and shelter, nutrition, etc.).

- Public providers in particular had large gaps in the areas of financial and emergency assistance and substance abuse prevention and treatment.

The needs assessors commented that a comprehensive and comparative NA for a large community represents a "formidable challenge" (authors' terminology). The size of the overall undertaking was immense, with the final report consisting of three volumes that totaled in excess of 520 pages of text and accompanying data. (It is interesting to note that Case Study 4, which was a community NA regarding health, also produced three separate volumes for its final report.) Thirty-one individuals were listed on the cover page of the final report as authors or contributors.

The authors noted that one option for NA would be to simply avoid getting into the complexity of data and tasks that situations such as this one required. On the other hand, they suggested that a better approach would be to seek practical ways of summarizing data and thereby creating information that is helpful in the real world of decision making.

Analysis of the Case

Identifying and analyzing needs in this case was a daunting task. The creation of the need-service gap approach was a sensible way of pulling together a tremendous amount of data and information from varied sources. The authors recognized that, when faced with the three volumes mandated by such a vast set of data, it was doubtful that decision makers, even with large blocks of time, would be able to digest and grasp the full implications of the report for resource allocation.

By developing tables that portrayed results in a visual, summarized, and easily inspected manner, Lipsey et al. (1997) were trying to facilitate the process of review and analysis of the findings. Their variation of GAS is tailored to UW and community organization work and should generalize to other communities as well as to other areas of need (education, health care, mental health, etc.).

Obviously, this NA was costly in terms of the number of people involved, the scope of the effort, and the organizational skills necessary to produce the final report and decision-oriented tables. Therefore, questions could be raised such as the following: Were data from some sources consistently better (more meaningful and utilitarian) than that from others? Would it have been possible to reduce costs by not including some sources?

CASE STUDY 3—MENTAL HEALTH NEEDS

Background of the Study

The purposes of this study were to identify mental health needs in the Canadian province of Ontario and to compare how mental health care dollars and services were distributed in accord with those needs. Such an NA, if carried out well, would establish a baseline for evaluating future efforts in mental health and would help the mental health care system to better deal with gaps in its own base of knowledge (Goering & Lin, 1996).

An Overview of the Methodology

To conduct the NA, the authors examined four existing sources of data. They were the Mental Health Supplement to the Ontario Health Survey; the National Physician Database (NPDB), with information pertinent to physicians in Ontario; data from provincial hospitals regarding admissions, discharges, and transfers; and data from the Canadian Institute for Health Information (CIHI) for general and specialty hospitals.

Immediately, it became apparent that although the data sources were relevant to the needs in question, they contained information collected for different reasons and that different methods had been used to obtain the data. For example, the purposes for collecting some data included research, billing, and administration with potentially subtle variations in definitions and subsequent coding. The methods also varied considerably, with the supplement employing a voluntary research survey (implemented through an interview procedure), whereas another source used clinical interviews. Sampling errors could easily come into play, which happened with the survey in which 76% of the households contacted agreed to participate.

The NA became even more complex due to other difficulties associated with the data sets. There were concerns about reliability and validity and the lack of standardization for data collection and entry across hospital and practice settings. To illustrate the validity problem, in some instances, a mental health diagnosis may be or may not be done correctly depending on who performs the diagnosis (psychiatrist or a general/family practitioner). Working with the four databases was further complicated by the manner in which they were organized, making it an involved task to extract the same or similar information from them.

Findings

Goering and Lin (1996) provided detailed results for each source and a synthesis of findings across them. Some key aspects of their findings, as well as some of the subtlety of the data, will be presented here. (Note: one consistent point in the article is that there are a large number of highly varied health services and record-keeping systems to deal with in this type of NA. This observation underscored the authors' comments and concerns about variability in definitions and data entry.)

For many areas of mental health, there was an inverse relationship between age and need (people in the age range of 15-19 years had the highest rate of mental health problems), and there were distinct differences in mental disorders between men and women in the data from the survey. The researchers cautioned about overinterpretation of the value of the survey data (self-report information) and further observed that questions could be raised about the efficacy of the survey technique when used with an elderly population (65 and older). They also concluded that there may be local unique patterns of need that could not be determined from the survey data to which they had access.

From other archival sources, they were able to estimate the provincial expenditures for mental health at 8% of the overall health budget. Problems abound here. The nature of outpatient services could not be sorted out in the data. The only clear information was in regard to inpatient services, which probably focused more on severe mental health problems as opposed to minor ones. Developing a comprehensive picture of treatment from this data was not possible.

Coding problems were inherent in the data from the physician database. For example, data were coded by the location of the physician, not that of the patient; thus, the data could not easily be related to local variations regarding the mental health needs of individuals (Level 1 needs) in the province. In addition, there was no mechanism to pick up mental problems in multiple diagnoses in which a physical ailment was given precedence over a mental health disorder.

When inpatient utilization (more severe cases) rates were examined, the authors found that many varied definitions affected how the rates were calculated. The definitions were not consistent or at times even close, leading to quite different utilization rates. For example, patients with long stays would increase utilization in one area when compared to another with different utilization policies. Rates also varied by type of hospital (general vs. psychiatric) providing service, whether the utilization was voluntary or involuntary, and the degree to which community placements were available.

Analysis of the Case

Goering and Lin (1996) did a thorough job of analyzing a mazelike set of information, piecing together as best they could a picture of the status of mental health needs and the provision of services with regard to those needs. The article is filled with carefully thought-out tables and caveats offered to help the reader interpret the meaning of tabularized data. It is, however, not surprising that the article concludes with the following statement:

"Still, there is an urgent need for more and better information along with more detailed studies of the appropriateness and effectiveness of services" (p. 16).

This work is analogous to other situations in which needs assessors will try to assimilate data collected and archived by different agencies and groups. Goering and Lin (1996) correctly alerted us to the assumptions that should be raised about how the data were created and entered into multiple databases. Problems encountered in these instances might be resolved by more cooperation (much more cooperation than ordinarily occurs) between agencies and by expending considerable effort to standardize definitions and data collection procedures.

One afterthought on the Goering and Lin (1996) study would have been to create operational definitions of the concepts and aspects of needs in concern. Then, instead of the authors doing the analysis, the definitions could be presented to individuals who regularly handle the databases, and they, in turn, would be asked to conduct the analysis. This action would tend to reduce any bias that might have slipped into the work, but at the same time it probably would increase the cost of the NA.

CASE STUDY 4—HEALTH NEEDS

Background of the Study

Health care is a major concern throughout the world. Dollars will only stretch so far, and many health organizations are conducting NAs to determine how to best capitalize on precious staff and monetary resources. Calgary (Alberta) Health Services is a community health organization that in 1996 undertook a comprehensive assessment of the health needs in Calgary and surrounding areas (Calgary Regional Health Authority [CRHA], 1996). The purposes of the assessment were the following:

develop a health profile of the region;

identify the community's views of health needs;

compile an inventory of health-related resources in the area.
  (CRHA, 1996, p. 1)

An Overview of the Methodology

To conduct the NA, the CRHA engaged in three main activities. First, by accessing existing records in the province and from telephone interviews of residents, CRHA developed an extensive *profile of the health* of the community. Examples of variables included in the profile were life expectancy, causes of death, reasons for hospitalization, and numerous other health concerns. The analyses of the data went into a great detail with, as would be anticipated, breakdowns by age groups, categories of health care providers, major diseases, and so forth. Second, key informants (health experts) were asked to review the findings and to express their views about them, raise issues, and make any suggestions that they wished. The goal of this latter activity was to produce a range of views about the data, not to gain a consensus.

The third source of data came from 56 focus group interviews (FGIs) conducted with nearly 500 people representing a variety of health and community organizations and the general public. The fourth source was an *electronic resource inventory* of health care organizations and providers in the area.

Collectively, the data were comprehensive in scope and required the efforts of a large project team to obtain, analyze, synthesize, and write the final report. Supporting documents for this NA indicated that there was an advisory committee of 17 individuals who undoubtedly were very active in all facets of the project and 4 key project staff members. It is of interest to note that the advisory committee was split into smaller working subcommittees, which fits with recommendations by us (Altschuld and Witkin) regarding how to work with a large committee. The report also contained the names of the key informants and the persons who participated in FGIs. Literally, input from hundreds of individuals was included in this NA.

Findings

The project produced three reports. One was a brief overview of its aims, methodology, and main findings. The second was a much longer presentation of key findings (Volume 1) from all parts of the project that was presented primarily in narrative form. The third product (Volume 2) contains many tables of the results that comprise the health profile.

The overview and Volume 1, in particular, provided very good descriptions of the purposes of the NA; its methodology, including specific questions asked and sampling considerations; and the nature of the results organized by data sources (health profiles, FGIs, etc.). In some instances, the data had been summarized across sources or different respondents.

The reports were well written, and it is apparent that a great deal of attention was paid to explaining the NA process and its results in a clear and readable manner. Numerous figures were used to show how the NA would relate to future health-planning efforts in the area and to depict health behavior. The overview noted that hundreds of suggestions had been obtained in regard to such features of health care as access, service delivery, education, and other related concerns.

Given the massive amount of data collected, the project staff correctly recognized that it would take time for the appropriate parties to digest the information in the overview and the two volumes. Therefore, they forwarded the report to key decision makers with the suggestion that it be carefully reviewed and studied. They also noted that cooperative (rather than single-agency) activity may be required to either resolve or attenuate some health problems.

Analysis of the Case

The data collected and the number of sources used fit what would be required for a comprehensive NA that focuses on health problems and related service delivery systems. These entities are complex and virtually demand that comprehensive data be obtained. The needs in health cannot be looked at through a single lens. Such an NA necessitates that there be a serious outlay of funds to support the endeavor. From our perspective, the costs of health care and of poor health are so great that it becomes absolutely necessary to have high-quality data to help in understanding needs and making decisions related to them.

One problem in the NA was that the volume of the data made it difficult for the project staff and advisory committee to pull together results into a fully integrated picture combining qualitative and quantitative sources. This is to be expected in NAs based on three or more sources of data and especially in cases in which the results from each source are very extensive. The NA conducted in Calgary should provide invaluable input into the health-planning process. It would be beneficial for other health jurisdictions to review their methodology and reporting format.

CASE STUDY 5—EVALUATION OF A NEW, NATIONAL INFORMATION CLEARINGHOUSE IN EDUCATION (A RETROSPECTIVE NA)

Background of the Study

In 1992, a new national information clearinghouse for education was established by the U.S. Department of Education, Office of Educational Research and Improvement (Klapper, Haury, & Buell, 1992). The clearinghouse, which was refunded for a second 5-year period beginning in the fall of 1997 (Simutis, Haury, & Tierney, 1997), is called the Eisenhower National Clearinghouse for Mathematics and Science Education (ENC).

The main purposes of the ENC are to develop and maintain a collection of instructional materials for K-12 public education mathematics and science instruction and to make a catalog of those materials available to all teachers, administrators, schools, and other interested parties in the United States free of charge. This clearinghouse is the only one of its type funded by the federal government with a main focus on instructional materials. To accomplish its goals, the ENC embarked on an ambitious program of collecting resources and developing products and services to assist educators in locating materials useful for mathematics and science classrooms. As a result of these efforts, the ENC produced 11 products and services (5 print products; 3 electronic products, including the catalog or resource finder; and 3 services, including technical help and reference services).

One of the activities specified in its first 5-year contract was that the ENC conduct a national evaluation of its work. Planning for the national evaluation was initiated toward the beginning of the fourth full year of operation, with the evaluation being carried out under the aegis of an external, national evaluation board (NEB) at the end of the fourth year and into the fifth year.

Although the main emphasis of this case was on evaluation, the evaluation contained an interesting feature that makes for its inclusion in this chapter. Due to the time necessary for start-up, ENC products and services had been available to educators for a relatively short 2 years prior to the national evaluation. Therefore, a part of the evaluation consisted of a retrospective NA in which the potential availability of various activities and resources to improve mathematics and science instruction was compared to their current availability. It is this part of the evaluation that will receive attention in the subsequent portrayal of the case.

An Overview of the Methodology

The evaluation used three methodological approaches—a nationwide mail survey of four different constituent groups, external expert panel reviews of a number of key products, and case studies of four sites actively engaged in educational reform. It should be stressed that the three methods were conceptualized and viewed as separate and independent studies, not ones designed for triangulation and/or corroboration purposes.

The surveys were administered to four separate randomly selected constituencies: teachers from a cross section of schools in the United States, principals from the same schools, users of products or services who had only one prior contact with the ENC, and users who had more than one contact with the ENC. For each constituency, different surveys were developed that were quite similar in content but tailored to the unique characteristics and background of the specific respondent groups (a form of a within-method NA). All surveys contained questions dealing with respondent familiarity with the ENC; how they learned about the clearinghouse; awareness of products and services, frequency of use, and evaluation of specific products and services; examples of how products located through the ENC were used; and suggestions for improving the service. Only the surveys mailed to teachers and principals contained the retrospective NA questions. Surveys were mailed from the mid-part of the spring until the end of May 1997. The return rate was in excess of 33%. (The return rate was affected by the late date of the mailing.)

The second part of the evaluation consisted of expert panel reviews of products conducted by mail. Panels of three individuals were sent products to review along with a protocol for conducting the review. The panelists, who did not know each other, were instructed to complete and return their written reviews within a 2-week period. The reviewers looked at the purposes of the product, its suitability for specific audiences for which it was intended, the clarity of information, the technical quality of the product, and the degree to which equity (fair representation of gender, freedom from stereotypes, etc.) was considered in the product. The panel reviews took place at the same time the survey was in process.

The third part of the evaluation was a geographically dispersed set of case studies of four sites that had been involved in mathematics and science education reform (Cullen, Denning, Haury, Herrera, Klapper, Lysaught, & Timko, 1997). The sites were selected based on a nomination process that began in the fall of 1996. Two of the sites (one urban and one rural) had been active in reform prior to 1994 and two after that date (again, one was rural and one was urban). A team of five to seven individuals visited each site and interviewed teachers and administrators in regard to the nature of the reform effort, factors that influenced how the effort was proceeding, the role of information (how it was obtained and used) in reform, and so forth. The interviews were semistructured, and all interviewers were free to probe responses as the interviews progressed. The case studies began in the fall of 1996 and were completed by the middle of the spring of 1997.

Several aspects of the case studies should be emphasized. They were funded and conducted by the ENC as a function of its internal evaluation unit and were primarily intended for ENC use only, not for the national evaluation. The purpose of the case studies was to study mathematics and science education reform, not to look at the use of ENC products and services. Early in the national evaluation process, the national evaluation board (NEB) took an interest in them, and they were subsequently included in the national evaluation. Thus, due to their origins, the case studies were not designed to corroborate the findings of the national evaluation generally or the NA part of it specifically. The internal evaluators of the ENC worked as an extension of the NEB and were part of the evaluation staff for all three methods. Thus, some of the individuals who visited sites also participated in other aspects of the overall evaluation effort.

Analysis of the data obtained from each part of the evaluation followed standard procedures. The surveys were analyzed by two members of the NEB and one member of the ENC internal evaluation team via existing and easily accessed statistical packages. The main outcomes of the analysis were descriptive results presented in tabular form and comparisons across different constituencies. The written reviews from the panels were summarized by two members of the NEB. The interviews from the case studies were transcribed and analyzed in accord with a standard qualitative analysis program (Ethnograph v5.0, 1998). Then, internal evaluators developed themes from the data and generated the main findings.

Findings

In the final evaluation report, the difficulty of pulling together fairly complex data produced from three relatively independent studies was clearly recognized. Furthermore, the entire evaluation effort took place in a setting that did not have established standards for success (e.g., how many respondents should be aware of the ENC after 2 years, and how many should have used its products and services?). Complicating the picture even more was the fact that the ENC was dealing with a highly varied national audience of educators—K-12 levels, rural and urban schools, technologically advanced sites as compared to those not equipped to handle fast-emerging technological changes, and so forth.

In regard to the retrospective NA portion of the survey, some data from the final report are provided in Table 8.3. In the table, activities and resources that would enhance change in mathematics and science educations are listed along with the difference between their desired and current availability. A traditional format for NA questions was used. The results shown are for teachers and principals, with the teachers feeling, for the most part, that there were considerably greater discrepancies than did the principals.

Similar data were also obtained from the case studies, although the original plan did not have provisions for the collection of such data. As the interviews progressed, it became apparent to the interviewers that teachers and administrators were having problems with the support for reform in many of the same areas as indicated by the survey data. With an emergent methodology, the site visitors probed such concerns in depth. The two sets of data were highly corroborative in nature.

Both studies also produced very similar conclusions about how teachers learn of new resources and activities that could be incorporated into their classrooms. Although various mechanisms provide them with information, the most prominent one highlighted in the survey data via an open-ended question was that of other educators (teachers, principals, curriculum specialists). Across all four case study sites, "other teachers" was the category mentioned most often as the key source of information.

The two data sets together provided a much stronger base for understanding how teachers obtain information and what might be critical considerations regarding how to disseminate information about new instructional techniques. In accord with other research regarding change, there appears to be a culture in schools that is characterized by an opinion leader or key informant whom other staff looks to for advice and ideas. How to reach this individual would be important in terms of dissemination.

Analysis of the Case

Case 5 is not particularly different from the ones previously described (i.e., the use of multiple methods enhanced the ability of the needs assessors to interpret the data). Seeing the same kinds of results from two distinct data sources added assurance that the results were truly identifying an underlying problem. Moreover, the fact that this result was obtained from methods not initially intended to corroborate each other tended to enhance the credibility of the finding.

The third source, the external panel reviews, afforded the needs assessors a quite different type of data. When they were reviewed in conjunction with the information from the surveys and case studies, the NEB was able to see some connections. Simplifying the design of some products and services or their dissemination would be helpful in terms of getting them used. As in the first case presented in this chapter, the results from the multiple methods were helpful in developing a more in-depth understanding of results.

One other comment is in order. Because the internal evaluators of the ENC were also involved in the national evaluation under the aegis of the board, it was possible that the case study procedures were contaminated by the survey questions and results. To some degree, the likelihood of this occurring was attenuated because the survey results were not available until some time after the case studies were completed. On the other hand, some contamination may have taken place. Ideally, it would have been better (but more costly) to have had independent bodies conduct each facet of the evaluation.

Table 8.3 Differences in Total Mean Scores Between "Potential to Improve" $(\bar{x}_1)$ and "Current Availability" $(\bar{x}_2)$ of Selected Information Sources and Supports as Reported by Principals and Teachers

Resource	Differences in Means[a]	
	Teachers $\bar{x}_1 - \bar{x}_2$	Principals $\bar{x}_1 - \bar{x}_2$
Regular printed updates on instructional materials and resources	.96	.35
Easily accessed catalogs/lists of materials	.09	-.28
School time provided to seek instructional materials and resources	2.12	1.10
School time available for individual planning	1.46	.85
School time available for group planning	2.13	1.35
In-school staff to assist with math and/or science instruction	1.62	1.34
In-school staff to assist in finding information	1.57	1.14
In-school staff to assist with computer use	1.23	.94
Computer support professional at the district level	.98	.67
In-service training	1.14	.57
Graduate-level university courses	.31	.01
Partnerships with business	1.55	.88
Information exchange with peers	1.08	.52

SOURCE: Altschuld et al. (1997). Reprinted by permission.
NOTE: The number of teachers responding to individual items varied from 163 to 174. The number of responding principals varied from 100 to 107.
a. Differences greater than 1.0 generally reflect large differences in excess of the standard deviation for the individual item.

CROSS-CASE ANALYSIS AND CONCERNS

The five case studies are excellent examples of multiple (mixed) methodology usage in NA. Major features (aspects or difficulties) that cut across the cases and commentary regarding those features are provided in Table 8.4. Collectively, the case studies encountered several common problems that help us to understand what is involved in undertaking such endeavors. The entries in the table are fairly self-explanatory and therefore will not be discussed to any extent in the text.

Instead, let us suggest a few concerns that we have. Keep in mind that we strongly believe in multiple-methods NAs and enthusiastically endorse their use in situations in which needs are complex and have to be considered from many vantage points. Within that framework, we see the advantages of qualitative and quantitative methods and wholeheartedly support the incorporation of both in NA, even though there will be problems in their use. Our concern rests with the escalation of costs in dollars and time involved when multiple-methods NAs are conducted.

Those concerns go something like this: "Might there be some methods that are better than others in helping to identify needs? Are some methods more cost-efficient than others, given the relative yield of information they produce? Is research available to help needs assessors with the choice of methods?"

In regard to these questions, literature sources and research provide guidance. Certainly other books (McKillip, 1987; Reviere et al., 1996; Witkin & Altschuld, 1995) offer good suggestions about the selection of methods. In terms of research related to cost-efficiency, Tweed and Ciarlo (1992) found that two key variables (the percentage of households composed of one person and the percentage of separated or divorced males older than age 15) were the best predictors of mental health needs within geographic areas. If a needs assessor were limited in terms of time and resources, he or she might reduce expenditures

Table 8.4 Cross-Case Analysis of the Five Multiple-Methods
Case Studies

Features Cutting Across the Case Studies	Comments
Size of the endeavor	Four of the five cases were extensive except for the one in nursing, which was a smaller research study. In general, multiple (mixed) methods in community, mental health, health, education, and other fields require larger NA teams, needs assessors with methodological skills that cut across methods, the generation of much longer reports, and greater expenditures of time and money.
Quality of the effort	Each case demonstrated careful attention to detail and thoughtfulness in trying to combine results from highly varied sources. The needs assessors are to be commended for undertaking multiple-methods NAs, persevering, and being patient in dealing with the methodological complexities that arose.
Problems with the quality of the data sources	All of the NAs encountered problems with the quality of the data sources. Needs had to be inferred from qualitative methods, return rates varied, archived data had been entered into records in accord with subtle yet meaningful differences in definitions of terms, and so forth. Validity and reliability of subsets of the data could be questioned.
Deriving meaning across sources	Consistently, the needs assessors had difficulty deriving meaning across the data sources. Indeed, in two of the cases, the data were not in agreement, and it became difficult to come up with a clear picture of needs.
Issues in reporting (length)	The four larger studies produced voluminous reports. Reading and digesting the amount of information presented would be a major time-consuming task, especially for busy managers or administrators. Summaries and different ways of portraying the results for decision-making purposes were needed.
Issues in reporting (orientation to decision making)	The needs assessors uniformly struggled in discussing where the results from individual methods supported those from others and where they did not. In many cases, it seemed as though separate studies were written and then somehow compared. The United Way NA report was best in overcoming this problem with its adaptation of goal attainment scaling. Perhaps all of the studies should have gone further in examining instances in which the data did or did not agree.

Features Cutting Across the Case Studies	Comments
Planning for comparison purposes	The nursing NA (Case Study 1) was a planned study about the extent to which methods would agree or disagree. In the clearinghouse evaluation (Case Study 5), three independent studies were carried out, with two of them corroborating each other. In the other three NAs, it might have been better to consider how individual methods would triangulate with or complement others. (This is not intended to detract from the commitment and quality of work of any of the needs assessors cited in the chapter. Instead, it is to suggest that even more thought should go into the use of multiple methods before an extensive amount of data is collected.)
Potential for contamination	Several of the NAs tried to deal with contamination as a source of invalidity by having members of the NA team independently implement each method. Others did not. Even with safeguards, some contamination across methods may have entered into the five NAs. A way to overcome this would be to have a separate group conduct data collection and analysis for each method. This strategy is prohibitively expensive and generally will not take place. Therefore, it is likely that some contamination will occur in most multiple-methods NAs. That contamination would generally be within tolerable limits.
Value of multiple methods	Whether stated directly or inferred from the documentation of the case studies, there appeared to be agreement that multiple methods were better than basing needs on a single data source. The needs being examined were complex, and a single source was insufficient for the job. The needs assessors gained greater insights from the data in the multiple sources, even if they had difficulty in collating and summarizing across them.

by limiting part of the NA to just looking at these two variables from census data or local databases.

If possible, try to build in funds for reviewing the literature (especially with an eye toward what methods would be best to use in a specific situation) prior to starting an NA. This expenditure tends to save costs in the long run. If you are embarking on a multiple-methods NA, we strongly encourage you to consult the literature.

Here are two other concluding thoughts across the five NA case studies. The importance of how findings are reported and communicated to key decision makers is underscored, especially in regard to complex multiple-methods studies. Utilization is the ultimate goal of the NA game, and needs assessors will have to think carefully about how to summarize and convey results. If budgets permit, short video presentations of the findings could be produced and used to facilitate the processing of the information by stakeholding groups. Lastly, it is easy to foresee other techniques becoming more prominent in future multiple-methods NAs. Electronic surveys, as one example, could easily be used with some populations. In other instances, ethnographic (naturalistic) techniques could be considered as candidates for the methodology of the NA. Over time, multiple-methods NAs will be more varied in structure and methodological choice as needs assessors become more sophisticated and creative.

CLOSING THOUGHTS

ANOTHER DIALOGUE BETWEEN TWO AUTHORS

This scene was repeated many times during the writing of two needs assessment (NA) books. The authors are in a large home office in Renton, Washington. His desk is neat with few notes or pieces of paper around. Her work area is drowning in a sea of Post-it notes and scraps of paper. Occasionally they glance at each other's space and wonder how anything ever gets done by the other person. Yet they enjoy the work and the support, friendship, and collegiality of their collaboration. He begins to speak.

He: You know, I've been thinking about something.

She: Congratulations, and it's about time! I'm glad that I'm having such a positive effect on you.

He: Oh, give me a break.

She: Okay, what's on your mind?

He: Well, thanks for the credit. This may sound strange, but every time I sit down to work on this NA stuff I have two conflicting thoughts. I've learned a lot about NA content and really do know a fair amount

235

about the process. And yet, at the same time, I'm uncomfortable and seem to feel that I really don't understand it at all.

She: What do you mean, what's the problem you're having? Tell me more about your thoughts.

He: It's hard to put them into words, but it goes something like this: Initially I viewed NA as rather straightforward—most of the methods used in NA and the general process have been known for years. I even started to wonder whether we would accomplish anything by writing these books. Maybe it's just writers' fatigue, but I get frustrated and I have the uneasy feeling that I really don't know anything about NA. I'm constantly seeing new ideas or issues at every step of the process. Things that I never questioned before I'm certainly questioning now. Did you ever have thoughts like this?

She: Before I answer, could you give me an example or two?

He: Sure. Here are a couple. NA data is more complex and filled with more problems than I ever imagined. And you'll recall that we've always talked about the use of multiple methods in NA, but that can be quite a can of worms.

Possibly it's just me, I'm tired today and out of sorts. I've been in the NA game for about 15 years, which may account for my feelings. I just haven't done as many of them as you have. You've been at this kind of work for a lot longer than I and are probably asking what has happened to this boy's mind. In any case, where are you in terms of NA? Do you have any questions like this?

She: Yes, I have often wondered about your *mind*. (Then after a pause, she continued with her response.) Kidding aside, I really feel the same way you do. After all these years, I feel that I know less than I did before, and many times I realize that I know very little about some aspects of NA. But that's what makes it fun and keeps us going.

Versions of this dialogue recurred over a 5-year period of summer work sessions together and innumerable long-distance phone calls. We probed each other's thoughts and ideas all the time. We debated and even argued over subtle points and concerns. That questioning attitude is what propelled the generation of two books and decisions about their content. That attitude, in concert with observations about the NA process, will guide our closing thoughts. Let's begin with observations.

OBSERVATIONS ABOUT NA

PROGRESS IS BEING MADE

There was joy in looking at the NA literature and seeing the efforts of colleagues in regard to using multiple methods, combining different types of information, and devising different and interesting ways of reporting NA findings. The number of studies that Witkin (1992) found in her 10-year historical analysis of NA activity from 1981 to 1991 was gratifying and provided concrete evidence that assessing needs was still an important activity.

Research about NA was of continuing interest, as noted in the work of Hamann and Altschuld (1997), Hansen et al. (1991), Penta (1994), Timko (1999), Fiorentine (1994), and a host of other individuals. The opportunities and need for research are obvious, especially if we are to advance in our knowledge of the NA process.

It was pleasing to see changes in NA. Numerous new techniques were included in this book based on both a review of the literature and different methods that we were using in our work. The multiple-methods case studies were exciting to examine, especially in relation to dealing with conceptually complex data sets. As more is written and enters the literature, NAs will improve and become increasingly useful for the development of organizational plans. With the passage of time, there should be larger numbers of individuals trained in advanced and sophisticated ways of conducting NAs.

IMPORTANCE OF NEEDS ASSESSMENT COMMITTEES

As the book progressed, the importance of the needs assessment committee (NAC) became more prominent in our thinking. NA is almost totally dependent on the work of the NAC, with the committee being the engine that propels the process to success or failure. The quality of people on the NAC, their ties to management, their formal and informal influence on the organization, how they relate to staff, the degree to which they are respected and seen as fair, the nature of

NAC leadership, and how NAC business is conducted all come together to form the infrastructure of the NA endeavor. A poorly constituted committee characterized by a lack of commitment and weak leadership will almost always lead to failure. This is a reasonable assumption, even if there is limited empirical evidence to support it.

Organizations frequently give inadequate consideration to which individuals should be chosen for the committee and how it should be led. A quick decision may be made to use internal staff for the leadership role—a decision that is easy to implement and lowers cost. The apparent ease and cost savings, however, may be "penny-wise but pound-foolish," especially if internal leadership deters a group from fully delving into the problems confronting the organization. In some cases, internal leadership will work, but in many others it probably will not.

Because of the importance of the NAC, careful thought must be given to why an assessment is needed and who might be the best individuals to carry out the process. An NA simply will not be successful without a concerned group that is solidly behind the endeavor and that has good leadership.

THE PROCESS IS MORE DIFFICULT THAN WE IMAGINED

It is painful to admit that neither of us fully appreciated the subtle landscape of NA. Our prior efforts concentrated on definitions of need, levels of need, and methods for collecting NA data. We looked at how to analyze data and transform them into NA indices. Causal analysis of needs was another aspect of NA that was emphasized. Much less attention was given to the detail of the three phases of the NA process. How could the process fail? How does it really get started?

The three phases are more involved than we originally thought. Often NAs do not move from the initial look at concerns and problems into the development of plans for action and their implementation. The work goes for naught. The NA just becomes an expensive exercise in futility that leaves a bitter taste. Working with complex data derived from mixed methods, carefully prioritizing needs against agreed-on criteria, and determining solution strategies for high-priority needs are more subtle, intricate steps than we first conceptualized them to be.

Now, based on our emerging views of NA, we are focusing on how management should be a part of the process and the criticality of staff buy-in and ownership. At its core, dealing with needs is part of a process leading to change. What should management's role be? How will it and the organization deal with potential changes resulting from the NA? What stance should management take in interacting with and supporting the NA process? Are there critical interface points between management and the NAC? Greater stress must be placed on communicating with staff, seeking their input, and developing the sense of meaning that the process and its results are ultimately important to them.

In addition, needs themselves are complex, particularly those that deal with social, educational, health, and mental health problems and programs. It is clear that viewing such needs from the unidimensional perspective of a single data source or group will no longer suffice.

Collectively, the above considerations tend to rule out *easy fixes* for the NA process. Sure, needs assessors should always strive for the simplest and most cost-efficient methods possible. Budgets will only stretch so far, and there will be limitations to what we can practically accomplish. On the other hand, the five multiple-method NAs described in Chapter 8 amplify the point that needs are embedded in the political and social fabrics in which organizations exist. Complex, sometimes intractable problems have to be probed in depth. Politics will come into play. NAs will not be easy, and they will require sizable expenditures of time and money.

COMMUNICATION

An NAC can get so involved in and enamored by the assessment process that it becomes isolated from the daily life of the organization. We do not think that this is a good outcome and strongly recommend that the NAC identify communication channels within the organization that are used throughout the NA process.

Communication could occur as a natural outgrowth of the collection of needs-related data from the staff of an organization or agency. After the data are analyzed and summarized, an excellent opportunity is there for keeping the staff up-to-date about what is taking place. Consider the following example.

Using NA Data to Initiate a Group Discussion

A federally funded national education center, which had been in operation for about a year and a half, wanted to examine its needs and future directions. As part of a strategic planning process, the center collected data from its managers about the various types of projects and programs being conducted under its aegis (Altschuld, Macce, & Forsythe, 1992). What sizes were the projects; who were the main beneficiaries; what goals were being achieved; what audiences were being reached; what were the side effects and/or unintended benefits; were the projects primarily research, development, service, or some combination; and so forth?

Data were collected and compiled into a profile of the organization's overall pattern of operation, which was then used as input for a strategic planning retreat. The profile was treated as an indication of the current organizational status in comparison to its mission and goals (the desired status). Moderate to sizable discrepancies (needs) were observed. The results were presented to approximately 10 important stakeholders (mostly managers) who attended a 1-day strategic planning retreat. The group forum proved to be an effective mechanism for communicating the findings and starting an introspective discussion of the discrepancies.

Findings and results should be communicated only when appropriate, not prematurely. Results were not given out prior to the meeting described above. Summarized profiles of the center on key variables were distributed at the retreat as a way of highlighting important findings. If preliminary findings or portions thereof were provided in advance of the meeting, they could have skewed what turned out to be a sincere analysis of the status and future direction of the center. The NAC, in conjunction with the needs assessor(s), should continually be alert to the need for communication with staff and management and should carefully select opportune times to do so on a frequent basis.

NEEDS ASSESSMENT AND THE DEMOCRATIC PROCESS

NAs work well in democratic organizations that value and use the opinions and ideas of internal and external stakeholders. Organizations characterized as open in terms of decision making and leadership style represent the best environments in which to carry out NAs that lead to change. By contrast, organizations that are tightly controlled from the top will be less inclined to meaningfully involve staff in the NA, especially in the decisions that affect who benefits and loses from the effort. In negative situations such as these, an NA could breed resentment and disenchantment.

Experienced needs assessors are aware of organizational dynamics, the fertile soil on which growth and change are predicated. If the context is not open, supportive, and empowering and if the needs assessors are external to the organization, they may be in a good position to press for as democratic an NA as possible. It is important that the press occur early in the NA so that a norm of conduct is established. Needs assessors must ever be vigilant in terms of monitoring the process and ensuring that a positive atmosphere is in place for the NA.

PROBLEMS OF INSTRUMENTATION

Problems abound in NA instrumentation. It is perplexing that the double-scaled format is used infrequently in NA surveys. Data obtained from single (preference) scale instruments fall short of what is required for an NA. Discrepancies cannot be determined from this type of data.

In addition, the wording of the questions and the structure of the surveys will affect the nature of responses. We often do not know the basis on which responses are made. Another complication associated with a survey is the fact that NA questions may require retrospective recall on the part of the respondent. The validity and reliability of retrospective responses are certainly circumspect and open to question.

In terms of data, we have consistently been troubled about the quality and accuracy of information culled from archived data (records). If records are considered to be a form of instrumentation, then how was the data in them generated and recorded? It seems as though records and the indices derived from them are taken as gospel, without thinking about the process of how that gospel was produced. Do the data abstracted from records represent the area of need? Are the data isomorphic with reality? The problem becomes staggering if the records were kept by different agencies in accord with policies, specific to each agency. The work by Goering and Lin (1996) underscores this nightmare as it confronts needs assessors in mental health.

Records are valuable and should continue to be a part of NA, but their use must be tempered by a healthy skepticism and questioning attitude. In some instances, making needs-based decisions on such data could be misleading.

Many other approaches to collecting data about needs do not directly lead to the measurement of discrepancies, the very essence of NA. If focus group interviews (FGIs), as a case in point, were thought of as an instrument, then we might have to expand the methodology to fit more closely with NA. An FGI that revealed a group was facing a number of major problems might be enhanced by asking participants to rank order the problems. Once the overall group rank order was established, the group could be queried as to what might have led to that particular ordering. Another possibility would be to quickly frame a small number of discrepancy-type questions as the interview was progressing. Then those questions could be incorporated into the interviews. The data so produced, although rough, would enhance understanding of needs.

In light of this discussion, should needs assessors become paranoiac about NA instrumentation? Should they give up their search for "truth" about needs? Will such a quest be in vain?

Discouragement is not our intent. We have brought the concerns forward for several reasons. First, not many individuals have been formally trained in the practice and art of NA. They are simply not aware of the nature and subtlety of problems in instrumentation that complicate the assessment of needs. Second, even those who have conducted many assessments may not be consciously thinking about these types of problems as they go about the business of NA. But certainly they have encountered many of them. It is hoped that we have not deterred experienced needs assessors but resensitized them to problems in instrumentation and the resulting NA data. We are confident that instrumentation will improve as the field moves ahead.

Observations such as those above have led us to feel that there are gaps in the literature of NA. Below is a brief discussion of a few areas in which the literature base could be enhanced.

THE NEED FOR MORE LITERATURE ON NA

RESEARCH ON NA INSTRUMENTATION

A particularly pressing concern is for research on the design instruments used for NA. What are good formats for and ways in which to word NA surveys? Can we achieve greater differentiation in responses to the "what should be" questions? Do we have enough understanding of the basis on which responses are made? How are responses to be interpreted? Are certain types of scaling approaches better than others? How do different types of NA surveys affect the response rates and the nature of responses made by the different groups who interact with them? Is it possible to ask for responses to three or four dimensions instead of one or two and still get meaningful data? Could we more often employ behaviorally anchored types of scales in our surveys?

Many subtle choices made by needs assessors in the design of the surveys are so commonly used in NA. More empirical research about format options in the NA context is needed and would be very helpful in guiding future endeavors.

MULTIPLE-METHODS USAGE

The use of multiple methods for NA holds great promise. The five case studies that were examined in Chapter 8 were very informative. But it was disappointing to see so few such approaches entered into the ERIC system or written about in journal articles. The literature continues to be dominated by single-method approaches. (And sometimes that domination could be characterized as having a numbers-only orientation to needs.)

It is suspected that many more multiple-methods NAs have been successfully conducted by needs assessors and that our knowledge base is considerably stronger than it currently seems to be. This is the file drawer problem of the NA field. Multiple-methods NAs are simply not entered into the literature. They should be, and needs assessors are encouraged to explain how they carried out such studies and what were their strengths and weaknesses. How did needs assessors overcome the problems in implementation and combining multiple sources?

PRESENTING NA DATA

We need to learn more about variations in summarizing and presenting data. Are some forms of presentation more convincing and utilitarian in NA situations? What kinds of needs data and information receive the most attention from decision makers? How do we deal with qualitative and quantitative data sources in general and in cases when they do not agree or when they might even produce conflicting results? What do we do with results collected from different groups that do not agree? How would we resolve conflicts in such situations?

PRIORITIZED, IMPORTANT VARIABLES

Are there some key variables in fields such as health, mental health, education, and others that have larger payoffs in terms of information yield in the particular areas of need being investigated? Is the collection of some data more cost-effective than others? How much do large-scale, multiple-methods NAs cost? (And, for that matter, what is the cost necessary for smaller NA efforts?) How long does it take to complete simple and multiple-methods NAs? Do long-term, in-depth NAs require so much time that organizational enthusiasm is dissipated? The field of NA would benefit from more being written about the costs of NA studies and alternative methods that generate information of reasonable quality although at much lower cost.

TRANSLATING NEEDS INTO SOLUTION STRATEGIES—THE PROCESS THING

The three phases of NA are, in our biased view, a good process for proceeding from the initial identification of needs to solution strategies that are eventually implemented. Yet in going to the literature, we found few examples of the entire process. How do organizations start looking at the problems facing them? How many of them form committees to investigate those problems? What activities do the committees carry out, what kinds of issues and difficulties do they run into, and how do they resolve them? Do groups and organizations go through a formal process of prioritization? Against what criteria are needs prioritized? What procedures are used for locating possible solutions and then finally choosing one? How are decisions made relative to the resources required for the NA?

The questions are exciting and show the complexity and subtlety of the NA process. Answering them offers high promise for how we can improve practice. In writing this book and the prior one, we pulled together information from many sources to develop the three-phase model. An honest admission is that we simply do not know the extent to which it mirrors reality.

Judging from the published literature, it does not. Judging from discussions with colleagues, we feel confident that many activities in the three phases are utilitarian and of value for the conduct of NAs. Most NA reports, however, give the impression that the process stops somewhere after the data were collected and analyzed. Problems with the data sets were usually well explicated.

What happened, then, in terms of decision making and organizational change? Did the NAs help the organizations to improve? Were important needs identified, and were decisions for actions made? How well did they work? Was any follow-up done? Did the needs assessors have a continuing role in the process? Were they funded for that continuing role?

Even in the extensive documentation of the five case studies, there was little explanation of the process beyond the collection and summarization of the data. Although the findings were explicit, did they have any instrumental or conceptual effects on the organization? Were they interesting exercises that slowly faded away? How did political factors enter into the use of results?

More extensive descriptions of what takes place throughout the NA process would be desirable. This would have to go far beyond what is ordinarily explained in current descriptions. In addition, it also would be very useful if there were more evaluations of NA processes, even if evaluation consisted only of capturing the informal ideas and thoughts of needs assessors shortly after NAs had been completed. What would they have changed and why? What are their perceptions of how NA reports and findings were received and used? Information generated in this manner would undoubtedly provide, if obtained and collated across a number of NAs, a set of categories depicting NA in use as opposed to a reconstructed logic of the process. Unique and valuable insights would be gained from such data.

COMMUNITY-BASED NAs

It was noticeable in some of the multiple-methods cases that the NA was community-wide in nature. The scope of activities necessary to assess needs was vast. How should needs assessors begin to conceptualize such an assessment? What are the pertinent variables to look at? How can the NA be focused? How do we develop a profile not just of existing services but of the quality and amount of services delivered? How do we sample within a community? From what groups and individuals should information be sought?

Perhaps what might be utilitarian are generic structures or models that would help in focusing an NA. We are not referring to a model of process such as the three-phased one. Instead, we are thinking about a model of context or environment. For example, if needs in education were to be assessed, how can we organize or think about the parameters of such an assessment in relation to the environment in which education exists? Who are the actors, who are the providers of services, what is the critical linkage between service providers, who are the recipients, where do funds come from, who are the important stakeholder groups, and so forth? It strikes us that it would be possible to come up with a generic structure of this type from an analysis of the NAs that have been conducted in education. The same idea would apply to NAs in health, mental health, social services, extension, and even to NAs in business.

Armed with generic structures, needs assessors and NACs could examine them against local situations to see what might be the best ways to focus the NAs. NAs will always have limited resources. With the structure or model in hand, the question is, Where would it be best to place our resources in this assessment of needs for the specific concern or problem of this specific NA? Would it be most advantageous to use a multiple-methods approach for only one key group, or would it be better to use the resources in two key clusters or areas of the model?

What triggered our thinking here is that there were similarities in the types of groups included in the multiple-methods cases studies and in the methods and general approaches of those assessments. If an analysis of many such cases were undertaken and the results were combined with other literature about environmental factors, some useful ideas for NA would surely arise. The structures or models

would not answer all issues of design and planning for NA, but the
would be helpful.

A FINAL NOTE

The first and last chapters began with a dialogue between two authors
A key refrain in our conversations was that we had more question
now than we ever did before. The questions exemplify our enthusiasm
about the new vistas that we see constantly emerging in NA.

The authors sincerely hope that other needs assessors share these
views and will continue to contribute to understandings about need
and NA. As a society, we must do our best to use resources wisely in
regard to the highest priority needs and where the most good can be
achieved. Well-planned and executed NAs are one way to accomplish
these ends.

GLOSSARY

Benchmarking   Comparing performance and strategies for achieving goals or resolving needs of one organization to that of an exemplary one.

Between-methods NA   An approach to assessing needs that employs different methods for the assessment.

Causal analysis   Examining needs in terms of their potential causes, particularly with regard to identifying those factors that can be changed by the organization and those that are not under its aegis.

Current need   A discrepancy between current and desired status, with the desired condition being anchored more in the present time or immediate near future (also see **Future need**).

Current status   The "what is" state, that is, the level of achievement or attainment for a specific area of the needs assessment. Indicators of current status can be obtained from records, unobtrusive measures, perceptions determined from survey responses, and so on.

Desired status

The "what should be" state, that is, the level of a required or desired end state or standard for a specific area of the needs assessment. Indicators of desired status come from norms, research, and perceptions. (If they are obtained from perceptions, the wording of questions—ought to be, should be, is required, is desired—will affect the determination of the what should be state.)

Discrepancy analysis

The process of determining the difference between current and desired status, usually resulting in a numerical index of need (needs index).

Double-scaled items

A format in needs assessment surveys that uses two scales—one for current status and one for desired status. (Most often, 5-point Likert-type scales are employed.)

Feasibility criteria

Criteria used in needs assessment to determine which needs are potentially most easily attended to or resolved. Feasibility criteria include costs, commitment of the organization, and the likelihood that an adult education intervention will have an impact on the area of need (Sork, 1995).

Force field analysis (FFA)

A procedure that requires identifying forces for and against a particular course of action and then comparing their relative strengths. FFA is particularly useful in the postassessment phase (Phase 3) of needs assessment.

Future need

A discrepancy between current and desired status in which the latter is temporally situated in the long term. All needs are rooted in the future, but in this type of need, the desired condition is anchored more in future time periods such as 5, 10, or more years ahead (also see **Current need**).

Goal attainment scaling (GAS)

A procedure for placing disparate entities on a common metric. For example, achievement for a math goal might be given a score of 3 on a 5-point scale, whereas achievement for a social studies goal might be given a 4 on the same 5-point scale. The values are judgments of the extent to which each goal was achieved. The *actual* amount of achievement for the content of each goal could be highly variable (see Chapter 4 for more discussion of GAS).

House of quality (HOQ)

A diagram in the form of a house that is a summary of the main aspects of the quality function deployment procedure for identifying design features with the greatest likelihood of resolving a set of needs.

Importance criteria

Criteria used in needs assessment to determine which needs are potentially of the highest importance. Importance criteria could include size of the discrepancy, number of people affected, relationship to organizational goals, and so on (Sork, 1995).

Incremental (slight) need

A need that requires minimal or small amounts of action to resolve (also see **Severe (major) need**).

Level 1 needs

Discrepancies between current and desired status for individuals who would be the direct recipients of services designed to alleviate the discrepancies. (Sometimes these are referred to as recipients' needs, primary needs, or performance needs.)

Level 2 needs

Discrepancies between current and desired status for individuals or groups who deliver services or implement programs designed to alleviate Level 1 needs. (Sometimes these are referred to as implementors', treatment, or secondary needs.)

Level 3 needs

Discrepancies between current and desired status for the organization (materials, facilities, support services, etc.). By determining Level 3 needs, the organization gains an understanding of what should be provided to service deliverers (Level 2) to assist them in implementing programs to alleviate Level 1 needs.

Maintenance need   A process, procedure, or activity that sustains the current *what is* status (Kuh, 1982). For example, it may be necessary to jog regularly to be able to run a mile in an average of 7 minutes. (That is, a need will emerge if adherence to the process does not occur.)

Marketing research   A process similar to needs assessment that ascertains the needs or wants (as is often the case) of a particular target group. Marketing research might be used to determine the styling, design, or appeal features for a product or process that relates to the wants of a target group. The wants may or may not be specific needs of the group.

Means-difference   A needs assessment analysis procedure that uses a
analysis   rough estimate of effect size, that is, the difference between the overall mean of the desired status and the overall mean of the current status for goals or areas of interest. This estimate or standard is then compared to the difference between the desired and current status of each individual goal. If difference exceeds the standard, it is considered to represent a need.

Mixed-methods NA   See **Between-methods NA.**

Multi-attribute   A small group procedure designed to compare alter-
utility theory   native solutions for a problem or area of need. The
(MAUT)   procedure requires that a group looks at each solution in terms of the probability that it will be able to satisfy weighted criteria. The probability of the solution meeting each criterion is multiplied times the weight of the criteria, and the resulting products are summed into an overall (utility) score. A solution with a higher sum would be favored over others.

Multiple   Different groups that have a stake in the outcomes of
constituencies   an NA in terms of making decisions about needs, delivering services, or receiving services.

Multiple-methods NA	See **Between-methods NA.**
Need	A measurable discrepancy between the current and desired status for an entity. (There are many ways to determine current status and many versions of desired—ought to be, expected, likely, required, normative, and so on—status.)
Needs analysis	A process of analyzing needs once they have been assessed to determine causal factors and potential solution strategies and then to select the most likely solution strategy for implementation. Needs analysis has been misinterpreted to be needs assessment, but it is impossible to analyze an entity that has not yet been identified (Rodriguez, 1988). Some needs assessment approaches embed needs analysis into their overall schema.
Needs assessment (NA)	The process of determining, analyzing, and prioritizing needs and, in turn, identifying and implementing solution strategies to resolve high-priority needs. (This general process is the one emphasized in this book.)
Needs assessment committee (NAC)	The group that oversees the conduct of all aspects of a needs assessment from Phase 1 to Phase 3, including the development of plans for resolving needs. (The NAC may also be involved in the implementation of needs assessment procedures and resultant solution strategies.)
Needs assessor(s)	The person or group charged with providing leadership for planning and implementing a needs assessment. Leadership includes guiding the NAC in deliberations about the focus and nature of the needs assessment process, designing instruments, implementing data collection activities, analyzing data, helping to set priorities, and so forth.

GLOSSARY

Needs-based priority setting	Numerous procedures employed to select needs of highest priority from a longer list of needs. A number of these procedures are multifaceted and require the specification of criteria for prioritization.
Needs index	The numerical discrepancy between current and desired status for an area of need.
Pattern matching	A needs assessment adaptation of a procedure used in concept mapping. The adapted procedure consists of a ladderlike figure in which the levels of desired status for goals or need areas would constitute one side of the ladder and the current status the other. The two sides would be connected by "rungs" (see Chapter 4).
Phase 1 NA	Initial phase in needs assessment consisting of numerous steps to focus the needs assessment and to collect existing data in regard to what is already known about the area of interest (usually leads to decisions about Phases 2 and 3 of the needs assessment process).
Phase 2 NA	Second phase of needs assessment consisting of numerous steps designed to formally collect, analyze, interpret, and prioritize needs assessment data. This phase, which may include a causal analysis of Level 1, 2, and 3 needs, sets the stage for Phase 3 of the needs assessment process.
Phase 3 NA	Third phase of needs assessment consisting of numerous steps primarily designed to select solution strategies for high-priority needs and to develop action plans for the implementation of the best solution strategy or strategies.
Preference items	See **Single-scale items.**
Priority screen	An ordered criterion used in the process of determining needs-based priorities. A set of criteria would be

placed in rank order, and each need would initially be examined in terms of the highest rank-ordered criterion or screen. Only those needs that pass that criterion would continue in the prioritizing process to the next highest-ranked criterion (screen) and so forth.

Proportional reduction in error (PRE)

An approach to analyzing responses from double-scaled NA items based on a matrix with two dimensions consisting of 5-point ranges (highest what should be status = 5 to lowest = 1; highest current status = 5 to lowest = 1). All cells in the matrix are compared to the cell with the highest *what should be* status and the lowest *current* one (cell 5,1). This cell has the greatest likelihood of being a need. Each cell in the matrix also has an assigned weight, and the value of the resultant PRE statistic is calculated using cell weights and the pattern of actual responses for each item to the double scales. The statistic goes from negative infinity through zero to +1.00. Higher values and those closer to a +1.00 indicate that the item has a higher probability of representing a need.

Quality function deployment (QFD)

A procedure primarily employed in business and industry for developing products that satisfy the needs of consumers or customers. The procedure requires identification and prioritization of needs, specification of design features that could affect needs, estimation of the impact of design features on each other, benchmarking against other organizations, and numerous other dimensions. The result of a QFD process is an HOQ diagram that identifies design features with the greatest potential for resolving needs.

Risk

The degree to which the problem represented by a need will escalate over time and the degree to which the NAC judges this situation to be a threat if allowed to go unresolved.

Risk assessment	The process of determining the amount of risk associated with a need. Risk could be established in a quantitative or qualitative manner.
Severe (major) need	A need of serious importance or one that will require that sizable actions be taken and extensive resources be committed to resolve the problem.
Simple multi-attribute rating technique (SMART)	SMART is a simplified form of MAUT. Some values for key criteria that are determined by consensus in MAUT are simply supplied to the decision-making group by the individuals leading the SMART process. The decision-making group would still determine the probability of each solution satisfying each of the key criteria (see Chapter 6 for more discussion of SMART).
Single-scaled items	Items that require respondents to rate items in terms of a single Likert-type scale. Usually the rating deals with the importance of an item. In needs assessment, single-scaled items may be referred to as "preference" items.
Tree diagrams	There are two forms of tree diagrams used in needs assessment work. One is a visual way of depicting statistical data for lay audiences so that they are more understandable than a summary index such as a correlation coefficient. The other form is a picture of major themes that arise during the early part of a QFD process.
Want	A want is a discrepancy in which the what should be state is beyond a reasonable or satisfactory level (Scriven & Roth, 1978). If a person has a million dollars and feels that they should have two million dollars, this is a want because the individual is already at a reasonable financial level. Wants are sometimes distinguished from needs in that individuals are almost always aware of wants (vacations, up-to-

date fashions in clothing), whereas they may not be aware of needs (problems in periodontia or in subtle, imperceptible shifts in vision).

Weighted needs index (WNI) An alternate procedure for arriving at a numerical index of need. The procedure is an adaptation of the PRE strategy and simply looks at only part of the what should be and what is a matrix. Weights for that part of the matrix are reversed from those of PRE. The WNI produces values from 0 to 5, with higher values indicating higher levels of need (also see **Proportional reduction in error (PRE)**.

What is status See **Current status.**

What should be status See **Desired status.**

Within-methods NA An approach to assessing needs that employs variations of a single method for the assessment (e.g., multiple versions of a survey or interview used to assess needs for different constituencies).

REFERENCES

Alford, R. (1999, January 19). School closing agenda in flux. *Columbus Dispatch*, p. A1.

Alstete, J. W. (1995). *Benchmarking in higher education: Adapting best practices to improve quality*. Washington, DC: George Washington University Graduate School of Education and Human Development.

Altschuld, J. W., Anderson, R., Cochrane, P., Frechtling, J., Frye, S., & Gansneder, B. (1997). *National evaluation: Technical report*. Columbus: Eisenhower National Clearinghouse for Mathematics and Science Education, The Ohio State University.

Altschuld, J. W., Berlin, D., Bohren, J., Cruickshank, D., Cyphert, F., Mayer, V., Shumway, R., & Zutell, J. (1985). *Evaluation of the chairperson* (A report to the chair of the Department of Educational Theory and Practice and to the dean of the College of Education). Columbus: College of Education, The Ohio State University.

Altschuld, J. W., Cullen, C., Thomas, P. M., & Witkin, B. R. (1996, November). *A needs assessment workshop: Toward needs-based decisions*. Workshop presented at the national and statewide conferences of the American Evaluation Association, Atlanta, GA.

Altschuld, J. W., & Kumar, D. D. (1995). Program evaluation in science education: The model perspective. *New Directions for Program Evaluation, 65*, 5-17.

Altschuld, J. W., Kumar, D. D., Smith, D. W., & Goodway, J. D. (1999). The changing countenance of context-sensitive evaluations: Case illustrations. *Journal of Family and Community Health, 22*(1), 28-41.

Altschuld, J. W., Macce, B. R., & Forsythe, M. (1992). *Strategic planning report*. Columbus: National Center for Science Teaching and Learning, The Ohio State University.

259

Altschuld, J. W., & Witkin, B. R. (1995, November). *Is what you want what you need?* Workshop presented at the annual meeting of the American Evaluation Association, Vancouver, British Columbia.

Altschuld, J. W., Yoon, J. S., & Cullen, C. (1993). The utilization of needs assessment results. *Evaluation and Program Planning, 16,* 279-285.

Anderson, C. L., Jesswein, W. A., & Fleischman, W. (1990). Needs assessment based on household and key informant surveys. *Evaluation Review, 14*(2), 182-191.

At your age with your high cholesterol, what's your risk of a first heart attack? (1997, July 28). *Time,* pp. 10-11.

Beman, D. S. (1995). Risk factors leading to adolescent substance abuse. *Adolescence, 30*(117), 201-208.

Berkowitz, S. (1996). Creating the research design for a needs assessment. In R. Reviere, S. Berkowitz, C. C. Carter, & C. G. Ferguson (Eds.), *Needs assessment: A creative and practical guide for social scientists* (pp. 15-31). Washington, DC: Taylor & Francis.

Brunner, M. L. (1987). A problem oriented assessment of continuing education needs of allied health department heads. *MOBIUS, 1*(1), 28-35.

Burns, R. (1992). To a mouse (stanza 7). In J. Bartlett (Ed.), *Familiar quotations* (16th ed., p. 361). Boston: Little, Brown. (Original publication 1785)

Calgary Regional Health Authority (CRHA). (1996). *Health Needs Assessment, 1996.* Calgary, Alberta: Author.

Calnin, G. T. (1998). *Laptop computers: Changes in teachers' practice.* Unpublished doctoral dissertation, University of Melbourne, Melbourne, Australia.

Camasso, M. J., & Dick, J. (1993). Using multi-attribute utility theory as a priority setting tool in human services planning. *Evaluation and Program Planning, 16,* 295-304.

Camp, R. C. (1989). *Benchmarking: The search for industry best practices that lead to superior performance.* Milwaukee, WI: ASQC Quality Press.

Campbell, D. T., & Stanley, J. C. (1963). Experimental and quasi-experimental designs for research on teaching. In N. L. Gage (Ed.), *Handbook of research on teaching* (pp. 171-246). Chicago: Rand McNally.

Caro, J., Klittich, W., McGuire, A., Ford, I., Norrie, J., Pettit, D., McMurray, J., & Sheperd, J. (1997). The West of Scotland Coronary Prevention Study: Economic benefit analysis of primary prevention with pravastatin. *British Medical Journal, 315,* 1577-1582.

Caruso, D. (1997, May 25). Revised statistics reporting favored. *Columbus Dispatch,* p. 1E.

Casey, M. A. (1988, October). *Focus group interviews with students: Overview and assessment.* Paper presented at the annual meeting of the American Evaluation Association, New Orleans, LA.

Chambers, D. E., Wedel, K. R., & Rodwell, M. K. (1992). *Evaluating social programs.* Boston: Allyn & Bacon.

Chuang, J. (1997, August 19). Calculating the traffic. *Seattle Times,* p. A6.

Claire, A., Dinan, D., & Wade, G. (1997, October). *Risky business: High-impact systems for identifying risk and improving accountability.* Paper presented at the 1997 Fall Training Conference of the National Legislative Program Evaluation Society, Jackson, MS.

Cullen, C. (1992). *Teachers' perspectives on accountability.* Unpublished doctoral dissertation, The Ohio State University, Columbus.

Cullen, C., Denning, R., Haury, D., Herrera, T., Klapper, M., Lysaght, R., & Timko, G. (1997). *Case studies: Teachers' perspectives on reform and sources of information* (Technical report from the Eisenhower National Clearinghouse for Mathematics and Science Education). Columbus: The Ohio State University.

Cummings, O. W. (1984, October). *Comparison of three algorithms for analyzing questionnaire type needs assessment data to establish priorities.* Paper presented at the annual conference of the Evaluation Network, San Francisco.

Cummings, O. W. (1985). Comparison of three algorithms for analyzing questionnaire type needs assessment data to establish priorities. *Journal of Instructional Development, 8*(2), 11-16.

D'Agostino, J. V. (1997, November). *A proactive approach to needs assessment for community development.* Paper presented at the annual meeting of the American Evaluation Association, San Diego, CA.

Demarest, L., Holey, L., & Leatherman, S. (1984, October). *The use of multiple methods to assess continuing education needs.* Paper presented at the annual meeting of the Evaluation Network, San Francisco.

Donnelly, J., & Florio, G. (1997, May). *Concept mapping in practice.* Workshop presented at the annual spring conference of the Ohio Program Evaluators Group, Columbus, OH.

Duff, C. (1997, January 16). Eyes on the price: Is the CPI accurate? Ask the federal sleuths who get the numbers. *Wall Street Journal,* p. 1.

Eastmond, J. N., Jr., Burnham, B. R., & Witkin, B. R. (1987, February). How to limit the scope of a needs assessment. In J. Buie (Ed.), *How to evaluate educational programs: A monthly guide to methods and ideas that work* (pp. 1-6). Alexandria, VA: Capitol Publications.

Edwards, M. M. (1997a, February 12). Closings part of broader review. *Columbus Dispatch,* p. 48.

Edwards, M. M. (1997b, December 5). Model-schools plan readied. *Columbus Dispatch,* p. 1A.

Ethnograph v5.0 [Computer software]. (1998). Thousand Oaks, CA: Scolari, Sage Publications software.

Fiorentine, R. (1994). Assessing drug and alcohol treatment needs of general and special populations: Conceptual, empirical, and inferential issues. *Journal of Drug Issues, 24*(3), 435-452.

Fisher, A. (1998, March 19). Honesty best policy on rapes, "gutsy" OU says. *Columbus Dispatch,* p. 1.

Fitzhugh, E. C., Wang, M. Q., Eddy, J. M., & Westerfield, R. C. (1993). A risk-related approach to a worksite health promotion needs assessment. *Health Values, 17*(5), 57-60.

Fitzpatrick, J. L. (1992). Problems in the evaluation of treatment programs for drunk drivers: Goals and outcomes. *Journal of Drug Issues, 22,* 155-167.

Fowler, F. J., Jr. (1993). *Survey research methods* (2nd ed.). Newbury Park, CA: Sage.

Gamon, J., Altschuld, J. W., Eastmond, J. N., Kirkhart, K., Morris, M., & Ory, J. (1992, November). *A focus group on using focus groups in the teaching of evaluation.* Workshop presented at the annual meeting of the American Evaluation Association, Seattle, WA.

Goering, P., & Lin, E. (1996). Mental health levels of need and variations in service use in Ontario. In *Patterns of health care in Toronto to the ICES practice atlas* (2nd ed., pp. 1-21). North York, Ontario: Institute for Clinical Evaluative Sciences.

Goodway-Shiebler, J. D. (1994). The effect of a motor skill intervention on the fundamental motor skills and sustained activity of African-American preschoolers who are at-risk. (Doctoral dissertation, Michigan State University, 1994). *Dissertation Abstracts International, 55,* 3781.

Greene, J. C., Caracelli, V. J., & Graham, W. F. (1989). Toward a conceptual framework for mixed-method evaluation designs. *Educational Evaluation and Policy Analysis, 11*(3), 255-274.

Guba, E. G., & Lincoln, Y. S. (1982). The place of values in needs assessment. *Educational Evaluation and Policy Analysis, 4*(3), 311-320.

Gutsche, S., Martin, D., Rumel, D., & Seaborn, J. (1996). *Health needs assessment, 1996.* Calgary, Alberta: Calgary Regional Health Authority.

Hale, K. M., Altschuld, J. W., Gerald, M. C., & Reuning, R. H. (1989). Assessment and comparison of interest in, commitment to, and perceived value of postbaccalaureate certificate and doctor of pharmacy programs. *American Journal of Pharmaceutical Education, 53,* 121-127.

Hale, K. M., Altschuld, J. W., Gerald, M. C., & Reuning, R. H. (1991). Pharmacy practitioner preferences for certificate structuring. *American Journal of Pharmaceutical Education, 55,* 335-338.

Hamann, M. S. (1997). *The effects of instrument design and respondent characteristics on perceived needs.* Unpublished doctoral dissertation, The Ohio State University, Columbus.

Hamann, M. S., & Altschuld, J. W. (1997, November). *Analytic techniques for assessing form and group effects in needs assessment surveys.* Paper presented at the annual conference of the American Evaluation Association, San Diego, CA.

Hansen, D. J. (1991). *An empirical study of the structure of needs assessment.* Unpublished doctoral dissertation, The Ohio State University, Columbus.

Hansen, D. J., Altschuld, J. W., & Sage, J. E. (1991, November). *Towards a general theory of needs assessment.* Paper presented at the annual meeting of the American Evaluation Association, Chicago.

Hauser, J. R., & Clausing, D. (1988). The house of quality. *Harvard Business Review, 66*(3), 63-73.

Herman, J. L., Morris, L. L., & Fitz-Gibbon, C. T. (1987). *Evaluator's handbook.* Newbury Park, CA: Sage.

Hildebrand, D. K., Laing, J. D., & Rosenthal, H. (1977a). *Analysis of ordinal data.* London: Sage.

Hildebrand, D. K., Laing, J. D., & Rosenthal, H. (1977b). *Prediction analysis of cross classifications.* New York: John Wiley.

Iutcovich, J. M. (1993). Assessing the needs of rural elderly: An empowerment model. *Evaluation and Program Planning, 16,* 95-107.

Kadlec, D. (1998, March 9). Measuring the new CPI. *Time,* p. 71.

Kaufman, R. (1992). *Strategic planning plus: An organizational guide.* Newbury Park, CA: Sage.

Kaufman, R., Rojas, A. M., & Mayer, H. (1993). *Needs assessment: A user's guide.* Englewood Cliffs, NJ: Educational Technology.

Kaufman, R., & Stakenas, R. G. (1981). Relating needs assessment, program development, implementation, and evaluation. *Journal of Instructional Development, 4*(4), 17-26.

Klapper, M., Haury, D., & Buell, L. (1992). *Technical proposal: Eisenhower National Clearinghouse for Mathematics and Science Education* (Proposal submitted in response to U.S. Department of Education RFP No. 92-032). Columbus: The Ohio State University.

Krueger, R. A. (1988, October). *Focus groups for community needs assessments: Overview and assessment.* Paper presented at the annual meeting of the American Evaluation Association, New Orleans, LA.

Kuh, G. D. (1982). Purposes and principles for needs assessment in student affairs. *Journal of College Student Personnel, 23*(3), 202-209.

Kumar, D. D., & Altschuld, J. W. (1995). *Evaluation of educational technology in preservice teacher education* (Final report of an NSF-AERA internship project submitted to the American Educational Research Association). Boca Raton: Florida Atlantic University.

Kumar, D. D., & Altschuld, J. W. (1999). Evaluation of an interactive media in science education. *Journal of Science Education and Technology, 8*(1), 55-65.

Laffrey, S. C., Meleis, A. I., Lipson, J. G., Solomon, M., & Omidan, P. A. (1989). Assessing Arab-American health care needs. *Social Science Medicine, 29*(7), 877-883.

Lagnado, L. (1997, April 17). Hospitals profit by "upcoding" illnesses. *Wall Street Journal,* p. B1.

Lipsey, M. W., Shayne, M., Cordray, D., Cottom, C., Derzon, J., Dimitropoulos, A., Maloney, E., Newbrough, B., Wilson, D., & Wilson, S. J. (1996). *Final report of the 1996 Nashville needs assessment: Vol. 1. Findings and analyses.* Nashville, TN: Center for State and Local Policy.

Lipsey, M. W., Wilson, D. R., Shayne, M., Derzon, J. H., & Newbrough, J. R. (1997, May). *Community needs assessment: The challenges of classification and comparison across diverse needs.* Paper presented at the Conference on Community Research and Action, University of South Carolina, Charleston.

Lyons, P., Doueck, H. J., & Wodarski, J. S. (1996). Risk assessment for Child Protective Services: A review of the empirical literature on instrument performance. *Social Work Research, 20*(3), 143-155.

McKillip, J. (1987). *Need analysis: Tools for the human services and education.* Newbury Park, CA: Sage.

Menzies, R., & Webster, C. D. (1995). Construction and validation of risk assessments in a six year follow-up of forensic patients: A tridimensional analysis. *Journal of Consulting and Clinical Psychology, 63*(5), 766-778.

Misanchuk, E. R. (1982). Analysis of multi-component educational and training needs. *Journal of Instructional Development, 7*(2), 28-33.

Misanchuk, E. R. (1985). On the appropriateness of certain algorithms for analyzing needs assessment data: A reaction to Cummings (1995) study. *Journal of Instructional Development, 8*(4), 25-28.

Mitra, A. (1994). Use of focus groups in the design of recreational needs assessment questionnaires. *Evaluation and Program Planning, 17*(2), 133-140.

Murgatroyd, S. (1993). The house of quality: Using QFD for instructional design in distance education. *American Journal of Distance Education, 7*(2), 34-48.

Nefstead, S. (1988, October). *Focus groups with educational programs: Overview and assessment.* Paper presented at the annual meeting of the American Evaluation Association, New Orleans, LA.

Ohio Department of Rehabilitation and Corrections. (1998). *Ohio parole board: Guidelines manual.* Columbus: State of Ohio.

Penta, M. Q. (1994, November). *Reassessing the comparability of three scoring methods for prioritizing areas of need: Implications for practice.* Paper presented at the annual conference of the American Evaluation Association, Boston.

Performance Management Committee. (1997). *Committee notes and minutes.* Columbus: College of Education, The Ohio State University.

Pitz, G. F., Heerboth, J., & Sachs, N. J. (1980). Assessing the utility of multi-attribute utility assessments. *Organizational Behavior and Human Performance, 26*, 65-80.

Pitz, G. F., & McKillip, J. (1984). *Decision analysis for program evaluators.* Beverly Hills, CA: Sage.

Posavac, E. J., & Carey, R. G. (1989). *Program evaluation: Methods and case studies* (3rd ed.). Englewood Cliffs, NJ: Prentice Hall.

QSR NUD*IST [Computer software]. (1995). Melbourne, Australia: Qualitative Solutions and Research, Sage Publications software.

Reviere, R., Berkowitz, S., Carter, C. C., & Ferguson, C. G. (1996). *Needs assessment: A creative and practical guide for social scientists.* Washington, DC: Taylor & Francis.

Rodriguez, S. R. (1988). Needs assessment and analysis: Tools for change. *Journal of Instructional Development, 11*(1), 25-28.

Royko, M. (1997, January 8). It's simple: Crime is down because prison population is up. *Columbus Dispatch,* p. 9A.

Sadowske, S. (1988, October). *Focus groups for state strategic planning: Overview and assessment.* Paper presented at the annual meeting of the American Evaluation Association, New Orleans, LA.

Salant, P., & Dillman, D. A. (1994). *How to conduct your own survey.* New York: John Wiley.

Schauerman, S., Manno, D., & Peachy, B. (1993, February). *Listening to the voice of the customer*. Paper presented at the CCBIA/League for Innovation in Community Colleges Conference, El Camino, CA.

Schauerman, S., Manno, D., & Peachy, B. (1994). Listening to the voice of the customer: Implementing quality function deployment. *Community College Journal of Research and Practice, 18*, 397-409.

Scissons, E. H. (1982). A typology of needs assessment definitions in adult education. *Adult Education, 33*(1), 20-28.

Scriven, M. (1967). The methodology of evaluation. In R. Tyler, R. Gagne, & M. Scriven (Eds.), *Perspectives of curriculum evaluation* (AERA Monograph 1, pp. 39-83). Chicago: Rand McNally.

Scriven, M., & Roth, J. (1978). Needs assessment: Concept and practice. *New Directions for Program Evaluation, 1*, 1-11.

Seidel, J., Friese, S., & Leonard, C. (1995). *The Ethnograph v 4.0: A users' guide*. Amherst, MA: Qualis Research Associates.

Shepherd, J., Cobbe, S. M., & Ford, I., et al. (1995). Prevention of coronary heart disease with pravastatin in men with hypercholesterolemia: The West of Scotland Coronary Prevention Study. In Y. Birnbaum & R. A. Kloner (Eds.), *Cardiovascular trials review* (pp. 310-311). London: J. Onwhyn.

Shillito, M. L. (1994). *Advanced QFD: Linking technology to market and company needs*. New York: John Wiley.

Siegel, P. (1997, July). *Benchmarking workshop*. Columbus: College of Education, The Ohio State University.

Simutis, L., Haury, D., & Tierney, R. (1997). *Technical proposal: Eisenhower National Clearinghouse for Mathematics and Science Education* (Proposal submitted in response to the U.S. Department of Education RFP Number 97-024). Columbus: The Ohio State University.

Smith, D. W., Steckler, A. B., McCormick, L. K., & McLeroy, K. R. (1993). Teacher's use of health curricula: Implementation of growing healthy, Project SMART, and the teenage health teaching modules. *Journal of School Health, 63*(8), 349-354.

Soriano, F. I. (1995). *Conducting needs assessments: A multidisciplinary approach*. Thousand Oaks, CA: Sage.

Sork, T. J. (1982). *Determining priorities*. Vancouver, Canada: University of British Columbia.

Sork, T. J. (1995, April). *Needs assessment in adult education*. Workshop sponsored by Faculty of Extension, University of Alberta, Edmonton, Alberta, Canada.

Sork, T. J. (1998, June). *Workshop materials: Needs assessment in adult education and training*. Workshop sponsored by the continuing education division of the University of Manitoba, Winnepeg, Manitoba, Canada.

Straw, G., Brown, H., Kutner, G., Marks, & Takeuchi, J. (1996, November). *Needs assessment and evaluation in a large non-profit: A tale of two programs*. Paper presented at the annual conference of the American Evaluation Association, Atlanta, GA.

Thomas, P. M., & Altschuld, J. W. (1985, November). *Needs assessment data from Delphi surveys: Collaborative procedures for transforming results of open-ended responses into questionnaire items for the second round.* Paper presented at the annual conference of the American Evaluation Association, Kansas City, MO.

Timko, G. M. (1999). *Student needs assessment in student affairs.* Unpublished doctoral dissertation, The Ohio State University, Columbus.

Trochim, W. M. K. (1989). An introduction to concept mapping for planning and evaluation. *Evaluation and Program Planning, 12,* 1-16.

Trochim, W. M. K., & Riggin, L. (1996). *AEA accreditation report: Draft.* Report submitted to the Board of the American Evaluation Association.

Turnbull, L. (1997, November 1). Columbus jams getting worse. *Columbus Dispatch,* p. A1.

Tweed, D. L., & Ciarlo, J. A. (1992). Social indicator models for indirectly assessing mental health service needs. *Evaluation and Program Planning, 15*(2), 165-180.

Van Voorhis, P., & Brown, K. (1996). *Risk classification in the 1990s* (Monograph prepared for the National Institute of Corrections). Washington, DC: U.S. Department of Justice.

Wald, M. S., & Woolverton, M. (1990). Risk assessment: The emperor's new clothes? *Child Welfare, 69,* 483-511.

Warheit, G. J., Bell, R. A., & Schwab, J. J. (1979). *Needs assessment approaches: Concepts and methods.* Rockville, MD: National Institute of Mental Health, U.S. Department of Health, Education, and Welfare.

Watson, E. (1997, August 19). Fast growth of Seattle causes the ouster of KBO head. *Seattle Times,* p. B3.

West of Scotland Coronary Prevention Group. (1996). West of Scotland Coronary Prevention Study: Identification of high risk groups and comparison with other cardiovascular intervention trials. *Lancet, 348*(9038), 1339-1342.

White, G. J., Murdock, R. T., Richardson, G. E., Ellis, G. D., & Schmidt, L. J. (1990). Development of a tool to assess suicide risk factors in urban adolescents. *Adolescence, 25*(99), 655-666.

Wickens, D. (1980). *Games people ought to play: A group process for needs assessment and decision-making for elementary and secondary schools* (Facilitator's manual). Hayward, CA: Alameda County Office of Education. (ERIC Document Reproduction Service No. ED 189 089)

Wilson, D. B., Shayne, M., Lipsey, M., & Derzon, J. H. (1996, November). *Using indicators of the gap between need for service and available service capacity as the basis for needs assessment.* Paper presented at the annual meeting of the American Evaluation Association, Atlanta, GA.

Witkin, B. R. (1975). *An analysis of needs assessment techniques for educational planning at state, intermediate, and district levels.* Hayward, CA: Office of the Alameda County Superintendent of Schools.

Witkin, B. R. (1984). *Assessing needs in educational and social programs: Using information to make decisions, set priorities, and allocate resources.* San Francisco: Jossey-Bass.

Witkin, B. R. (1992, November). *A qualitative analysis of needs assessment in the 1980s: The state of the art.* Paper presented at the annual meeting of the American Evaluation Association, Seattle, WA.

Witkin, B. R. (1994). Needs assessment since 1981: The state of the practice. *Evaluation Practice, 15*(1), 17-27.

Witkin, B. R., & Altschuld, J. W. (1995). *Planning and conducting needs assessments: A practical guide.* Thousand Oaks, CA: Sage.

Witkin, B. R., & Richardson, J. (1983). *APEX: Needs assessment for the secondary schools* (Manual). Hayward, CA: Office of the Alameda County Superintendent of Schools.

Witkin, B. R., Richardson, J., Sherman, N., & Lehnen, P. (1979). *APEX: Needs assessment for secondary schools* (Student survey). Hayward, CA: Office of the Alameda County Superintendent of Schools. (APEX consists of survey booklets for students, teachers, and parents, and an administrator's manual.)

Witkin, B. R., & Stephens, K. G. (1973). *Fault tree analysis: A management science technique for educational planning and evaluation.* Hayward, CA: Office of the Alameda County Superintendent of Schools.

Yoon, J. S., Altschuld, J. W., & Hughes, V. (1995). Needs of Asian foreign students: Focus group interviews. *Phi Beta Delta International Review, 5,* 1-13.

INDEX

ABOUT THE AUTHORS

James W. Altschuld is Professor in Quantitative Research, Evaluation, and Measurement in Education at The Ohio State University (OSU) and has also served as the evaluation coordinator for the National Center for Science Teaching and Learning at OSU. He has been an evaluator for the Columbus (Ohio) public schools, a supervisor in the Delaware Department of Public Instruction, and a research specialist at the Center for Vocational Education at OSU. His teaching, research interests, extensive publications, and conference presentations focus on needs assessment, evaluation methodology, and the development of evaluation as a field. In 1995, he coauthored (with Belle Ruth Witkin) *Planning and Conducting Needs Assessments: A Practical Guide.* Published articles and presentations include "The Utilization of Needs Assessment Results," "Needs of Asian Foreign Students: Focus Group Interviews," and "Teaching of Needs Assessment Across the Disciplines." In 1994, he coedited an issue of *New Directions for Program Evaluation* devoted to "The Preparation of Professional Evaluators: Issues, Perspectives, and Programs." He has served as president of the Ohio Program Evaluators' Group and as chair of the Topical Interest Groups, in teaching of evaluation and needs assessment, of the American Evaluation Association (AEA).

He currently is chair of the AEA task force on evaluator certification. He has received major state and university awards for his teaching and his work in evaluation. He received his doctorate in educational research and evaluation from OSU.

Belle Ruth Witkin (1917-1998) had been a visiting scholar in the Department of Speech Communication at the University of Washington. She was engaged in research, teaching, and consultation on needs assessment, program planning, and evaluation beginning in 1996, when she joined the staff of a regional educational planning agency in Alameda County, California, of which she later became director. There she designed and field-tested several models of needs assessment, directed needs assessments in educational and community settings, and convened the first national conference on needs assessment. She was codeveloper of the first applications of systems safety analysis to planning and evaluation in education and the social sciences. She served as a consultant on needs assessment and evaluation for school districts, universities, corporations, and government agencies, including the U.S. Department of Agriculture and the National Institute of Education. Her first book, *Assessing Needs in Educational and Social Programs* (1984), became a major resource in the field. In 1995, she coauthored (with James W. Altschuld) a second book titled *Planning and Conducting Needs Assessments: A Practical Guide.* She also published a book chapter and many articles on needs assessment in professional journals, including "Needs Assessment Since 1981: The State of Practice." She was president of the California Association for Program Evaluation and served on the editorial review board of *Educational Planning* and *Evaluation Practice.* She received her doctorate in speech science from the University of Washington, where she taught communication courses for several years. Her interest in communication, particularly group processes and listening, was continually reflected in her applications of communication theory to needs assessment.